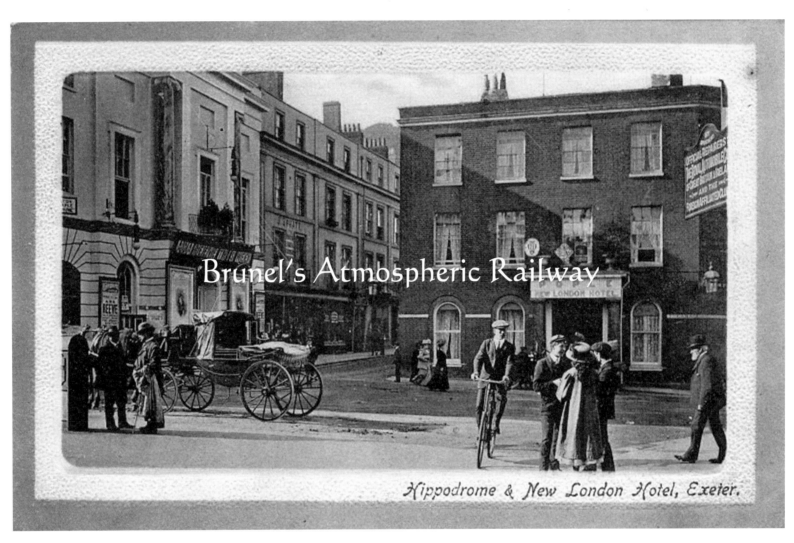

Hippodrome & New London Hotel, Exeter.

New London Inn Square, Exeter, 1911

To the left is the Hippodrome Theatre, converted in 1908 from the former Royal Public Rooms, which dated from 1820, whilst opposite stands Pople's New London Hotel, built in 1794. The third house down the street receding into the distance is number 7 Northernhay Place, where William Dawson painted his superb set of watercolours in 1848. The Hotel was demolished in 1936 and everything else in this picture was destroyed in the blitz of 4th May 1942.

Photo: www.exetermemories.co.uk.

First published in 2013 by:

The Broad Gauge Society

in association with

The Friends of Devon's Archives

ISBN   978-1-84785-037-9

Reprinted 2013

———————————

Distribution on behalf of the Friends of Devon's Archives:
Stevensbooks, Taddyforde House South, Taddyforde Estate, New North Road, Exeter EX4 4AT.
Tel 01392 459 760, www.stevensbooks.co.uk.

Also available through the Broad Gauge Society:
publications@broadgauge.org.uk.

———————————

Design and layout: Paul Garnsworthy and Mike Middleton.

Printed by:
Short Run Press Ltd, Bittern Road, Sowton Industrial Estate, Exeter, EX2 7LW.
Tel 01392 211 909, www.shortrunpress.co.uk.

Brunel's Atmospheric Railway

Featuring the Contemporary
Watercolours of William Dawson

edited by
Paul Garnsworthy

22" diameter atmospheric tubes preserved at Didcot. Wikipedia – GNU free documentation.

Page 3

www.broadgauge.org.uk

Formed in 1980 to promote the research and modelling of the 7ft 0¼in gauge railways of Britain, which operated from 1838 until 1892. Activities have expanded to cover model engineering and industrial archaeology. Certain members have gone further, to recover historic trackwork and construct replica rolling stock and the steam locomotive 'Fire Fly'.

The Society has over 350 members, a modest membership fee, holds meetings, field trips, regularly attends modelling exhibitions, and has a web-site and e-mail group. New finds, photographs, research and articles on operational details of the Broad Gauge railways are presented in the Society's magazine *Broadsheet*, along with articles on modelling this era. The Society also publishes a regular News-Sheet giving news of forthcoming meetings, new drawings, model kits, and other items of interest.

Exeter

Editorial

The 'Western Times' of 5th August 1848 reported that "*Mr Dawson, the talented surveyor of Northernhay Place, has completed a series of watercolour drawings of views of both sides of the line of the railway from Exeter to Totnes*". A very limited number of extracts have appeared in works over the years, and invariably in monochrome. For the 150th Atmospheric Railway and Watercolours anniversary in 1998, the Broad Gauge Society published our booklet "The South Devon Atmospheric Railway". For the first time, the full set was printed together, and in colour. Modest printing methods kept the cost within the means of anybody who was interested, and the booklet sold out within weeks.

During the intervening years we have received numerous requests for a new version, to modern standards. Taking up the challenge, we obtained high resolution images from the Institution of Civil Engineers, and chose a larger format to do justice to the fine detail. Soon after this, we received an approach from the Friends of Devon's Archives, proposing a joint venture. The Friends were keen to expand the content of the book, which has resulted in several new chapters as outlined above. As a consequence of the increased size and number of pages, we decided with some reluctance to split and re-arrange the watercolours, so that all the views face in the same direction.

We are grateful to the Friends for their support, to all those who have contributed to the written content, or have provided images for reproduction. Particular thanks are due to Peter Kay for permission to incorporate his scholarly work on the history of the Atmospheric system on the South Devon. Finally, Mike Middleton is to be congratulated on his outstanding work in laying out all the pages, annotating images and re-working older drawings to modern standards.

We hope that William Dawson would feel that we have done justice to his original handiwork. Perhaps initially attracted by the application of the latest technology right on his doorstep, Dawson soon found himself recording a great white elephant and a curiosity for generations to come.

Paul Garnsworthy

Contents

www.foda.org.uk

Founded in 1998 with the aim of promoting the preservation and use of historical records throughout Devon, and to raise public awareness of their importance for research and education.

Financial support is provided for the acquisition of documents relating to Devon. Close liaison is maintained with the local record offices in Devon, to improve standards of care and availability of the county's written heritage.

Regular events arranged by the Friends include:-

- Annual conferences in Exeter in October and Plymouth in November.
- An opportunity to work with archives.

Totnes

The Development of Atmospheric Propulsion

The use of atmospheric power was already a reality at the dawn of the railway age. James Watt's first beam engine design of 1765 featured a separate condensation chamber. Steam propelled the piston upwards, after which the supply was cut off and a valve opened to the condenser which was kept cool. The steam condensed, thereby reducing in volume and creating a partial vacuum. The greater atmospheric pressure above the piston drove it downwards. Transportation on the early waggonways was provided by horses on the level sections, later supplemented by primitive steam locomotives, whilst transfer between levels was by means of rope-worked inclines, powered by stationary steam engines. Many engineers and inventors were drawn to explore improved alternatives and atmospheric power was a popular theme.

George Medhurst Proposal, 1810 - 1827

In 1810 George Medhurst proposed to convey goods in trucks running on rails within an iron tube 12 square feet in area, propelled by compressed air. In 1812 he suggested twin iron tubes, six feet high by five feet wide, within which carriages having an inch clearance all round the tube might run on rails, carrying goods or passengers.

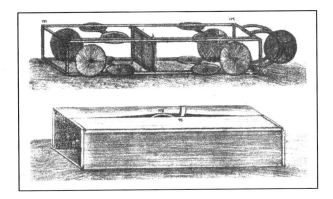

By 1827 his ideas had changed to a goods truck running within a tube, connected to a passenger carriage outside, both moving together and driven by very low pressure compressed air. There would have been a lifting iron plate on the top of the tube to allow the connection.

The truck which George Medhurst proposed to run in an iron tube; a road carriage which would be connected to the tube below ground.

John Vallance worked on similar lines to Medhurst. In 1812 he suggested iron tubes of 11½ feet in diameter (later reduced to 6 feet in diameter), within which trucks fitted with a backboard almost the same size as the tube would convey passengers or goods, being propelled on rails by very low atmospheric pressure of about 2 inches of vacuum. He actually built a mock-up, 8 feet in diameter by 150 feet long, within which a carriage 22 feet long by 5' 6" wide was steadied by lateral wheels. In 1826 and 1827 it carried up to 20 passengers at a time, at speeds of 2 miles per hour.

John Hague in 1827 patented a system by which a partial vacuum in a tube was connected to the cylinders of an engine, the pistons being moved by air pressure. The system found actual application in powering cranes and machine tools.

Henry Pinkus Proposal, 1834

Henry Pinkus proposed in 1834 to lay atmospheric railways on the country's principal roads, with rails integral with tubes of 30 to 40 inches in diameter. The valve was to take the form of a cord, which would be lifted over the governor carriage and then pressed down again afterwards. In 1836 he suggested tubes of 10" diameter, stiffened by circular fins on the outside. This time the valve would be formed by two curved sheets of polished metal, with their top edges pressed together. The vacuum was to be used to drive the cylinders of an atmospheric locomotive, rather than powering the train directly. A model was made and a short test track commenced but not completed.

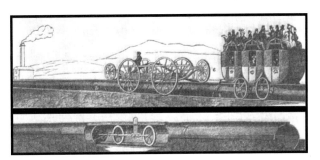

The piston within the tube is connected by a bar to the governor which draws the train. The valve is carried up over the vehicle before being pressed down again.

Samuel Clegg, Jacob & Joseph Samuda, patent of 1838

The breakthrough came on 3rd January 1838, when Samuel Clegg, Jacob Samuda (who had been an apprentice of John Hague) and Joseph Samuda took out patent no. 7920. This suggested the use of a hinge of leather, plated with iron, the lower plate convex to fit the circular tube, sealing composition and a heater. A model was set up at the Samudas' ironworks in Southwark. This drew two men weighing 18 stone in a carriage weighing 160 lb. up a 1 in 10 incline 180 feet long at 7 m.p.h., using a tube of 3⅝" diameter exhausted by a steam engine, and 8 inches of vacuum. Agreement was reached with the partially-built Birmingham, Bristol & Thames Junction Railway, whereby the patentees would lay down 1¼ to 1½ miles of line near Wormwood Scrubs, supplying rails, apparatus and Ballast. The experimental section was only half a mile long in the end, running from just south of the Great Western line, alongside Wormwood Scrubs to the Dalgarno Gardens bridge, the Engine House being on the Scrubs side of the line just north of Scrubs Lane bridge. Old rails from the Liverpool & Manchester Railway were re-used, a 9" diameter tube, with vacuum created by a 16 h.p. steam engine and an air pump with a 37½" diameter cylinder. The first test took place on 11th June 1840. Using the piston carriage alone or with one coach, the greatest speed attained was 36 m.p.h., weight moved 11½ tons and number of passengers carried 76.

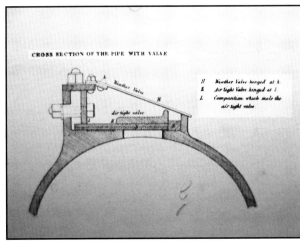

The principles of the Clegg & Samuda system, including leather valve with iron plates, angled coulter, composition heater and weather flap. The S.D.R. did not bother with the latter two refinements; the heater was not found to produce any benefit, but to omit the weather flap on a railway built next to the sea seems a classic case of false economy.

The Samudas reported to the *Railway Times* that the advantages of Atmospheric traction were the absence of excess weight to be hauled compared with locomotives and of the weight and friction of rope compared with rope haulage; safety, since collisions were impossible; the ability to work steep gradients; and the cheapness of fixed engines compared with locomotives.

The tests ran every Monday and Thursday, from 3 to 5 p.m., with the public being allowed to ride on the trains. A distinguished group attended the tests on 16th July 1841, including James Pim, Charles Vignoles, Macneil the engineer. and Lord Morpeth, all connected with the Dublin & Kingstown Railway, plus Mr. McMullen of the Grand Canal, Johnson of the Forth & Clyde Canal, and Baxendale, chairman of the South Eastern Railway. The test track was in poor condition by then, but speeds of 25 m.p.h. were attained despite the conditions. As a result it was determined to use the system for the D.&K.R. extension to Dalkey, which lead to further installations on the London & Croydon and Paris à St. Germain, as described on pages 99 – 101, and eventually the South Devon Railway itself, which forms the subject of this book.

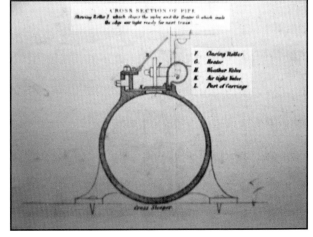

The Work of William Dawson

William Dawson was a talented and thorough land surveyor, born in London near the start of 1790, who was living and working in Exeter during the Atmospheric era. The Devon Heritage Centre holds several examples of surveys which he carried out, including the following:-

QS/DP/118: Honiton and Ilminster Turnpike Branch Roads, 1835, 6½" to the mile.

QS/DP/121: Road from Upottery to Seaton, 1835, 6½" to the mile.

QS/DP/136: Amendments and Extensions of Turnpike Roads in Parishes of Upottery and Yarcombe, 1838, 6½" to the mile.

QS/DP/138: Honiton and Ilminster Turnpike Roads, 1839, 10" to the mile.

In addition to these professional commissions, Dawson also produced limited edition works for sale to the public, when suitable subjects presented themselves. On the evening of Christmas Day 1839, a great landslip occurred at Bindon, near Axmouth. A book about this landslip published by subscription a few months later, was written and illustrated by the eminent geologists Dr. Buckland and Rev. W.D. Conybeare, together with technical and artistic illustrations by William Dawson and Mrs. Buckland. This was the first landslip ever to be described in a thoroughly scientifically manner. Dawson's contributions included several longitudinal sections (featuring his unique marker seagulls), plus three artistic views.

This was obviously successful, for a decade later Dawson undertook a much more extensive work – a complete record of the Atmospheric railway under construction between Exeter and Totnes. This totalled 25 sheets, each including a strip plan of a mile and a quarter of railway, a longitudinal section, and sketch views to either side of the line. This was advertised for sale in 1848. Thankfully a full set has survived in the possession of the Institution of Civil Engineers, and this forms the basis of the current book.

A planned second volume never materialised, due to abandonment of the Atmospheric, but a few individual paintings were made available as lithographs, showing trains now in the charge of steam locomotives.

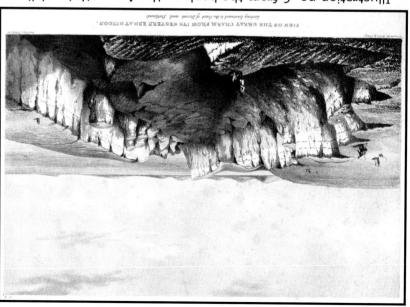

Illustration no. 6 from the book on the Axmouth Landslip, published in 1840.

Reproduced by kind permission of Devon Heritage Centre, ref. SC.0052.

William Dawson & His Family

Kelley's Directory of 1866 records William Dawson as an architect, living in Cathedral Yard, Exeter, whilst the Morris & Co. Directory of 1870 describes him as a surveyor, still at the same address. White's Directory of 1878-9 lists the Executors of William Dawson in Cathedral Yard.

The 1861 return also records him as a land surveyor, born Southwark, Surrey, living in The Close, aged 71. The 1871 return again records him as a surveyor, born Southwark, Surrey, living in The Close, aged 81.

Taken with the dates on his gravestone, the possible range for his day of birth runs from 13th June 1789 to 31st March 1790.

His wife, Caroline, was born in Exeter, and was stated to be 30 in the 1841 Census, 43 in the 1851 Census, 53 in 1861, and 63 in 1871, the latter ages corresponding with the dates on her gravestone.

His eldest child, Sarah, is stated to be 20 by the 1841 Census. In the 1851 Census, she is recorded as having been born in Kennington, Surrey, and aged 33. She was living elsewhere by the time of the 1861 and 1871 returns.

His second child, Elizabeth, is stated to be 20 by the 1841 Census. In the 1851 Census, she is also recorded as being born in Kennington, Surrey, and aged 31. On the night of the 1861 Census, she was away from home, but the 1871 Census records her, now aged 51.

His third child, Mary, is stated to be 15 by the 1841 Census. She was away from home on the night of the 1851 Census, but the 1861 Census records her as having been born in Kennington, Surrey, and now aged 39. The 1871 Census records the same birth place, and gives her age as 49.

His fourth child, Emma, is stated to be 15 by the 1841 Census. She was away from home on the night of the 1851 Census, but the 1861 Census records her as having been born in Kennington, Surrey, and now aged 37. She was living elsewhere by the time of the 1871 return.

His fifth child, John, is stated to be 9 years old by the 1841 Census. The 1851 Census records him as an assistant surveyor, aged 18, and having been born in Exeter. He was living elsewhere during the 1861 and 1871 returns.

His sixth child, Caroline, is recorded as 7 years old by the 1841 Census. The 1851 Census shows her as a scholar, aged 17, having been born in Exeter. In 1861 she is still at home, aged 27. Following her marriage in 1864, she died before her parents. She does not appear in the 1871 return. Her gravestone recording the date of birth as 27th September 1833 and her death as 11th March 1874.

Others appearing in the Census returns include a visitor in 1851, and two servants each in 1851, 1861 and 1871. It would appear that Elizabeth, Mary, and perhaps Emma, never married. It may well be that descendants of Sarah, John and Caroline still live in the area today. Four paintings by Dawson were bequeathed to the Royal Albert Memorial Museum, Exeter, by the late Mrs. Kate Dawson in 1929. She may well perhaps have been a daughter-in-law to John Dawson.

Exeter Cathedral Records show that Dawson's funeral was held in the Cathedral on 18th June 1877, when he was recorded as 88 years old. His gravestone in Exeter Higher Cemetery confirms the final age, but records the date of death as 12th June 1878, which is presumably the correct date.

The funeral of his wife, Margaret Caroline Dawson, was also held in Exeter Cathedral, on 10th October 1876, when she was recorded as 68 years old. Her gravestone gives the dates of her birth as 13th November 1807 and death as 5th October 1876.

The Cathedral Records note that his daughter, Caroline Dawson, married John Woodman, a surgeon in St. Sidwell's, Exeter on 6th July 1864. Woodman's father, William Woodman, was also recorded as a surgeon. The gravestone, located next to her parents, gives Caroline's date of birth as 27th September 1833 and death as 11th March 1874.

From the ten-yearly census returns, it would appear that Dawson had four children born in Kennington, Surrey, from a previous marriage (Sarah, Elizabeth, Mary and Emma being only 10, 12, 14 and 16 years younger than Mrs. Dawson), and two in Exeter from his current marriage. Each census applied to the night of 31st March / 1st April, and details of the family from the various returns are as follows, although ages given seem to have been rounded off in the case of the 1841 census. All the addresses are in the professional district of Exeter. William Dawson is recorded in Northernhay Place by the 1841 Census (as also stated in the 1848 newspaper report on his watercolours), and is described as a civil engineer, aged 50. The 1851 return gives him as head of household, a land surveyor living in Dix's Field, aged 60, and born in Southwark, Surrey.

The cross was erected first, for the burial of Dawson's youngest daughter Caroline in 1874. The second simpler stone was added in 1876, when Margaret Caroline Dawson died, but touchingly close to her daughter. William Dawson's name was added in 1878, his young grandson Arthur in 1880, his son-in-law John Woodman in 1903, and finally the latter's second wife Katharine Louisa in 1916.

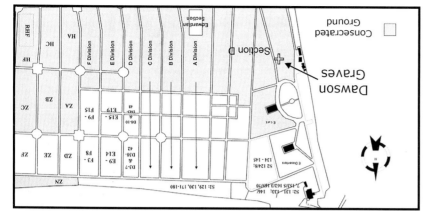

W. Dawson April 1848

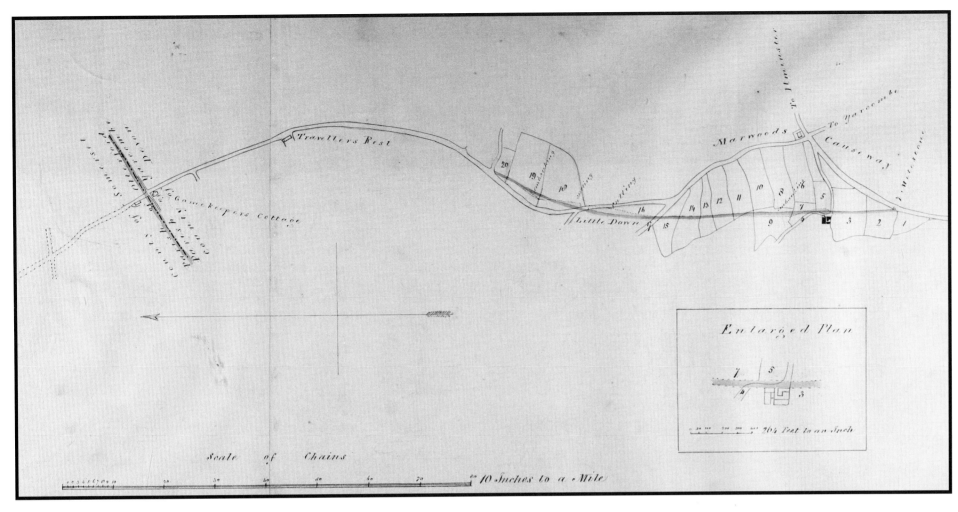

The Honiton and Ilminster Turnpike Trust

The Honiton and Ilminster Turnpike Trust was created to build a new road down the hill east of Monkton. This new route to London (now the A303) connected the old road through Chard (A30) from Devonshire Inn Junction to the existing turnpike at Ilminster.

Part of the Turnpike (A303) can be seen at the right-hand end of this extract. Dawson's drawing of 1839 sets out the route of a proposed branch of the Turnpike, which would have made connection with Taunton.

The road improvements shown on Dawson's drawing were not actually made, and the route of the current B3170 remains much as shown here.

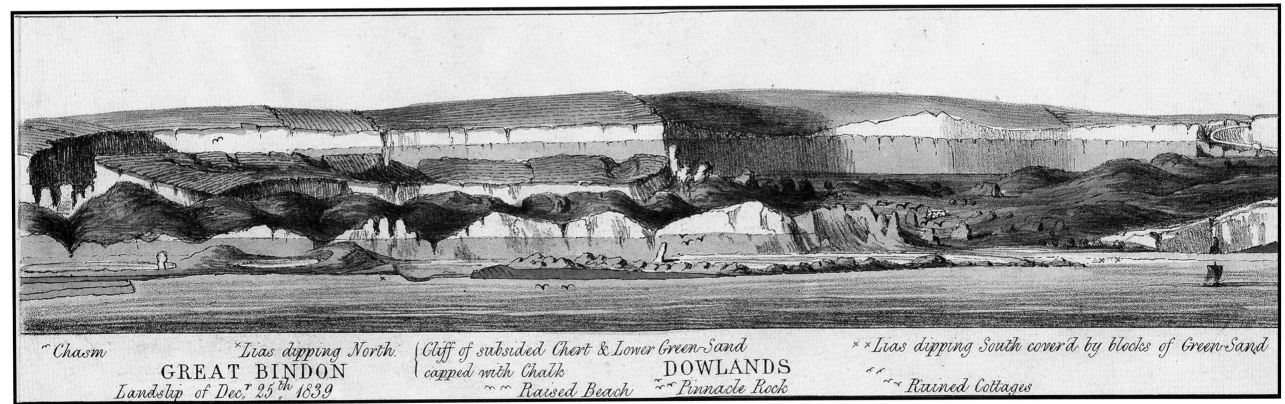

Geological View of the Coast from Lyme Regis in the County of Dorset to Axmouth Harbour on the East Coast of Devon

This extract covers three quarters of a mile, approximately one ninth of the total length of Dawson's magnificent strip view of what we now know as the "Jurassic Coast". The original consists of one large sheet, 752mm wide by 227mm high, with the coastal views running across it in three panels. It is in colour, with the sea and vegetation represented naturally, but the rock faces colour-coded to represent the different geological strata, based on information supplied to Dawson by The Revd. W.B. Conybeare. The book was published in 1840 by J. Murray of London and includes a list of the subscribers. The selected extract includes the Great Bindon landslip of 25th December 1839, and so relates to the View of the Great Chasm on the preceding page.

The Clegg and Samuda System in South Devon

15 inch Diameter Pipe and Piston Frame

It is not thought that any of the 15 inch diameter pipes used between Exeter and Newton still exist. The drawing is based upon surviving 22 inch pipes, with the dimensions adjusted accordingly. The mountings would have been approximately 5 inches below rail level, necessitating some scalloping to the top surface of the transommes. The cranked coulter can be seen passing through the slot in the tube, within which it is fixed between the two bars of the piston frame. The top of the coulter is fixed to a hinged mechanism suspended from the axle-hung mounting frame on the piston carriage. Within the tube, one of the specially shaped wheels can be seen in end view behind the coulter, in the act of raising the continuous leather and iron valve.

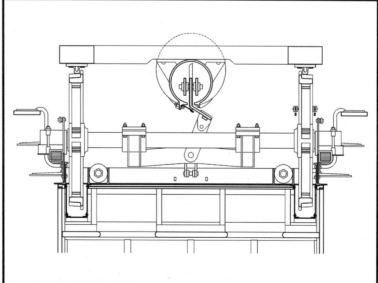

Drawing: Paul Garnsworthy

Separating or Equilibrium Valve

Jacob Samuda's following words, describing the action of the valves at the end of each three mile pipe section, repay careful study. There may have been modifications before installation in South Devon:-

"The main valve is divided into two sections of about 3 miles each, by separating valves opening in the direction in which trains move. The entrance valve (A, Fig. 5,) is opened by the wheel of the leading carriage, which depresses a lever outside the pipe, thus disengaging a catch, which allows a weight to fall and to move a slide valve across two openings in the side of the valve box, on either side of the seat of the valve (B). This causes the air in the chamber (C) to rush into the exhausted tube (D), and the valve (B), which is attached to the same fulcrum as the valve (A), being then in equilibrium, it immediately opens by the external pressure upon it. The disc (B) is rather larger than the valve (A), and thus keeps it closed until the slide is moved as described, in consequence of the superior surface it exposes to the pressure of the external atmosphere. A weight is attached to the fulcrum of the valve itself and is disengaged by the action of the wheel. Its object is to open the valve, in case of any obstruction or impediment to the proper action of the slide.

An exit valve is placed about 30 feet beyond the branch pipe leading to the exhausting apparatus, and thus, when the travelling piston has passed this branch, its advance diminishes the space between it and the valve, and there being no outlet for the air in the pipe,

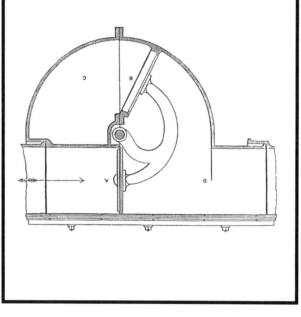

its density is increased as the space is reduced, until the pressure inside the pipe is greater than outside, and the valve opens. A double set of these valves is employed, where it is necessary to use the same main, for travelling in both directions."

The chairman of the meeting was William Cubitt, who was not only vice president of the I.C.E. but also engineer to the atmospheric London & Croydon Railway. It is good to hear Jacob speaking. He was evidently the principal engineer behind the Atmospheric, but by the end of the year he was dead, killed by a burst steam pipe at Blackwall.

22 inch Diameter Pipe

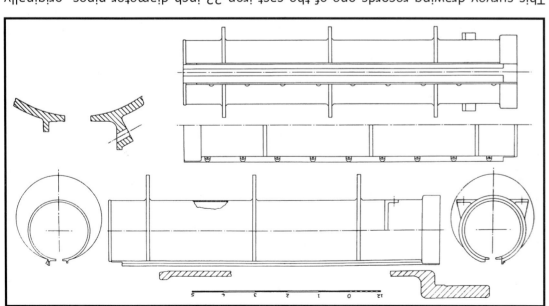

This survey drawing records one of the cast iron 22 inch diameter pipes, originally laid between Newton and Totnes, and now preserved at Didcot Railway Centre. Note the mounting brackets at one end only, next to the socket. These would have been approximately 12 inches below rail level, so the transommes were presumably fitted below the longitudinal baulks on the line west of Newton. Further timbers were fixed on top of the transommes, connecting to each baulk, but leaving a gap in the middle for the pipe, as seen on page 77. Massive stiffening rings, 33 inches in diameter, kept the tube in shape after the valve slot was ground out.

Drawing: Mike Jolly

Clegg and Samuda's Piston Arrangement

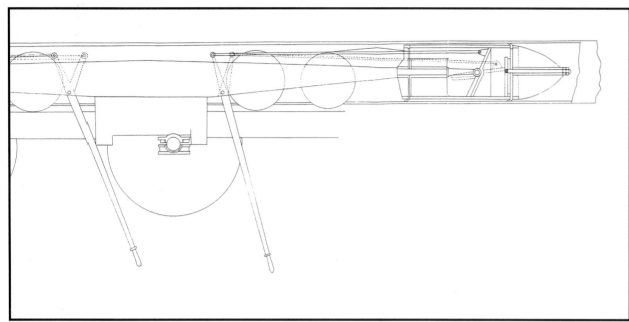

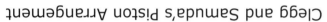

This is an extract from one of eight drawings which formed part of Clegg and Samuda's patent no. 10,167 of 1844. It shows the piston head as a cylinder, with cup leather rings at each end and a streamlined guide at the front. A valve within the piston is opened and closed by a lever within the cabin. Drawings of London & Croydon Railway piston carriages show a similar lever in the cabin, but it is not known if they were used on the South Devon. The basic construction of the piston may however be regarded as typical.

J. & J, D'A. Samuda's Specification.
Patent no. No. 10,167, 30th April 1844.

Drawing and commentary: 14th May 1844, Address to the Institution of Civil Engineers,
"The Atmospheric Railway", by Jacob Samuda, Assoc. Inst. C. E.

The Decision to Go Atmospheric

The S.D.R. had been promoted, engineered and passed by Parliament as a double-track locomotive-worked line. But it was no surprise, in retrospect, that it should have been changed to an Atmospheric line. Brunel, committed to technological progress, had taken interest in the Atmospheric experiments being carried out since 1840 at Wormwood Scrubs on the West London line, which seemed to show signs of at last lifting the Atmospheric idea out of never-never land and into practical working. In July 1840 Brunel had in fact considered, but rejected, the possibility of Atmospheric traction on the Box incline. Then Charles Vignoles decided to adopt the Atmospheric on the Kingstown & Dalkey Railway near Dublin, which began trial running in August 1843 (the public opening was in March 1844). Brunel visited it in November and, like most visitors, was much impressed. In January 1844 Brunel's name appeared as Engineer to the Atmospheric Gravesend, Rochester & Chatham Railway; and in May he appeared in support of the Croydon & Epsom in Parliament, their Committee hearings having become a sort of test-case for the Atmospheric idea in general. After this the Atmospheric began to take off very quickly; something of a national fervour for Atmospheric railways was evident by the time the S.D.R. act was passed in July 1844, and this reached a peak in 1845.

When Brunel was preparing the S.D.R. plans in the autumn of 1843, he was only "seeing the possibility" of Atmospheric working, and perhaps only on the inclines at that. Had he *known* the line was to be Atmospheric, he would have arranged some sections differently[1]. In May 1844 he was asked about the possibility of the Atmospheric on the S.D.R., and replied evasively "I have not been called upon to recommend it or not". In fact he must have been pretty decided by then. At their meeting of 5th August 1844, the S.D.R. Board had before them a letter from Jacob & Joseph Samuda, the Atmospheric patentees. (Jacob, the greater engineer, was killed in an accident in November that year and so was never involved in the S.D.R. work). We may assume Brunel was involved in the appearance of this letter; he reported very quickly on the matter, in favour of the Atmospheric, and a few days later Gill and other directors were off to Ireland to join the growing list of distinguished visitors at Dalkey. Gill was not in on the plot; he went there "prejudiced against the Atmospheric system", but returned impressed. At their next meeting on 19th August the Board resolved to adopt Atmospheric working; and the first Shareholders' meeting on

28th August confirmed this unanimously. It was a glorious month for the Samudas, for at this same time the Act for the Epsom line, and the Atmospheric 'third line' on the Croydon line, was passed. Work on the Croydon therefore began at the same time as on the S.D.R. It was the start of the Atmospheric Age.

Brunel's August 1844 report was quite firm in its advocacy of the Atmospheric, which, he stated, would be cheaper in both initial construction costs and subsequent working costs. The greater part of the supposed saving in construction costs was, however, due to comparing a double-track locomotive line and a *single*-track Atmospheric line, on the claim that the latter would have the same capacity as the former. This dubious notion was not challenged at the time. The working costs Brunel guessed would be £8,000 per annum less than a locomotive line.

Other advantages claimed by Brunel for the Atmospheric (and largely proved correct) were higher speeds, greater freedom from accident, improved travelling conditions for passengers, and the ability to run more trains at very little extra cost. In a sentence that he was to come to regret profoundly, Brunel concluded the report:-"I have no hesitation in taking upon myself the full and entire responsibility of recommending the adoption of the Atmospheric system on the S.D.R., and of recommending in consequence that the line and works should be constructed for a single line only".

It should *not* be thought that Brunel wanted the Atmospheric purely because of the gradients west of Newton. He was supporting the Atmospheric for more level lines also; and locomotives were now showing on the 1 in 37 Lickey Incline that they could surmount very steep gradients. In Parliament in April 1844, Brunel was non-committal as to whether assistant stationary power would be necessary for locomotive working on the S.D.R. inclines (although when doing the costings to support the Atmospheric in August, he conveniently assumed that it *would* have been!).

By the end of the year the S.D.R. had deposited a Bill for Atmospheric extensions to Torquay and Tavistock, and the Cornwall Railway had also agreed to adopt the Atmospheric. At the February 1845 Shareholders' meeting Gill enthused that "there was little doubt that there would be an Atmospheric line of railway from Exeter to the Land's End". The only dissentient voices came from the G.W.R.; its Chairman Charles Russell (who had also visited Dalkey, with Daniel Gooch, in September) wrote to Gill in December 1844 to say that the G.W.R. Board entertained "very grave

apprehensions" over the idea of an Atmospheric single line, and pointing out that the September 1843 agreement *required* a double line. But as that agreement also required that Brunel should be the S.D.R.'s Engineer, and Brunel had recommended the very course objected to, the G.W.R. was in rather a weak position!

After the decision to adopt the Atmospheric, Brunel made several changes in the constructional details of the line. The headroom of the over-bridges was reduced by 18" (although locomotives *could* still pass under them); the under-bridges were given one ring less thickness; and 50 lb rails were specified instead of the 70 lb used on the G.W.R. The track was also laid with transoms at 10 ft. intervals to fit the pipes.

There is not space here to go into the history of the development of Atmospheric railways, or of the detailed methods of working of the various systems; for this the reader must refer to Charles Hadfield's *Atmospheric Railways* (David & Charles – reprinted by Alan Sutton Publishing, Gloucester 1985). It may, however, be helpful to reiterate briefly the facts of Clegg and Samudas' system, as adopted on the S.D.R. (and the other working lines). Stationary engines situated beside the line, at intervals of several miles, worked vacuum pumps which exhausted the air from a continuous pipe laid between the rails, so creating a (partial) vacuum in the pipe. In the top of the pipe was a continuous slot, normally sealed by a continuous leather 'longitudinal valve' hinged on one side and held down by iron weights. Trains were headed by a 'piston carriage' which had fixed underneath it, at the head of a 10 ft. long iron plate, a 'piston' which fitted tightly inside the pipe. On the upper side of the plate were small wheels which pushed up the leather

valve immediately behind the piston, so allowing air to rush into the pipe. Because of the vacuum in front of the piston, the Atmospheric pressure exerted by the air on the back of the piston drove the train forward. The power available to propel the train was in proportion to (a) the size of the pipe – a larger pipe meaning a larger piston surface area for the air to press against – and (b) the level of vacuum in the pipe in front of the train.

The Pipes

The first step taken to bring the Atmospheric to reality on the S.D.R. was the invitation of tenders for the pipes. A four-page specification was issued in 21st October 1844, and tenders sought for 4,400 tons of 13" diameter pipes, enough for the Exeter to Newton section. At this stage Brunel was anticipating 13" pipes on this section, 15" pipes generally west of Newton and 22" pipes on the inclines, using an 'expanding' piston[2]. (The Dalkey and Croydon both had 15" pipes throughout). The pipes were a difficult precision job, and the S.D.R. found that many firms did not want to tender, some having just had trouble from their Croydon tenders. The Land & Works Committee therefore had only two tenders before it at its meeting on 17th December; Thomas Guppy of Bristol was offering £8 17s 6d per ton, and George Hennet £8 per ton provided that the S.D.R. furnished the iron at 70s per ton. "After much discussion" (probably because Hennet did not actually *own* a foundry!) they agreed to let Brunel conclude a contract with Hennet[3].

Hennet's (unwritten) contract was actually for 12,000 tons for the whole distance to Plymouth, and included the *laying* of the pipes, at a further price to be decided by Brunel. Hennet bought and improved a foundry at

---

Specification of **4400** *Tons of Pipes for the Atmospheric Apparatus.*

October 21, 1844.

CASTINGS.

THE pipes are to be 13 inches internal diameter, and to be cast according to the form and thickness shewn in drawings, Nos. 1 and 2, and in every respect of workmanship fully equal to the samples exhibited at the Great Western Railway Station, Paddington, and marked "Castings S. D. Ry.;" they must be perfectly straight, and their inside diameters smooth and cylindrical. Two gauges will be furnished; one, 12⅞ inches diameter, and one 13 1/16 inches diameter: the smaller one must pass through every pipe, and the pipes will be rejected as too large, if the larger one passes.

The cores must be perfectly cleaned out, and any sharp projections of metal removed.

All the pipes are to be proved with a pressure equal to 150 feet head of water, in the presence of a person appointed by the Company, and none will be received except so proved, and marked accordingly.

The socket to be of the internal diameter shewn in the drawing, and perfectly concentric with the interior of the pipe.

The thickness of the pipes, throughout, must correspond with the drawings.

The iron used must be good sound metal, run from pig-iron, and not from the stack.

Bridgwater, and Shapland (a Director) took charge of obtaining pig-iron to Hennet. By the summer of 1845 Hennet had made 1,592 13" pipes (685 tons or 3 miles). Brunel then decided that 13" pipes would be inadequate, and that 15" pipes would have to be used between Exeter and Newton as well.

In November the 13" pipes were dumped in a field at Temple Meads which Hennet owned and agreed to rent for only 1s per annum. A few months later a no-doubt-embarrassed Brunel was asked by the Board whether anything useful could be done with the 13" pipes, or whether they should be broken up.

Hennet then started on making 15" pipes instead, and subsequently 22" pipes (the first 22" pipe was made in July 1846). By April 1846 the total production was 16 miles of 15" pipe; by February 1847 it had increased to 22½ miles of 15" pipe (11,885 pipes) and 5 miles of 22" pipe (2,600 pipes).

Laying of the pipes could not of course start until the permanent way was laid. It began, from the Exeter end, in mid-December 1845. (One assumes that the pipes were brought from Bridgwater by rail). The first long pipes must have been difficult things to handle. Progress seems to have been made at about 150 yards per day. At the August 1846 Shareholders' meeting Brunel was able to report that the pipes were laid up to the then end of the track at Hackney. Despite the false start, therefore, the pipe production had no part in the delays to the Atmospheric.

The Leather Valve

This had to be obtained from Samuda. By a contract of 20th February 1845, 52 miles was to be supplied (21 miles by 1st July, the remainder as required by Brunel), at £2.13s per chain on delivery, 18s per chain for fixing and a final £1.9s twelve months after the Atmospheric came into use (Samuda being required to maintain the valve during the first twelve months). In the event seven miles were delivered by June and all the initial 21 miles by September. It therefore arrived long before it could be fixed, which had unfortunate effects as described later. Fixing to the pipes began late in 1846 and was completed as far as Teignmouth by March 1847. Samuda also had to be paid for **patent rights**. An agreement dated 22nd March 1845 provided for £250 per mile to be paid on the Atmospheric coming into use, and a further £250 twelve months later. Had all this money been paid, it would have totalled some £86,000.

The Stationary Engines

Tenders for the engines (and vacuum pumps) were invited from 23 firms late in 1844 and opened by the Land & Works Committee on 7th January 1845. It was decided that Boulton & Watt, and J & J Rennie and Scott Sinclair & Co should do three pairs each. Scott Sinclair then pulled out and after further discussion, in the course of which Brunel decided that eight Engine Houses rather than nine would suffice for the Exeter-Newton section, it was decided that Boulton & Watt and Rennie would still do three pairs and Maudslays (who were building the Croydon's engines) would do two pairs. The prices varied between £4,250 and £4,725 per pair. All the engines were 40hp verticals (giving 80hp per Engine House), but the manufacturers were left to produce their own designs. Each Engine House also had two small 12hp engines to pump water for the boilers etc. The engines were all completed by the end of 1845, but could not all be delivered then as the Engine Houses were not sufficiently complete.

The **boilers** for the Engine Houses were delivered from May 1845. The first two arrived at Topsham by ship and Margary was told to have them thrown over the side of the vessel, tow them up the river and land them on

The Engine Houses

Engine House	Location	Date of Commencement of Work on Building	Engine Supplier	Date Engines Started	(Large) Engines Sold	Engine House Demolished
Exeter	194m 04ch, south end of St. David's Station, Up Side. (OS 911932)	June 1845	Boulton & Watt, Smethwick	August 1846 (but not used for pumping until December)	One sold February 1853 to Mr. West (for £1,650 with Turf). Other not known.	1983 (Exeter Panel Box site, opened 1st April 1985).
Countess Wear	197m 22ch, south of C/W Turnpike Bridge, D/Side. (OS 941890[1])	June 1845	J & G Rennie, London	23rd February 1847	1st sold Jan 1850 (unknown buyer); 2nd sold Apr 1853 (unknown buyer) for £450[4].	1859
Turf	199m 60ch, south of Turf L.C., D/Side. (OS 962858)	June 1845	Boulton & Watt, Smethwick	4th February 1847	One sold February 1853 to Mr. West (for £1,650 with Exeter). Other not known.	Circa 1860[6]
Starcross	202m 43ch, south of station, Up Side. (OS 977817)	August 1845	Boulton & Watt, Smethwick	23rd March 1847	October 1856, to Cwm Celyn Ironworks (for £650).	Still standing
Dawlish	206m 06ch, east of station, Up Side. (OS 965768)	Circa January 1846	Maudslay, Sons & Field, London	11th February 1847	1853, to Samuda Brothers, London.	1873
Teignmouth	208m 75ch, adjacent to station, Up Side (OS 942731)	Spring 1846	J & G Rennie, London	3rd June 1847	October 1853, to Mr. Guppy (for £850).	Circa 1856
Summer House[2]	212m 13ch, Down Side (OS 892728)	Summer 1846	Maudslay, Sons & Field, London	Autumn 1847	1853, to Samuda Brothers, London.	1855
Newton	214m 05ch, east of station, Down Side. (OS 868714)	Autumn 1846	J & G Rennie, London	27th August 1847 (?) (some doubt as to exact date)	February 1853, to Samuda Brothers, London (for £800)[3].	1893 (?)
Dainton	218m 01ch, west of Tunnel, Down Side. (OS 850661)	Circa May 1847	Boulton & Watt, Smethwick	Installed but never started	August 1849, to Mr. Hill (for approximately £3,000)[5].	1850s (?)
Totnes	222m 62ch, adjacent to station, Up Side. (OS 802610)	Summer 1847	Boulton & Watt, Smethwick	Largely installed but never started	January 1853, to Mr. West (for £850).	Still standing
Rattery	227m 24ch east of Rattery Mill, Down Side (OS 734606)	January 1848	Harvey & Co, Hayle	Never installed (building never completed)	Parts delivered to Totnes sold January 1853, to Mr. West (for £200).	Reduced and converted to cottages c.1850.
Torquay	218m 13ch, ¾m north of (Torre) station, Up Side. (OS 900661)	Summer 1847	Boulton & Watt	Never installed	------	Still standing

Notes

1. MacDermot and Hadfield wrongly state that Countess Wear was on the Up Side.
2. Often referred to as 'Wear' or 'Ware' prior to opening; the name "Summer House" was presumably settled upon to avoid confusion with Countess Wear.
3. It is not wholly clear that Samuda bought both the Newton large engines, but both were sold at this date.
4. The January 1850 minute only refers to "one Rennie's engine", but this is the only Rennie engine not referred to elsewhere and so is presumably the one there referred to.
5. According to Clayton the Dainton engines went to the Plymouth Ironworks, Merthyr Tydfil.
6. Chimney only left standing until 24th August 1882. Stone from Engine House used to build outbuildings at Exewell Barton.

the west bank at Countess Wear. Margary did not think much of this idea and contrived a trip to Bristol to get Hammond's superior authority for the alternative plan of landing them on Topsham Quay. This was done on 6th May, aided by a 'grab engine' loaned by Carpenter the line contractor. Another ship arrived at Topsham in July. In October the boilers were still sitting on Topsham Quay and Margary decided that it was time to move them to the Engine Houses, but it is not recorded *how* this was done. The next delivery in August was by rail.

The Engine Houses
In the spring of 1845 Brunel fixed the sites of the eight Engine Houses for the Exeter-Newton section and drew up plans for them. They were positioned at roughly three-mile intervals from Exeter (the exact spacings were 3.2, 2.5, 2.8, 3.5, 2.9, 3.2 and 1.9 miles). Each Engine House consisted of a tall Engine Room, a lower Boiler House, a chimney and store sheds; although the ground plans varied from one site to another. In contrast to the Croydon's Gothick, Brunel chose an Italianate style, with the chimneys designed as Campaniles, all of them different in detail. Earlier Engine Houses were built in various stone, the later ones of grey limestone[6], all had Bath stone window surrounds and 'Italian Tile' roofing.

A reliable source of water was needed at each Engine House. At Countess Wear, Turf, Teignmouth, Summer House, Newton (and Dainton) large open-air reservoirs were constructed, fed by nearby streams. Starcross had an underground reservoir immediately south of the building. Exeter had a well but the arrangements at Dawlish are uncertain[7]. Each Engine House also required a short siding for coal trucks.

Exeter, Countess Wear and Turf Engine Houses were built by Carpenter, starting in June 1845, under Margary's supervision. The day *after* work began at Turf, Brunel paid a visit to South Devon and decided that it should be relocated 150 yards nearer Exeter! The chimney here was found to be a little out of line when completed, and a buttress had to be built. Starcross was commenced in August, probably by Carpenter; again there was a last minute change of plan, but this time only to have the north wall 30ft from the Courtenay Arms instead of 15ft. The chimney at Starcross, built on riverbed mud, had to be completely taken down after it was finished, due to inadequate foundations. It was rebuilt 'thinner and lighter' on piles. At the February 1846 S.D.R. meeting, an angry shareholder asked Brunel "why they are taking the Engine Houses down again". Even after the second attempt, the Starcross chimney developed a very bad lean[8].

There was then a long delay before work began at Dawlish, Teignmouth, Summer House and Newton, started at various dates in 1846. Some of these later Engine Houses were built by Hennet[9].

Preparing for Operation
The Croydon was running atmospheric trains in August 1845, and public services began in January 1846. The S.D.R., starting work in the same month in 1844, did not run a test train until March 1847 and did not start public services until September 1847. Admittedly the S.D.R. was a wholly new line and a longer route; but it is doubtful if this was in fact the cause of its slowness.

In the optimism of 1844 it was assumed that the line would be worked Atmospherically from the start (and this at a time when a July 1845 opening was being spoken of). At the February 1845 meeting Gill told the shareholders that they would have the chance, before the next meeting in August, of "testing the Atmospheric system in a ride from Exeter to Newton". However it should have been obvious by then that there was no likelihood of the Atmospheric being ready for summer 1845. Only the pipes and valves had been ordered early enough for a possible 1845 start. The engines might have been ready to work by the *end* of 1845, *if* the Engine Houses had been ready to receive them. But the one precluding factor, that ruled out any chance of an early start of Atmospheric working, was the 10 month delay in starting on the Engine Houses. Even worse, the *further* delay until Spring 1846 in commencing Teignmouth Engine House subjected the whole system to a delay for public Atmospheric service, as Exeter to Teignmouth was regarded as the minimum sensible distance for the start of Atmospheric working. It is difficult to see why the Engine Houses could not have been started in 1844, had Brunel put his mind to it.

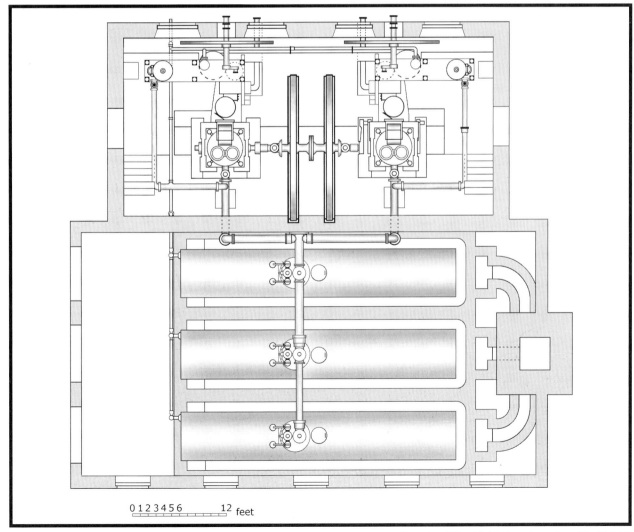

Engine House Plan
Boulton & Watt produced two sets of standard drawings for their vertical engine houses, showing left and right handed versions to suit different sites. In the event, Exeter, Turf and Starcross were all built to the same handing as shown here. The chimneys were however built at the junction between boiler house and engine house, rather than in the middle of the boiler house end wall. In the case of Starcross, the boiler house was also set at 90 degrees to the engine house, due to the constricted nature of the site. Steam supply to the engines was provided by three Lancashire boilers, each approximately 35 feet long by six feet in diameter.

Far from seeking to make up for these delays, Brunel had decided by the summer of 1845 to delay all details of the Atmospheric in order to profit from the Croydon's experiences. This was made public at the August meeting. By the February 1846 meeting, the decision had been made to open the line using locomotives; and all that Brunel could say about the Atmospheric was that there would be "considerable delay" but "you will be perfectly satisfied with the result". The Board expressed their 'undiminished confidence' in the Atmospheric. But by this date a considerable current of local criticism of the Atmospheric idea was becoming evident (albeit emanating in part from those who would by nature have been opposed to all new-fangled ideas anyway). It was also becoming clear that the capital costs of the system would be far above Brunel's estimate; the S.D.R.'s 1846 Act added a further £611,666 to the company's authorised capital to cope.

Boulton & Watt's foreman, a Mr Turner, arrived in Devon on 15th November 1845 to supervise the erection of their engines at Exeter (which was progressing some way in advance of the other locations) and Turf; and Rennie's foreman arrived at much the same time to start preparation at Countess Wear. There was then a dispute as to whether the S.D.R. or the manufacturers were obliged to supply the labour for erection! By April 1846 the engines at these three locations were nearly complete, and erection at Starcross and Dawlish began in the summer. In August the Exeter engines were tried, and found to run very roughly. Now it was Brunel's turn to get impatient, for whilst the manufacturers could justly complain of being delayed in starting erection, Brunel considered that they made an extremely long job of it when they *did* start. There were far more problems with the engines, when testing began, than there ought to have been; especially from the Maudslay engines at Dawlish, which had major defects delaying their full commissioning.

The Croydon's Atmospheric opening in January 1846 was followed by a number of breakdowns, and then a complete shutdown in June-July whilst the valve was modified. The national fervour for Atmospheric railways began to take a downward trend, the delays on the S.D.R. doing nothing to help. As 1846 passed by and there was still not a whiff of smoke out of their chimneys, the S.D.R. Board began to fret. Brunel was now regularly failing to attend Board meetings, and in July 1846 the Board appointed a special Committee of Directors to pursue him and establish the exact state of progress on the Atmospheric. At the August 1846 shareholders' meeting Brunel promised Atmospheric trains "in a few weeks", and Samuda proclaimed that "the triumphant success of the Atmospheric principle is now put beyond all question".

0 1 2 3 4 5 6   12 feet

Drawing Mike Middleton, based on Hadfield tracing and Boulton and Watt original of April 1845

Test Running (February to August 1847)

At the end of 1846, Samuda, feeling no doubt that the Exeter engines were now working satisfactorily, moved to South Devon and took up residence in the 'Board House' in Dawlish, from where the successes and failures of the Atmospheric trains could be observed directly. Progress was now much more noticeable. The Exeter engines were now working satisfactorily, and in December 1846 experiments were conducted in exhausting the pipe between Exeter and Countess Wear, a vacuum of 25" being achieved (more than was needed for service running). At various dates in February / March 1847, the Countess Wear, Turf, Starcross and Dawlish engines were started: however the Countess Wear engines broke their eccentrics and could not be used for the first test trains, and the Dawlish engines proved very unsatisfactory.

Then, on 25th February 1847, the first piston carriage was delivered at Exeter; and at 6pm that same day it was sent down to Turf, towing a locomotive behind it[0], to clear the water and dirt out of the pipe. What was clearly regarded as the first official Atmospheric test train ran when Brunel came down. Margary was awoken at 6.30am by the arrival of a note telling him to "get steam up at the Engine House for Mr Brunel". The train left Exeter for Turf at 12.30pm and then made two further trips, Exeter and Turf exhausting a double length of pipe

because of Countess Wear being out of action. All seems to have gone well. After this there were trips to Turf almost every day. On 11th March the piston carriage was towed to Starcross and then ran back atmospherically to Dawlish, but regular trips to Starcross did not begin until after the Starcross engines were started on 23rd March. Meanwhile, on 22nd March, the 'Fire Ball' locomotive towed the piston carriage from Starcross to Dawlish and back, clearing out "a great quantity of water in the pipe". Atmospheric test runs to Dawlish seem to have been delayed until May[11]. Brunel was making frequent visits at this period to carry out experiments. The Flying Post reported in March that the test trains had "caused much curiosity" locally, and "excited no little wonder and surprise".

26th June saw Samuda promising the line would be ready in two weeks', providing faults in the Dawlish engines were rectified. They were given new steam pipes and condensers, and seem to have worked tolerably well after this, although always underpowered. On 3rd August Brunel told the Board that things would be ready "in a few days", and his suggestion was approved that several Atmospheric trains should be run in addition to the normal timetable.

In the meantime came the shocking news that the Croydon had abandoned Atmospheric working on 3rd May. Although this was due to the Croydon having been taken over by the anti-Atmospheric Brighton company, and not to any upsurge of failures in working, it must nevertheless have left the S.D.R. feeling uncomfortably isolated. But at a special shareholders' meeting on 22nd May the Board still pledged its support for the Atmospheric. A side-effect of the Croydon abandonment was a letter from the Secretary of the L.B.S.C.R. asking if the S.D.R. wanted to buy any of the Croydon's Atmospheric equipment; they did not.

The Ghost Service (August to September 1847)

From Monday 16th August 1847, two Atmospheric trains were run each way between Exeter and Teignmouth, stopping at each station on a timetabled basis in order to test the system realistically, but not carrying ordinary passengers. Some goods trains were also run atmospherically from this date. At the end of the month Brunel reported "The tube and valve appear in good order, and the whole has worked well". But it was only at this period that the details of the starting arrangements at the stations, and other traffic matters, were worked out. Or, as the anti-Atmospheric Woolmer's Gazette put it in a piece entitled "Atmospheric Vagaries" on 28th August, "every day brings forth new obstacles, which are only overcome by fresh mechanical contrivances". This column became a regular feature of the paper as it dredged up every incident it could get hold of, and made up others.

The Start of Public Service (September 1847)

The 'ghost service' was running sufficiently well for Brunel and Samuda to decide after only three weeks that it should become an advertised public service as from Monday 13th September. The timings were 3.10pm and 6.0pm from Exeter, and 10.45am and 4.0pm from Teignmouth[2]. Samuda had given instructions that he was to be notified immediately of any delays to Atmospheric trains, but at the end of the first week there had not been any. Even Woolmer's had to concede that the passenger service had been "tolerably successful", and reported a failure on a goods train. As a result of this success, three of the ordinary trains (the 9.50am down, and 8.20am and 12.30pm up) were transferred to Atmospheric working (between Exeter and Teignmouth) as from 20th September, and more followed in October. The piston carriages remained in the train as far as Newton, where there was a long booked stop anyway, to save station time at Teignmouth.

There were no public celebrations, but on 7th September the S.D.R. Engineers organised a little celebration of their own, a Ball in Sea Lawn House; "a very brilliant achievement... a suite of three rooms was appointed to the dancing, which was sustained with unwonted animation until long after daylight on Wednesday morning... the ices, confectionery, and wines were of the most recherché description... the decorations, lights and furniture for the occasion were supplied by Mr Tapper of Dawlish, by whose taste the whole interior assumed the splendour of fairy magnificence". All the main figures attended, except that Brunel was (as ever) occupied elsewhere, Mrs Brunel having to come on her own. Invitations also went out to many of the gentry of the neighbourhood.

Despite this progress, the Board's dissatisfaction with Brunel reached new heights in April 1847. They demanded a Resident Engineer who would be more readily available. They also wanted some definite answer from Samuda on when public services to Teignmouth could begin. Samuda attended the 11th May Board Meeting and stated that the Dawlish to Teignmouth pipe was now being connected to the Engine Houses, the Teignmouth engines would be started on 22nd May, and the line to Teignmouth ready for traffic on 15th June. In the event, the Teignmouth engines complained (Rennies complained that the S.D.R. had failed to supply any coal!) and regular test running then began to Teignmouth.

Reporting to the August 1847 shareholders' meeting, Brunel absolved Samuda of any blame, being, "I am not surprised that the public and proprietors have become impatient" he continued. The satisfaction of seeing the Atmospheric at last completed was tempered by a weariness of it created by the long delays, and this was not to be without influence on its ultimate fate.

Drafting the August 1847 report, Brunel also included the admission "the delays and difficulties - have been so wearying and incessant, that I have myself more than once repented having made the attempt". The last thirteen words were crossed out before the report was printed, and so the shareholders never heard them, Brunel no doubt feeling the admission inappropriate at that stage. But we can still read them.

Engine House Cross Section

One of the two 40hp engines is seen in end view, with its vertical steam cylinder sitting at floor level and vacuum cylinder sitting on top of a cast iron frame 20 feet above, where a separate pump room was created. A substantial crosshead, mounted on the piston rod between the two cylinders, drove two huge connecting rods which turned a crank shaft below floor level. This was solidly mounted in the foundations and smooth running was ensured by an 18 feet diameter flywheel. One of the two secondary 12hp engines is seen alongside, with its flywheel against the external wall. The flywheel shaft passes through the wall to the exterior, so the engine could possibly have supplied mechanical power and vacuum.

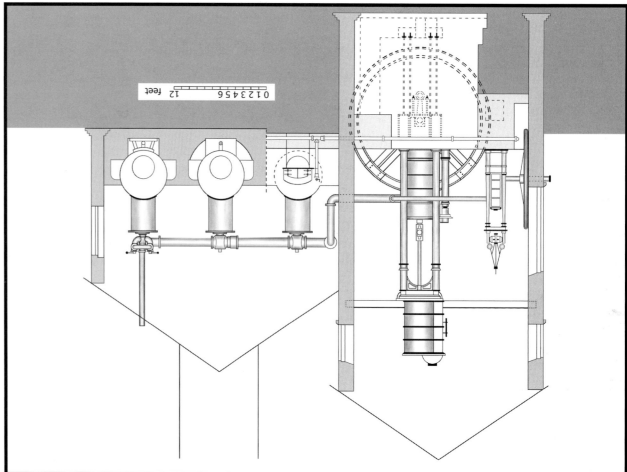

0 1 2 3 4 5 6   12 feet

Drawing Mike Middleton, based on Hadfield tracing and Boulton and Watt original of April 1845

Exeter St. David's

Exeter Engine House is seen in 1909, when it was used to produce gas for coach lighting. Ventilation louvres and chimneys have been added to the boiler room roof, whilst gasometers and various outbuildings have been erected. The engine room has been strengthened to support the locomotive depot water tank, fed by pumps located in a new brick building to the left of the boiler room. Water was obtained from an adjacent well. To the left is the overall roof of the substantial new Bristol and Exeter Railway station of 1862-1864, designed by Bristol architect Henry Lloyd and B.&E.R. engineer Francis Fox.

P.H.

An opportunist shot through the window of a moving train, showing a loco coming into Exeter depot, the photographer was probably quite pleased to get it even this sharp. His photo of 8th August 1963 has however captured a unique close-up of the former Engine House. Aesthetically, the water tank fitted very well over the corbelled stonework of the original eaves; luckily the previous tiled roof had been hipped, so the corbels extended all the way round. Steel strengthening plates can be seen in the walls, and the tank still seems to be full of water, judging by the float positions. 7022 Hereford Castle was a B.R. built engine, running from 1949 until 1965.

Exeter St. Thomas

Originally known as St. Thomas, the station was renamed St. Thomas (Exeter) in April 1853, and Exeter (St. Thomas) in May 1897. In 1861 the viaduct was widened on the west side (away from the city), and a second track brought into use which necessitated the construction of a separate Up platform. A new train shed was built across both lines, with stone walls and wood and iron roof structure. It is seen here circa 1920, with maintenance work in progress. There are ladders up to the roof from each platform, scaffolding and netting within. The glazing was removed in the 1950s, but the basic structure of the train shed remained intact until demolished in 1971. The wide space between the tracks bears witness to the line's Broad Gauge origins.

G.S.

Also in 1861, in connection with the doubling of the viaduct and erection of the new train shed, elegant new two-storey buildings were built on the city side of the viaduct. The South Devon Railway only had access rights to St. David's, whereas St. Thomas was their own property. The station was therefore styled to enhance the S.D.R.'s status within Exeter. Rendered walls featured semi-circular arched windows, much in fashion at the period. The station was partially unstaffed from 3rd May 1971, only being manned on summer weekends. The buildings have been let out for commercial use. As seen here, they are currently used as a Chinese restaurant and in immaculate condition.

Starcross is the most familiar of the surviving Engine Houses, being prominently situated in the main street, adjacent to the station and opposite the ferry landing from Exmouth. The soft red Breccia stone used for the walling has weathered significantly, lending an air of history to the structure, but the Bath stone window and door surrounds and corbelling to the eaves remain crisp.

The building acted as a museum to the Atmospheric Railway from 1982, but this has subsequently closed. The grade 1 listed structure was purchased in 1993 by the Starcross Fishing and Sailing Club. Dingy storage facilities opened in 1994, followed by the new Brunel Tower Clubhouse on the upper floor in 1997. Surviving features include a massive water tank below ground level.

Photo: Rob Speare

"in acknowledgement of the many kind instances of hospitality" which the Engineers had enjoyed from them. This was a time of optimism for the Atmospheric cause, the only cloud on the horizon being the possibility that the system might not be extended beyond Totnes. A large new Atmospheric staff of engineers, stokers, valve men and greasers had been appointed in recent months, headed by James Pearson who was made Atmospheric Superintendent in September (at £300 per annum). Pearson had been in charge of the engines on the Croydon (under Hensman, the Croydon's Atmospheric Manager, who was also now in South Devon but working as Samuda's assistant, not as an S.D.R. employee). The newly-appointed Atmospheric staff had not endured the worrying delays of the previous three years, and were no doubt keen to prove the practical success of the system. The public also took to the Atmospheric trains, thanks to the more comfortable ride and absence of smoke and cinders. "Master piston is getting a general favourite", reported one local correspondent, and another noted that "the pleasure of travelling is much increased by this mode – you can write while the speed is 50mph or more".

Atmospheric Service to Newton
(December 1847)
Following the completion of the Summer House and Newton engines (the former were given the same improved pipes and condensers as at Dawlish, and never seem to have caused any trouble) trial running to Newton began in November 1847. All proving well, those ordinary trains that were being worked atmospherically

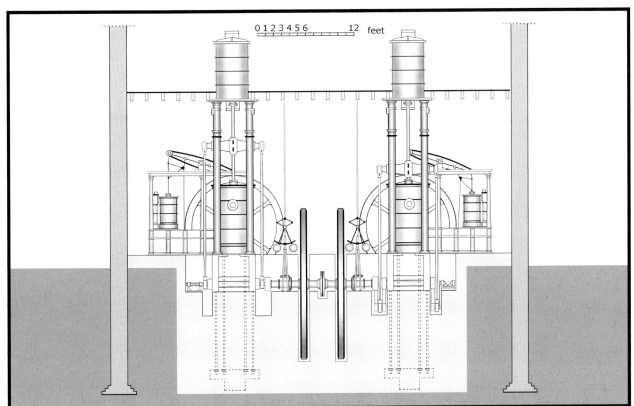

were so worked through to Newton as from 17th December. From 10th January 1848 *most* trains were worked atmospherically through to Newton[13].

The Full Atmospheric Service
(February 1848)
The Board had decided in August 1847 that, as soon as it was felt practicable, the *whole* service between Exeter and Newton should be worked atmospherically, in order to give a full trial to the system. Accordingly Brunel was asked on 15th February 1848 to "arrange the removal of locomotive engines from the line above Newton". This was arranged quickly, full Atmospheric working beginning on Wednesday 23rd February. The Engine Houses now had to work 20 hours a day. It is noticeable, incidentally, that *all* the major developments in bringing the Atmospheric into use took place a few days before the February and August shareholders' meetings!

Punctuality and Problems
On the whole, the working of the Atmospheric seems to have been as good as many a contemporary locomotive-worked line; probably *better* on most days, but, like modern electric traction, the Atmospheric was more subject to serious disruption in extreme weather than was the steam locomotive. However, the S.D.R. Atmospheric was subject throughout its life to a "regular system to depreciate it", especially the "false and malicious charges" in *Woolmer's* (as Gill called them in August 1848). So all its *faults* tended to be prominently reported, and this created in later minds a false picture of continual chaos[14]. The S.D.R. never had cause for Atmospheric

working to be suspended (except for a few trains on some days of heavy frost), nor did any of the stationary engines (despite their inadequacies) break down in service, as the Croydon's had. At the February 1848 Shareholders' meeting, Thomas Woollcombe, a leading Director, reported a survey (taken from the guards' journals) of 884 trains run by Atmospheric power between 13th September 1847 and 18th January 1848. As far as net running times were concerned, this showed that:-

30 trains had gained 11-15 minutes on schedule.

327 trains had gained 6-10 minutes on schedule.

57 trains had lost 1-5 minutes on schedule.

8 trains had lost 6-10 minutes on schedule.

1 train had lost 11-15 minutes on schedule.

3 trains had lost 16 or more minutes on schedule.

10 trains had failed.

This was "an able defence of the Atmospheric", thought the *Western Times*. Unfortunately, a defence of the punctuality of the Atmospheric had become very necessary. There had been bad frosts on many days in December to February, and this had affected the valve (preventing it from closing properly, and so leaving the pipe non-airtight) causing serious delays. The worst day was Tuesday 18th January; *Woolmers* described the scene at Teignmouth (hopefully not wholly untruthfully):-

"In the station yard were congregated Porters, Policemen, Engine drivers, Omnibus drivers, guards, passengers, and a host of idlers, talking of valves frosted, grease frozen, no vacuums.... in the office stood numerous passengers with indigo faces, chattering teeth, and benumbed fingers, all pressing as close to the counter as possible, inside of which was a warm stove for the benefit of the clerks, whose fiery eyes were stuck on the telegraph dials – "Train Stuck?", "How is your vacuum?", "Where's the Express?", "Have you got an engine?", "Is the line clear?".... the excited clerks scarcely knew what they were about.... the half past 8 came down at length at ½ past 10, and the ½ past 10 came down at ½ past 12...."

Engine House Longitudinal Section
The heavily engineered foundations are particularly apparent in this view, extending over 16 feet below floor level. The crank shafts of the two principal engines are mounted 3'6" below floor level and fitted with coupling plates so that the two engines can be run together if necessary. The long crossheads driving the pairs of connecting rods are prominent. From the size of the cranks the stroke can be measured at six feet. In the background, it can be seen that secondary power is supplied by two small beam engines. These have 12 feet diameter flywheels and the steam cylinders can be seen mounted on iron platforms near the outer ends of the room.

Even on this day, though, "all was well" by the afternoon. The frequent problems in these weeks nevertheless had a bad impact on the credibility of the Atmospheric just when it was beginning to seem a success. "We hope the Directors are well founded in their continuing enthusiasm for the Atmospheric", wrote the by no means anti-Atmospheric *Western Times* on 12th February, "because the hindrances and irregularities which occurred during the late frost were such as to have demanded their serious attention". 'Vacuum' seems to have become something of a joke-word locally; one Teignmouth correspondent reported having heard a 'coal-heaver' ask an exhausted mate "How's your vacuum?"

After February, though, the frosts vanished and confidence returned for a while. In March the *Plymouth Herald* reported "the regular and perfect daily operations of the Atmospheric", and *Woolmer's* could not find an anti-Atmospheric story for many weeks running. All remained well until May, when the valve began to cause problems again, as described later.

Working the Atmospheric
Very little information is available on the details of how S.D.R. Atmospheric trains were actually worked. All Brunel's records of the Atmospheric were destroyed; there is nothing in the S.D.R. records beyond odd references in the minutes; and the enormous national interest in the Atmospheric was dying out by the time the S.D.R. actually began working, so there are no journal articles of use. The picture has to be reconstructed from (often exaggerated) press descriptions of times when things went wrong, and the pro- and anti- Atmospheric pamphlets printed in December 1848. All that is known about some aspects of working is that Brunel *said in 1845* that they would not cause any difficulties!

Shunting and Forming Trains
At an Institution of Civil Engineers debate in February 1845, Brunel stated that he "anticipated doing all the station work with as much facility as with locomotives, and even *more* conveniently". But he did not explain *how*. Atmospheric power was for all practical purposes incapable of carrying out any shunting; piston carriages could not reverse, and there were no pipes in the station area in any case. However, one must look at things in the context of the 1840s, when vehicles were normally pushed by hand at stations anyway; so this defect of the Atmospheric was not of much concern then. There were also always locomotives available at Exeter and Newton, where the change of traction took place. The S.D.R. was the only railway that ever ran *goods* trains by Atmospheric power. Apart from the fact that the daily goods had sometimes now to be run in two

SDR Timetable from 20th September 1847

Down	Weekdays										Sundays					
	Mail									Goods	Mail					Goods
Class	1,2	1,2,3	1,2	1,2	1,2	1,2	1,2,3	1,2	1,2		1,2	1,2,3	1,2	1,2,3	1,2	
	Steam	Steam	Atmos	Steam	Steam	Atmos	Steam	Atmos	Steam	Steam	Steam	Steam	Atmos	Steam	Atmos	Steam
	am	am	am	pm	pm	pm	pm	pm	pm	pm	am	am	pm	pm	pm	pm
Exeter	4.15	7.50	9.50	12.00	2.20	3.10	5.40	6.00	10.10	10.20	4.15	7.45	3.10	5.40	6.00	10.20
Starcross	4.32	8.12	10.12	12.22	2.42	3.29	6.02	6.19	10.32	-	4.32	8.08	3.29	6.03	6.19	-
Dawlish	4.42	8.22	10.22	12.32	2.52	3.40	6.12	6.30	10.42	-	4.42	8.19	3.40	6.14	6.30	-
Teignmouth	4.52	8.32	10.32	12.42	3.02	3.50	6.22	6.40	10x52	11x05	4.52	8.30	3.50	6.25	6.40	11x05
Newton	5.10	8x50	10x50	1x00	3.20	-	6.40	-	11.10	11.50	5.10	8x50	-	6.45	-	11.50
Totnes	5.40	9.20	11.20	1.30	3.50	-	7.10	-	11.40	am 12.20	5.40	9.20	-	7.15	-	am 12.20

Up	Weekdays										Sundays					
								Mail		Goods					Mail	Goods
Class	1,2,3	1,2	1,2	1,2	1,2	1,2	1,2	1,2	1,2,3		1,2,3	1,2	1,2	1,2	1,2	
	Steam	Atmos	Atmos	Steam	Atmos	Atmos	Steam	Steam	Steam	Steam	Steam	Atmos	Atmos	Atmos	Steam	Steam
	am	am	am	am	pm	pm	pm	pm	pm	pm	am	am	pm	pm	pm	pm
Totnes	6.20	8.20	-	10.25	12.30	-	3.55	7.20	8.00	9.30	6.15	8.20	-	-	7.15	9.30
Newton	6.50	8x50	-	10x55	1x00	-	4.25	7.50	8.30	10.15	6.45	8x50	-	-	7.45	10.15
Teignmouth	7.02	9.02	10.45	11.07	1.12	4.00	4.37	8.02	8.42	11x45	6.57	9.03	10.45	4.00	7.58	11x45
Dawlish	7.12	9.12	10.53	11.16	1.22	4.08	4.47	8.12	8.52	-	7.07	9.14	10.53	4.08	8.09	-
Starcross	7.23	9.23	11.03	11.26	1.33	4.18	4.58	8.23	9.03	-	7.18	9.26	11.03	4.18	8.21	-
Exeter	7.50	9.50	11.25	11.50	2.00	4.40	5.25	8.50	9.30	12.30	7.43	9.55	11.25	4.40	8.50	12.30

Notes: All trains stop at St. Thomas, except the 4.15am down.
Crossing of trains shown: X.
Classes carried on Sundays are estimated.

Times of Goods trains not definitively known at this date – times shown are taken from Goods bill dated 1.12.1848, Devon County Record Office Doc. 39562.

portions to keep train weights down, the goods workings do not seem to have caused any problems. Of course the S.D.R. goods traffic was very limited in quantity at this date, and Teignmouth was the only station where hand-shunting could not be supplemented by locomotive shunting if necessary. In addition to the public goods traffic there were coal trains for the Engine House sidings, and these were also atmospherically powered (and, presumably, shunted by hand).

The piston carriages were always detached (down) and attached (up) at Newton, although most trains ran beyond. On arrival at Newton (or Exeter) the driver had to 'wind up' the piston. It is typical of our ignorance of working details that even this piece of information is derived from a casual reference in a newspaper report; we may *guess* that the S.D.R. piston carriages had a piston at each end, and that the other one was lowered for the return journey[15]. The piston carriages were presumably pushed by hand off and on to the trains.

Starting Trains from Stations

Because the pipe could not be run through points, it had to stop short of the station throats beyond the loop points, and this created problems in starting trains away from the stations. St. Thomas was an exception, as there were no points and no break in the pipe, the station being in the middle of the Exeter to Countess Wear pipe section. Accordingly there were no problems in starting here; one simply had to release the brakes. The suburban-passenger-only Croydon had started trains by gravity, the stations being built on top of artificial gradients; but this was impracticable on a main line like the S.D.R.

Two methods of starting trains were used on the S.D.R:-

(1) Starting Ropes.
A separate piston working in an auxiliary 8" pipe outside the rails had a rope attached to it, the other end of which was hooked to the train. This auxiliary pipe ran for some 100 yards to the start of the main pipe, at which point the driver released the rope. No further hard facts are available, but the accompanying drawing attempts an explanation. This system was definitely used at Starcross, Dawlish and Teignmouth (and we may *assume* that it was used at Exeter). It is no surprise that the ropes were prone to breaking. On 9th November 1847 David Drake, an S.D.R. labourer, was busy barrowing coals from trucks to the Engine House at Starcross, when the 3.10pm down Atmospheric train arrived. When this train was signalled to start, it did not move, and "all available porters and policemen were called to push it". It was then noticed that the rope had broken; unfortunately Drake had been passing at that moment, and was found "lying on the ground frightfully injured from concussion". He later died from his injuries. On 1st January 1848

a similar incident at Teignmouth resulted in a valveman having his legs broken, rendering amputation necessary. A rope-break at Dawlish had more amusing effects; the piston shot through the pipe on its own and out into the air at the far end "making a pretty bobbery". *Woolmer's* thought that wire ropes would be better. A different kind of danger was revealed at Starcross on 4th March 1848, when Porters Field and Collings left the down end rope lying across the lines, resulting in the 10.45am up train hitting it and the piston carriage being derailed "and the piston much injured". Pearson was instructed to "place a guiding bar on the platform to mark the proper direction for placing the rope".

(2) Separate Lengths of Main Pipe.
By January 1848 experiments were being carried out on an alternative system (which may have been used at Newton from the start) in which separate lengths of 15" pipe were laid between the rails in the station area for use by the normal piston. Again details are unknown; one assumes that these pipes stopped short of the loop points and that trains had to coast over the points to the start of the section pipe. After the March 1848 derailment, Brunel was asked to "expedite the arrangements for dispensing with the towing ropes at Dawlish and Starcross". This may mean that Dawlish and Starcross were by then the last places still using ropes; in any event there were no further reports of rope accidents after this.

Gauges were provided for the drivers to ascertain the level of vacuum in the pipe ahead, so they would not attempt to leave a station if there was not yet sufficient vacuum.

Stopping Trains at Stations

The initial braking, prior to the train leaving the main pipe at the station throat, must have been done against the Atmospheric power, making judgment more difficult than in the case of locomotives. At St. Thomas, the *whole* braking had to be done against the Atmospheric. On both the Croydon and the S.D.R., the Atmospheric trains had a reputation for overshooting the stations; one wonders if this was because the drivers were frightened of stopping short, which would have left them stuck helpless, and so tended to err in the opposite direction? Trains on locomotive lines also frequently overshot at this period, but they could reverse back into the station, whereas an Atmospheric train could not and its passengers had to climb down onto the track where it stopped[16].

All this was naturally made much of by the anti-Atmospheric faction. *Woolmer's* reported, possibly truthfully, that on 29th January 1848 "the 9.50am down train refused to be brought up at the St. Thomas station, nor was a check to its speed effected until it had got about ¾ mile beyond.... Several passengers were waiting at the station, and they refused to wait two hours for the next train. The only alternative was to bring back a first class carriage by manual propulsion. Into this, passengers of all classes were closely padded, and then, by the united aid of policemen and porters, the carriage was pushed back on to the train, which was quietly waiting amid the bleak air of the marshes".

Other instances reported were of a down train at Teignmouth that only stopped at Shaldon Bridge (".... off started the porters in their best Sunday suits, and after a lapse of 30 minutes the carriages were pushed back singly into the station at a funeral-like pace"), a down train at Dawlish stopping in the Kennaway Tunnel, and a piston carriage running alone on test shooting past St. David's and only coming to a halt "....half way to Cowley Bridge".

When the train overshot to the extent that the piston entered the next pipe section, the braking would again have to be done against the Atmospheric power[17] and the train might start *accelerating* again if the brakes were in a poor way. This happened to the 4.00pm up on 24th August 1847 which was not supposed to be carrying passengers, (but clearly was, suggesting that the 'ghost service' was less ghostly than it should have been !) There was a large party on board going to dine in Dawlish, but as the train approached there was consternation at its pace. "Hollo !" shouts one, "Where the ***** are you going?", "Stop ! Stop !"

SDR Timetable from 5th May 1848

Down

	Weekdays											Sundays					
	Mail	Exp						Exp	Goods			Mail					Goods
Class	1,2	1,2,3	1,2	1,2	1,2	1,2	1,2,3	1,2	1,2	1,2		1,2	1,2,3	1,2	1,2,3	1,2	
	Atmos	Atmos	Atmos	Atmos	Atmos	Atmos	Atmos	Atmos	Atmos	Atmos	Atmos	Atmos	Atmos	Atmos	Atmos	Atmos	Atmos
	am	am	am	pm	pm	pm	pm	pm	pm	pm	pm	am	am	pm	pm	pm	pm
G.W.R. dep. London	pm 8.55				am 9.50	am 7.45		am 10.15	am 2.00	am 5.30		pm 8.55					
B.&E.R. arr. Exeter	am 4.05				pm 2.15	pm 2.40		pm 5.25	pm 8.50	pm 10.00		am 4.05					
Exeter	4.15	6.50	9.55	12.00	2.00	3.00	5.20	5.45	8.55	10.05	10.20	4.15	6.50	12.00	5.20	5.45	10.20
Starcross	4.32	7.09	10.14	12.19	2.39	3.19	5.39	6.04	9.14	10.24	-	4.32	7.09	12.19	5.39	6.04	-
Dawlish	4.42	7.20	10.25	12.30	2.50	3.30	5.50	6.15	9.25	10.35	-	4.42	7.20	12.30	5.50	6.15	-
Teignmouth	4.52	7.30	10x35		3.00	3.40	6.00	6.25	9.30	10x45	11x05	4.52	7.30		6.00	6.25	11x05
Newton	5.05	7x45	10.50	12x55	3.15	-	5.15	6x40	9.50	11.00	11.50	5.05	7.45	12x55	5.15	6x40	11.50
Totnes	5.30	8.15	-	1.25	3.45	-	→	7.10	-	11.25	am 12.20	5.30	8.15	1.25	→	7.10	am 12.20
Laira	6.30	9.20	-	2.20	4.45	-	→	8.15	-	am 12.20	1.50	6.30	9.20	2.20	→	8.15	1.50

Up

	Weekdays												Sundays					
											Mail	Goods					Mail	Goods
Class	1,2,3	1,2	1,2	1,2	1,2	1,2	1,2	1,2	1,2,3	1,2	1,2		1,2,3	1,2	1,2,3	1,2	1,2	
	Atmos	Atmos	Atmos	Atmos	Atmos	Atmos	Atmos	Atmos	Atmos	Atmos	Atmos	Atmos	Atmos	Atmos	Atmos	Atmos	Atmos	Atmos
	am	am	am	am	am	am	pm	pm	pm	pm	pm	pm	am	am	pm	pm	pm	pm
Laira	-	7.30	-	-	9.35	11.30	-	2.55	5.10	-	6.25	8.00	7.30	11.30	5.10	-	6.25	8.00
Totnes	-	8.25	-	-	10.30	12.25	-	3.50	6.05	-	7.20	9.30	8.25	12.25	6.05	-	7.20	9.30
Newton	7x45	8.55	9.30	-	10x55	12x55	-	4.15	6x40	7.20	7.50	10.15	8.55	12x55	6x40	7.20	7.50	10.15
Teignmouth	7.57	9.07	9.42	10x45	11.07	1.07	4.00	4.27	6.52	7.32	8.02	11x45	9.08	1.07	6.55	7.33	8.02	11x45
Dawlish	8.07	9.17	-	10.53	11.17	1.17	4.08	4.37	7.02	7.42	8.12	-	9.19	1.17	7.04	7.44	8.12	-
Starcross	8.18	9.28	-	11.03	11.28	1.28	4.18	4.48	7.13	7.53	8.23	-	9.30	1.28	7.13	7.55	8.23	-
Exeter	8.40	9.50	-	11.25	11.50	1.50	4.40	5.10	7.35	8.15	8.50	12.30	9.55	1.50	7.40	8.20	8.50	12.30

	Exp					Mail							Mail			
		pm												pm		
B.&E.R. dep. Exeter	-	10.00 12.00	-	-	5.30 (Swindon)	-	-	9.00	-		-		3.45	-	-	9.00	-
G.W.R. arr. London	-	pm 4.50 4.30	-	-	-	-	-	am 4.15	-		-		am 10.30	-	-	am 4.15	-

Notes:
- All trains stop at St. Thomas, except the 4.15am down.
- Crossing of trains shown: X.
- Intermediate stops Totnes - Laira not shown.
- Passengers change at Exeter on all services.
- Times of Goods trains not definitively known at this date – times shown are taken from Goods bill dated 1.12.1848, Devon County Record Office Doc. 39562.
- The 5.20 and 5.45pm down combine at Newton.

---

screams another, but all to no purpose, on - on goes the gimcrack into the next 'pipe', and with accelerated speed vanishes the hope of dinner; in due course the train reaches Starcross where, more obedient, the breaks did their purpose. Neither bus nor fly was to be had, nor any down train expected...."

Entering and Leaving the Pipe

At the ends of each 3-mile-long pipe section, there were automatically-worked valves which served to keep the pipe airtight when they were shut, but which had to open briefly to allow the piston to enter and leave the pipe. (These valves are not to be confused with the leather longitudinal valve). The piston did not *hit* these valves; when entering the pipe it worked a trip which opened the valve by cutting off the air supply to it, and when leaving the pipe it pushed open the valve by air pressure (the remaining air in the pipe being compressed into the ever-decreasing distance between the piston and the valve until the pressure was sufficient to force open the valve)[18]. At the intermediate Engine Houses (Countess Wear, Turf and Summer House) trains passed from one pipe section to another at full line speed. Although this was not good for the piston, it *worked*. There must have been a gap of several yards where the siding points were, over which trains had to coast.

Maintenance of the Longitudinal Valve

Great trouble was experienced in keeping the longitudinal leather valve in good order. Samuda had designed a 'weather cover' for the valve, but this was not used on the S.D.R. either because of the additional cost, or perhaps in the fond belief that the Devon climate was too mild to justify it. If it *had* been installed, much trouble might have been avoided. Firstly, the 'composition' used to seal tight any gaps between the pipe and the leather valve (on its opening side) failed to act effectively. A lime soap was used initially, which went hard, obliging the S.D.R. to employ staff along the line to follow each train and apply more composition where necessary. Subsequently a mixture of cod oil and soap was used; this was more fluid, but tended to get sucked into the pipe as a result.

Secondly, the leather valve had its natural oils sucked out by the vacuum in the pipe, leaving it pervious to air (affecting the seal) and water (which froze in winter, preventing it from shutting effectively) both of which affected the vacuum adversely. To combat this, the 'greasers' along the line had to continually apply oil to the leather to replace the natural oils.

Water getting into the pipe, especially overnight, provided an obstruction to the piston and reduced the speed of the trains. A piston carriage was run along the line first thing each morning, to drive the water out of the pipe. The further problems that affected the valve in the summer of 1848 are noted later.

Engine House Pumping

Each Engine House pumped for trains coming towards it. (In theory it was also possible for an Engine House to pump for trains going away from it[19], but this was not sensible because it would have meant pumping having to cease the moment the train entered the section, so that the vacuum would have decreased as the train proceeded, and, given the leaky valve, the train might not have made it). Pumping began 5 to 8 minutes before the train left the previous station, because it took longer to get a good vacuum at the far end (where the train was) than at the rear end, and continued throughout the passage of the train through the section. Brunel had originally anticipated that only 3 minutes' pumping before departure would be needed, but in practice the valve leakage increased this. Until the Telegraph was installed (see later) pumping had to start in time for the train's *scheduled* departure from the previous station, and carry on until the train actually appeared; but after the Telegraph was available, the start of pumping could be delayed until the time appropriate to be ready for the likely *actual* departure of the train, as advised.

It was possible for an Engine House to pump the two sections of pipe either side of it simultaneously, but this was only occasionally necessary, as there were no *booked* crossings anywhere between Exeter and Newton in the Atmospheric period, and comparatively few non-booked trains about. (Brunel said in 1845 that one of the Engine Houses between Exeter and Newton would have "water power in addition to steam power" to enable it to regularly pump both ways so that trains could be crossed there; but this was never done). It was also possible for an Engine House to be cut out of circuit altogether, but this was undesirable in service due to the longer time needed for the other Engine Houses to get a vacuum in a *double* length of pipe, and the only record of it happening on the S.D.R. is when Countess Wear was out of action in the test period. A further possibility envisaged by Brunel in 1845, but never heard of in practice, was for the *two* Engine Houses in advance of the train to exhaust six miles of pipe together simultaneously. The workload of the Engine Houses varied considerably, primarily in relation to the lengths of pipe either side, as shown in the Table. Ideally the Engine Houses would have been equally spaced, but this was impossible due to it being necessary to have an Engine House at each station. Hence the Starcross – Dawlish – Teignmouth sections were dictated; this meant a high workload for those Engine Houses, but it would have been quite uneconomic to build intermediate Houses between them. There were also variations in the numbers of

trains. Exeter and Newton, which generally pumped in one direction only had the easiest task. The engines and vacuum pumps were underpowered for their job, primarily because they had been designed for a 13" pipe rather than 15" (100hp instead of 80hp would have been appropriate for 15" pipes). As a result they had to be overworked, although this was an economic problem rather than one that affected the train service. It was also often necessary to work at higher vacuums than intended (20" instead of 15") due to the high valve leakage. Merthyr steam coal was used, delivered to Bridgwater by sea, and thence by rail.

Speeds

Speeds of up to 70mph were achieved when all was working well, but the *usual* running speed seems to have been nearer 40 mph. Speed was very much affected by train weight; some amateur train-timing in September 1847 over the level mile between MP197 and MP198 revealed 68mph from a 30 ton train, 60 mph from a 50 ton train, and 34 mph from a 100 ton train. The 1848 watercolours show trains of 5 coaches behind the piston coach, probably weighing 60 tons at most. The scheduled timings of the Atmospheric trains – 40 minutes to Teignmouth, 55 to Newton – were the same as those of locomotive-hauled trains in the years either side; but it seems from Woollcombe's figures that the Atmospheric had about 5 minutes in hand on these schedules.

Some very fast start-to-stop timings were reported from light test trains, thanks to quick acceleration. On 25th September 1847 there was a 17-minute run from St. Thomas to Teignmouth (14 miles). According to the *Western Times*, there was a 20-minute run from Newton to Exeter on 19th January 1848, and a 21½-minute return on the 20th, the timings of the latter given as Exeter 9.50am, Starcross 9.57am, Teignmouth 10.05am and Newton 10.11½am[20]. Whatever the exact figures, it seems likely that the S.D.R. Atmospheric trains were capable of faster start-to-stop times than any other form of transport then known. Because the wheels were not engaging in traction, and because the piston in the pipe provided a steadying effect, the motion of the Atmospheric trains was much smoother than that of a locomotive-hauled train, and curves could be taken faster. However, when leakage in the valve was very bad, progress could be very irregular, and speeds might be reduced to a crawl.

Atmospheric trains were free from the possibility of that class of collision which most vexed the minds of passengers of the time, that is, one train running into the back of another travelling in the same direction between stations. Samuda also told the Parliamentary Committee that "it is impossible that we can have trains travelling in opposite directions on the same length of tube"; but that is clearly not strictly true – all trains that overshot the stations and ran on into the next pipe section would obviously have hit any train coming the other way at the time, and it was only thanks to the lack of booked crossings that this never happened. The Starcross derailment was the only train accident under the Atmospheric. For workers on the line, though, the Atmospheric trains were very dangerous. They made little track noise, and the only warning of their approach was the blowing of a horn. "The Policemen complain that they cannot hear the horn", reported *Woolmer's*. Two greasers were run over and killed by trains (although one was drunk and had fallen asleep!).

The Atmospheric Beyond Newton

The question of the Atmospheric beyond Newton is so closely linked to the fate of the system as a whole that it cannot be ignored here. Brunel seems to have decided, at an early stage, to put off any work on the installation beyond Newton. Eventually, in April 1846, the Board raised the subject. This resulted, in August, in their approving the order of six pairs of engines from Boulton & Watt. These were to be of a new design, a 68hp (136hp per pair) horizontal engine based on the 50hp and 82½hp horizontals that Boulton & Watt were then making for the Croydon's Epsom extension, and incorporating many improvements over the existing S.D.R. engines. When the Croydon cancelled its order following the abandonment of Atmospheric working there, the S.D.R. (in June 1847) agreed to take three pairs of these engines also. In the end one pair of the earlier order was cancelled, and Boulton & Watt were left to produce eight pairs of engines, on top of which a further two pairs were ordered from Harveys of Hale in 1847. In February 1847 the Board prodded Brunel about the Engine Houses west of Newton; there was also now Torquay to consider. By April plans were being drawn up for Dainton and Torquay; and on 26th May Brunel made a visit and settled the positions of Totnes, Rattery, Wrangaton and Ivybridge. These were noticeably further apart than the Engine Houses east of Newton, the distances being 4, 4¾, 4½, 4½ and 3½ miles. Nothing was ever settled for beyond Ivybridge[21].

Construction of Dainton, Totnes and Torquay Engine Houses began in the summer of 1847. The engines (a 68hp pair) were in at Dainton by summer 1848, but were never started. Some equipment, including parts of the engines, was installed at Totnes. Torquay was completed as a shell, but nothing was ever installed. Finally, work began at Rattery in January 1848; the buildings were never completed, although the engines were delivered (to Totnes, by sea). These Engine Houses beyond Newton were also in Italianate style, but rather different in appearance to those built east of Newton, as the use of horizontal rather than vertical engines meant that the Engine House proper was much lower and longer. In the summer of 1847, work also began on laying the 22" pipes west of Newton. This was completed as far as Totnes in 1848.

The first nail in the coffin was in August 1847. The day before the shareholders' meeting, the Board had a deputation from George Hudson and other Directors of the Midland (who, as successors to the Bristol & Gloucester, had a sizeable shareholding in the S.D.R., but had not yet obtained a seat on the Board. They wanted any expenditure on the Atmospheric *west of Totnes* to be held back until after the next (February 1848) meeting.

At this stage there was such support for the idea that the Atmospheric must be tested on Dainton incline that nobody sought to suggest halting of expenditure on the Newton to Totnes section. As there was as yet nothing being done west of Totnes anyway, the Board accepted the Midland request; although they managed to evade it somewhat by getting approval for a resolution that expenditure should not be incurred west of Totnes *excepting to provide additional power up the two inclines, which will be necessary in any circumstances.* This enabled work to be undertaken at Rattery and Hemerdon, as well as carrying on at Dainton, Totnes and Torquay, and remained the official line, up to the summer of 1848. At the February 1848 meeting, Brunel stated that Atmospheric working between Newton and Totnes would begin in about "3 or 4 months".

The next nail was driven on 28th March 1848 when the Board told Brunel to arrange for the suspension of work on the engines, except for Dainton, Totnes, Rattery, Hemerdon and Torquay. Finally, on 20th June 1848 the Board asked for the engines (with these exceptions) to be *disposed of* when complete. This was the first action that assumed that there would *never* be any general Atmospheric working west of Totnes. But until August 1848 it was still being assumed that the Atmospheric would be commissioned shortly to Totnes and Torquay, and then as assistant power on Rattery and Hemerdon banks.

The Telegraph Fiasco

The shareholders were no doubt expecting Brunel to report on the successes and problems of the Atmospheric at their February 1848 meeting, now that six months' practical experience had been gained. Instead he told them that he was "refraining from offering any observations" on it, because the *absence of the Telegraph* in the Engine Houses meant that the engines were having to work twice as long as necessary, resulting in excessive fuel consumption. "Only when this evil was removed" he said, "would the Atmospheric become the subject of actual experiment.... to test the economy of working". It was really quite extraordinary that, after six months' trials, the Engineer should suddenly invent some wholly new technical-sounding excuse for refusing comment, and admit at the same time that the proprietors' money was being wasted daily on useless fuel consumption! Unfortunately none of the shareholders seem to have had the acumen to ask Brunel *why* the Telegraph had not been installed, and whose fault it was. One is forced to the conclusion that it was Brunel's fault, and that the matter had simply been sitting in Brunel's in-tray. The Telegraph was an obvious necessity for the efficient working of an Atmospheric railway, primarily to inform Engine Houses when trains were running late to avoid wasteful pumping, but also because they had to

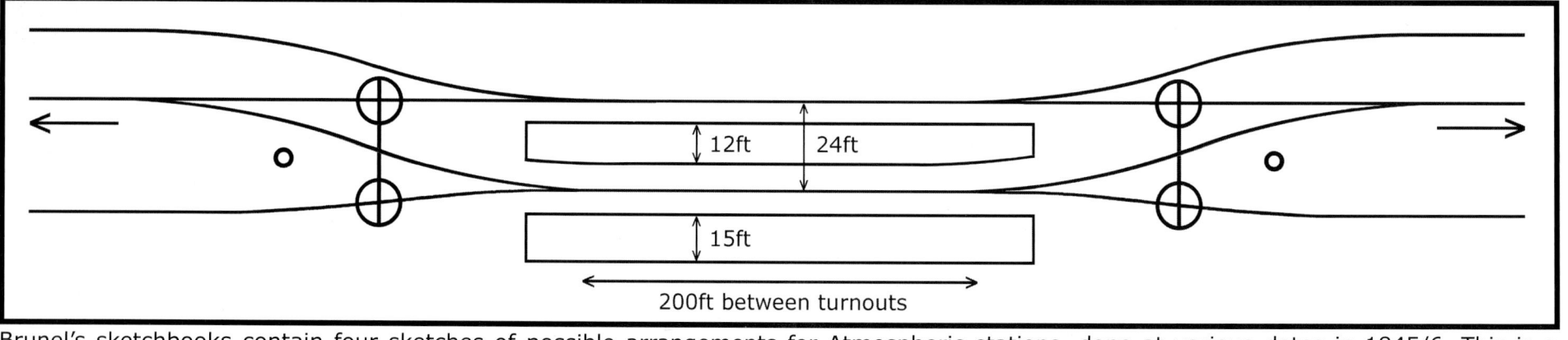

Brunel's sketchbooks contain four sketches of possible arrangements for Atmospheric stations, done at various dates in 1845/6. This is a redrawing of the most detailed of them (which is undated). It matches Brunel's report to the Parliamentary Committee on the Atmospheric in April 1845 stating that S.D.R. stations would have a loop and two platforms. The stations as actually built incorporated the loop but had only one platform. Neither the turntables nor capstans shown were actually provided. The S.D.R. stations ended up having conventional layouts not specially arranged for Atmospheric working, and no particular problems arose from this.

Starcross

This 1936 view of the Engine House from the pier shows the lean of the tower very clearly. The building had been built on poor foundations and, despite two subsequent reconstructions, the tower developed a dangerous list after a few years, putting stress on the engine room walls. To reduce this adverse effect the chimney was soon reduced in height to 56 feet. The lean-to shed to the left of the tower was used by the local permanent way gang. The G.W.R. signal box to the left dated from 1918, and replaced the Saxby and Farmer box of 1874.

The former engine room was used as a Wesleyan chapel from 1867 to 1958, and is seen in this guise in 1936. The intermediate floor has been removed, creating an imposing space appropriate for religious use. The clerestory lighting afforded by the former pump room windows accentuated the effect, whilst of course the building did already have its own bell tower or 'campanile'. By contrast, the former boiler room found more prosaic use, being taken from 1868 by W.H. Parkhouse, coal, potato, hay and manure merchant, where he remained until his death in 1940 at the age of 95.

Dawlish

The earliest close view of the station, taken about 1862. The train shed is seen end on, apparently supported by a large strut. Separate flights of steps serve the booking hall and platform. The water tank was erected around September 1853. It provoked complaints in the local papers about its "horribly vulgar style", and only lasted until 1872. The down platform shelter is visible behind it. The goods shed can be seen behind the station building, and the tower of the former Engine House looms above all. It was demolished in 1873 to release siding space for the new station, but the back wall survives, built into the cliff face.

Not the best of prints, but this is the only known close-up photograph of Dawlish Engine House, dating from about 1866-67. The pale limestone walls of the chimney contrast with the red quoins. The Roman-tiled hipped roof of the boiler room can be seen in front of the campanile and the gabled roof of the taller engine room beyond it. Both seem to be in natural clay tiles, not the black-glazed type unearthed at Turf. In front of the boiler room is George Hennet's coal shed of 1851, demolished in 1868. In the background the train shed and original platform of 1846 are visible. The second platform of 1858 for the down line is also in place, but difficult to pick out. Between the station and the Engine House is the timber-built goods shed of 1849.

Newton is seen from the north on 17th July 1889, with the station pilot, 'Hawthorn' class 2-4-0 Wood in the foreground, dating from January 1866 but in immaculate condition. The main train shed of the station is to the right, built in 1861 to replace the three smaller train sheds from Atmospheric days. The down line is in the centre and the shed on the left used for storing carriages. Part of the works can be seen behind the locomotive.

No complete close-up photos of Newton Engine House are known to survive, but we found this sketch which appeared in the G.W.R. Magazine, probably made around 1890, for it is thought that the Engine House was demolished soon after the end of the Broad Gauge in 1892 in connection with general improvements. The sketch was in newsprint so this image has been re-touched by P.R.G. The chimney may appear squatter than other examples, but the railway is on an embankment, so there is another storey below rail level. The hipped roof of the boiler room can be seen in the foreground, at right angles below the campanile; it appears that the engine room roof has been laid in the usual Roman tiles. Behind the campanile, it appears that the engine room roof has been replaced with a water tank, as was done at Exeter. This tank is also visible in the photo on page 102.

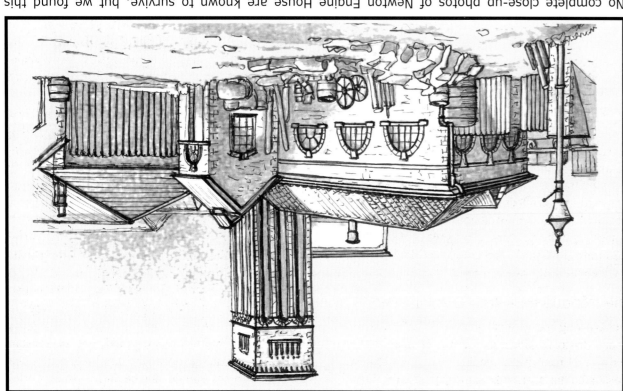

Newton

This view shows the opposite end of Teignmouth station on 11th March 1894, just days before its final demolition. The middle siding has been removed and the down line is being re-laid to a straighter alignment in cross-sleepered track. The goods line crossing at right angles is being removed. The platform to the right had a lifting section to permit wagons to be transferred to the goods shed seen on the right.

Looking west from Myrtle Hill Bridge, Teignmouth station was recorded in the last week of May 1893. The broad gauge baulk road had been converted to narrow gauge in the previous year, providing the opportunity to rebuild the station. Dismantling of the old structure is just commencing in this view. The left-hand train shed is the original from 1846, with the separate up platform and second shed to the right being added as early as 1848. The goods line crosses at right angles beyond the station, with the goods shed roof just seen to the left.

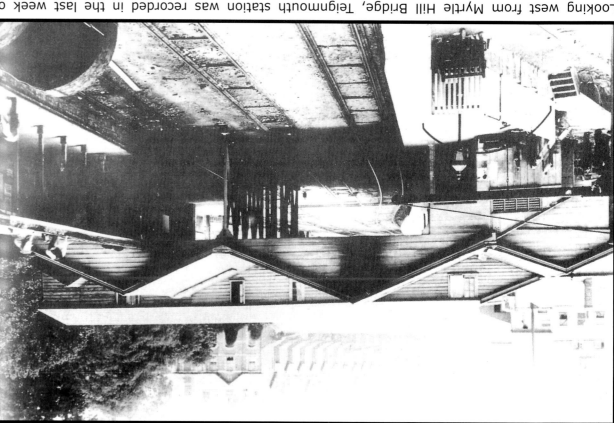

Teignmouth

be told when trains were running in the wrong order (when it might be necessary to pump *in the opposite direction* to the timetabled situation). The Dalkey and Croydon had it in their Engine Houses, Brunel had allowed for it in the S.D.R. Atmospheric costings, and Samuda had asked Margary to install it in the S.D.R. Engine Houses back in January 1847. As the S.D.R. *already* had a Telegraph system, the only action needed was the purchase of eight additional instruments and their fixing in the Engine Houses, a few weeks' job. But nothing was done about it.

The S.D.R. Atmospheric Department must have been relying on porters running between stations (which all had a Telegraph instrument in the office) and the Engine Houses, when any major disruption occurred; but clearer, nobody was bothering to run out to the Engine Houses when trains were merely 5 or 10 minutes late. How the remote Countess Wear, Turf and Summer House ever knew what to do when the timetable went astray, one does not know! Brunel promised that the problem would be "speedily remedied", and indeed the *Plymouth Herald* reported work under way in March. But it was not until 2nd August that the job was completed. Even then Brunel said on 19th August that the Telegraph was only being used during the day (he hoped that night use might start that week); possibly this was due to some staff not being trained. By the time the Telegraph was installed, it was too late for its beneficial effects to influence the fate of the system.

The Working Cost Factor

Up to the end of 1847 the S.D.R. had been preoccupied in getting the Atmospheric to *run*; and, whilst there had been concern over the escalating capital costs, the question of working costs had probably been put to the back of people's minds. Nevertheless, it had always been pointed out in the railway press that Atmospheric railways needed to prove themselves economically as well as technically; and during the spring of 1848 some of those in positions of influence in the S.D.R. began to experience a growing feeling that the Atmospheric might *not* be acceptable on working cost grounds, even if it was running successfully. On the S.D.R. the underpowered engines, valve problems and lack of Telegraph were of course making the economics that much worse.

In December 1847 the Board asked Pearson to supply weekly figures of the cost of Atmospheric working, but we need not regard this as more than intelligent housekeeping at this stage. It was at the February 1848 shareholders' meeting that the working costs question first assumed prominence, but the Directorate continued to express confidence publicly. In April *Woolmer's* started spreading rumours that the coal costs alone of the Atmospheric were greater than the S.D.R.'s revenue (a gross exaggeration, but making a point). In May there was a large fares increase, which must have added to such rumours. By June it was clear to those in the know that the S.D.R. was likely to make a loss in the first half of 1848, due to the high costs of the Atmospheric. Nevertheless, throughout 1848 the Atmospheric Department was gradually succeeding in *bringing down* the weekly working costs (see table), as more experience was gained, and as the Telegraph came into use. By the late summer costs were down to 62% of the January figures.

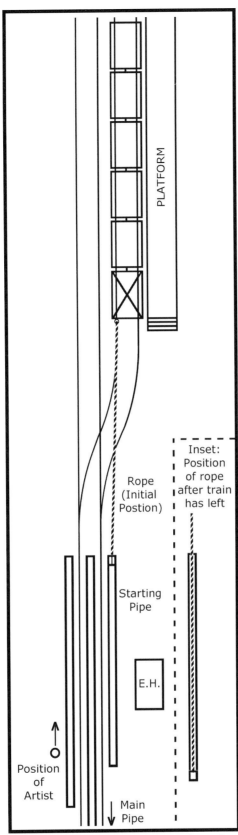

PLATFORM

Inset: Position of rope after train has left

Rope (Initial Postion)

Starting Pipe

E.H.

Position of Artist

Main Pipe

The drawing attempts an explanation of how the starting rope system might have worked, shown arranged as at Dawlish, and may be compared with the painting on page 70. The pipe on the inland side is limited in length, has a capped end and no slot, so would appear to be the 8" diameter starting pipe. The pipe on the other side continues along the line and so is presumably for vacuum distribution.

But some became convinced that, despite these impressive reductions, the working costs of the Atmospheric could *never* be brought down to those of locomotive working. From May 1848 there was a revised timetable, increasing the number of passenger trains over the Exeter to Newton section from 9 to 10 each way.

The Decay of the Valve (Summer 1848)

When warm dry weather came in at the start of May 1848, the leather of the valve began to dry up and shrivel in the heat. It was then unable to close down properly, and excessive air leakage occurred. Water was sprayed on to the valve from a tank in the piston carriage, and this helped a little, but the leather also started to *tear* at the joints between the iron plates that weighed it down when shut. The iron was rusting and corrupting the leather; also, the rivets joining the iron to the leather were being loosened by the rusting, so creating play and the potential for tearing. These troubles did not occur on other Atmospheric lines, and it seems that the leather and iron may have started deteriorating during the long period they were kept in cases after delivery. Additionally, the salt air on the S.D.R. cannot have done the valve any good; between Starcross and Teignmouth it must have been subjected to regular drenching by salt water and spray (which had probably not been anticipated, given Brunel's confidence that the sea would not touch the line). Samuda also claimed that the S.D.R.'s greasers had not been applying sufficient oil. Once the valve tore, it had to be replaced; by June 1848 over two miles had been replaced at a cost of £1,017, debited to Samuda's account under the 12 months' maintenance obligation. When the valve tore it was hardly possible to maintain a vacuum at all, and from May *Woolmer's* was able to start telling stories of dreadful delays again. On 5th May the 10.05pm down stuck at St. Thomas and did not reach Starcross until 2.00am, and the last up train (or so it was claimed) did not reach Teignmouth until 6.00am. On 13th May an up goods stopped on the viaduct north of St. Thomas, and horses had to be brought out to bring it into St. David's. So the tales continued until the end. Sometimes improvisation saved the day; on 4th August the 8.55pm down got stuck at Dawlish after the previous train had torn the valve, but a policeman held his coat over the tear to get a vacuum! But (as in the winter troubles) there was no overall disruption to the service; even in the worst week (14th to 20th July), when 83 trains lost time by an average of 8 minutes, 53 trains were punctual or gained time.

The Dénouement (May to August 1848)

It must have long been evident that the G.W.R., Bristol & Exeter and Bristol & Gloucester railway companies, who enjoyed a 11/21 majority on the S.D.R. Board, had never had the same enthusiasm for the Atmospheric as the 'Local'

Directors and the shareholders at large; but they had been unable to resist the mania for Atmospheric railways in 1844/5. By 1848, though, the Atmospheric was a fad of the past in the public mind, and a movement to abandon it on the S.D.R. might stand some chance of success, providing of course that at least some good reasons could be demonstrated.

By the summer of 1848 there were in practice nine 'Associated Companies' Directors (the two B & G Directors had gone and not been replaced when that company was taken over by the Midland), and nine Local Directors (Lord Seymour never attended meetings). The Local Directors all remained committed to the Atmospheric, which they must have felt a personal responsibility for, and none more so than Thomas Gill the Chairman. To get a majority for abandonment, one of the Local Directors had to be won over to the other side. In determining the outcome, the two most important figures were Brunel and Thomas Woollcombe, both of whom effectively 'changed sides' in August.

We can now take events in chronological order:-

23rd May – Following a complaint (from an unspecified source) about "recent irregularities in the working", the Board set up a Committee to investigate the working of the Atmospheric, comprising Gill, Woollcombe and Derry, all *Local* Directors[22].

20th June – The Atmospheric Committee report back to the Board, concentrating on the decay of the valve. The Board asks Brunel to report on the valve problems.

4th July – The Committee report to the Board on the financial aspects of Atmospheric working (the *loss* was indubitable now). The Board asks Brunel to meet the Committee at Plymouth one day next week.

18th July – Brunel having failed to reply, and showing no sign of coming to Plymouth, the Board appoints a heavyweight deputation - Gill, Russell (Chairman of the G.W.R.), Buller (Chairman of the B.&E.R.) and Woollcombe - and instructs Brunel to meet them in London on the 21st, and to send a written report. The meeting takes place, but the report does not arrive until the 31st.

31st July to 19th August – Brunel sends in three versions of his report, basically the same but including several vital changes of emphasis, reflecting a growing feeling in his mind that it might be best to kill off the Atmospheric. In the *first* version, Brunel stated that fuel costs might be reduced by expenditure on modifications to the engines, and that the valve problems could probably be solved by painting, zincing or galvanising the iron plates (albeit the *whole* of the existing valve would need replacing). All this might reduce the working expenses to 1s per train mile "which may make it worth the while to continue the working of the line between Exeter and Newton". Dainton Engine House should be completed, but as assistant power for the incline only (the first suggestion that Newton to Totnes should not be fully Atmospheric).

Working of the Engine Houses

Engine House	Number of minutes needed for pumping prior to departure of train from previous station/Engine House[1], plus number of minutes train pumping whilst train in section[2].		Number of scheduled passengers trains pumped for per week[3].	Length of pipes either side (combined)[4].		Number of hours actually pumped sample week[5].	
	Down Trains	Up Trains			Order		Order
Exeter[6]	-	6+7	65	3m 18ch	7	62¼	7
Countess Wear	6+6	5+7	130	5m 56ch	4	83¾	4
Turf	6+6	6+6	130	5m 21ch	5	69¼	5
Starcross	8+8	6+6	130	6m 23ch	2	87¾	3
Dawlish	8+8	8+8	130	6m 32ch	1	105¼	1
Teignmouth	8+8	6+8	124	6m 10ch	3	90¼	2
Summer House	8+9	5+4	118	5m 10ch	6	62¾	6
Newton[6]	6+4	-	59	1m 72ch	8	52½	8

Notes: 1. Figures given by Pearson in Gill December 1848 pamphlet. These times were increased when the Engine valve was in particularly bad condition.

2. Estimated from timetables.

3. There were goods and special trains on top of this. These figures show the proportional differences between the Engine houses' train numbers.

4. These are actually the distances between the Engine House and those either side; the pipe sections were several hundred yards shorter than this.

5. These are half the figures given by Pearson in Gill pamphlet for the sample fortnight 8th–21st June 1848, which was a comparatively good period for valve leakage. Longer hours were necessary when the valve was particularly bad.

6. Figures given on assumption of pumping in one direction only. Pearson does actually give pumping times for down trains from Exeter (5 minutes) and up trains from Newton (5 minutes). Even in June, when the telegraph was probably in partial use, the actual hours worked were between two and three times what was theoretically necessary for the pumping times and train numbers in question.

Although far from enthusiastic, this was certainly not recommending abandonment of the Atmospheric. In the *last* version, however, Brunel made the recommendation that Atmospheric working be continued between Exeter and Newton *conditional* on Samuda agreeing to renew the valve and maintain it beyond the originally agreed 12 months. On 19th August Brunel sent a note to Samuda requiring him to "put the valve in thorough repair". After this events move very quickly. There were two main reasons for the haste. Firstly, there was a shareholders' meeting coming up on 29th August, where there was bound to be acrimony over the £2,487 loss shown in the accounts for the first half of 1848 (there had been £5,000+ profits in previous half-years). This the anti-Atmospherics could take advantage of to persuade the shareholders (whose authority was of course needed for such a move) to vote for abandonment. Secondly, on 13th September the S.D.R. would be obliged to pay Samuda the £7,500 due for the final instalments of the payments for the valve and patent rights – perhaps not a large sum in the context of the total capital costs of the Atmospheric, but nevertheless 15% of the company's annual receipts at a time when finances were becoming grim. The S.D.R. would also have been obliged to maintain the valve at their own expense from this date.

23rd August – Gill meets Samuda to discuss the latter's proposals in relation to Brunel's conditional recommendation.

26th August – Samuda makes a formal offer to Gill – for £210 per mile he will install a new valve to Brunel's specification between Exeter and Newton, and maintain it for the next 12 months. Gill was certainly keen to accept this offer, but Russell and Brunel now demanded that Samuda enter into a contract to work the line at his own risk (which they knew he would not agree to).

28th August (Monday) – In the morning Gill and Woollcombe meet Samuda, and draft a Report to the Board (which they hope the other two members of the Board might accept) proposing that an agreement be made with Samuda. Later in the morning the Atmospheric Committee meet in Teignmouth[?]. Brunel suddenly says that he is not convinced that Samuda could succeed, by the means suggested, in "making the valve what it ought to be". (Samuda was in fact proposing to do what Brunel's report had recommended!) Brunel is also generally more anti-Atmospheric than before, although he tries to deny it when Gill points this out. Upon hearing Brunel's views so expressed, Woollcombe decides that he can no longer support Gill, and agrees to a rival Report to the Board prepared by Russell and Buller advocating abandonment. Gill refuses to sign this, so the Committee members submitting their separate views to the Board.

29th August (Tuesday) – In the morning the Board meeting continues. Gill proposes an agreement with Samuda, but cannot get a seconder. Lord Courtenay (whose exact role we have to guess at) then proposes four resolutions which are carried by eleven votes to seven (the remaining seven Local Directors abstaining).

1. That the employment of the Atmospheric be suspended; but ~
2. That if Samuda wished to make further improvements and continue Atmospheric working, he should be allowed to do so if he made an agreement by 6th September to "undertake the expenses of working the line at a defined cost per train mile".
3. That in the absence of such an agreement, the line should be worked by locomotives from 9th September.
4. That the Board should not be precluded from assisting Samuda financially to improve the Atmospheric system.

Gill insists that he must put *his* case to the shareholders, but is silenced by a resolution that "all discussion of the Atmospheric and locomotive system should be avoided" at the meeting. In the afternoon, the shareholders' meeting is held. As the Board's report has not been printed and circulated in advance as usual, the whole thing comes up as a surprise to the shareholders. They now find themselves told that:-

"Your Directors, without pronouncing any judgement as to the ultimate success of the Atmospheric system, and whilst they are prepared to afford to the patentees and other parties interested in it the use of the machinery for continuing their own experiments, have arrived at the conclusion, with the entire concurrence and on the recommendation of Mr. Brunel, that it is expedient for them to suspend the use of the Atmospheric system until the same shall be made efficient at the expense of Mr. Samuda".

The meeting, not surprisingly, was "one of the most spirited on record". But the high feelings were not due to any argument between pro-Atmospherics and anti-Atmospherics; not a single voice seems to have been raised in defence of the Atmospheric, only universal criticism of Brunel and the Board for having adopted the Atmospheric in the first place. The Board's report was greeted by cries of "Hear! Hear!" There was *loud cheering* when Ellis of the Midland said that he was "exceedingly disgusted with the Atmospheric bubble"; and *loud and protracted cheering* when someone proclaimed that "the idea of continuing such a system one moment longer appears to ALMOST BORDER ON INSANITY!"; and *an outburst of tremendous cheering* when Samuda was insulted as "as wild a visionary as ever existed". Finally, the Board's recommendation was approved unanimously, just as it had been in August 1844. Although the words were conciliatory, it is clear that the anti-Atmospherics were confident that they had killed off the system for good.

The £2,487 loss which caused the wrath was in fact a false figure; it was subsequently amended to a £2,009 *profit*. The reason was an unpaid sum due from the Post Office for the carriage of mails, which was actually mentioned in a footnote but hardly in a way to be noticed. Moreover, the Board must have known by August that there was going to be a large profit in the second half of 1848: the revenue had greatly increased since the opening to Laira in May 1848 but this had only increased working costs a little. In the event there was a £18,217 profit for the second half, three times any previous profit, and that under Atmospheric working to September. So the picture given to the shareholders was far from the whole truth. However, this must not distract us from the fact that the Atmospheric was still costing more than locomotives, and hence *reducing* the profits. But it never really caused a loss, and was becoming more economical by the week. The anti-Atmospherics would never again have had such an easy wicket, had they not succeeded in killing the system in August 1848.

The Last Days of the Atmospheric (September 1848)

The Atmospheric staff did not appreciate the threat until too late. They were feeling pleased at their success in reducing costs, and maintaining the service despite the valve problems (which diminished in August). On August 3rd they had a celebratory dinner at Newton for the opening of the new Atmospheric workshops there. Later in August, a new design of rubber valve was tried out, and there were reports of 22" pipes being delivered to replace the existing 15" pipes. Then came the shock. Someone soon rushed from the shareholders' meeting to Laira station bringing the news: the clerks rushed to telegraph it up the line; and we may imagine it being shouted out at every station. "Great was the

consternation and surprise all along the line", reported *Woolmer's*. It was soon all over. The Atmospheric Committee met again on Wednesday 6th September as planned, to consider Samuda's response to the Board's resolutions; it was deemed unsatisfactory; and they resolved to introduce locomotive working on Sunday 10th (not the 9th as originally planned). The Atmospheric staff were given their notice, and an order made to cut off coal supplies to the Engine Houses. And so it happened; the Atmospheric continued in regular operation up to the arrival of the up goods in Exeter at about 12.30am on Sunday morning, and the Engine Houses were then shut up, never to work again. The 4.15am Down Mail left St. David's under its own power, as has every subsequent train[24].

Reaction
(September 1848 to January 1849)
"The change did not occur without an expression of deep regret on the part of a large number of persons who have been accustomed to the Atmospheric traction", reported the *Western Times*, noting also "We travellers, all the time being of the uninitiated, little dreamed of the vast expense which the project was entailing on the company. We knew nothing but the rate of speed attained, and the diminution of irregularities, which seemed to set the seal of success upon it". The abandonment was the talk of the area, and the railway press, for a couple weeks, and then, in the way of things, it was forgotten about by most people. Anti-Brunelites and old reactionaries had a field day. But some began to wonder whether the decision was a little hasty. A letter in the *Railway Chronicle* demanded to know why the Directors' Report had not mentioned the increased reliability of the system in later weeks. Gill was not willing to let things lie, and was approached by others who regretted the lack of information provided on 29th August. On 7th November Gill told the Board that he was resigning the Chair so that he could speak out publicly against the decision, and on 28th he published a lengthy pamphlet addressed to the shareholders. At a meeting in Bristol on 5th December he succeeded in getting enough signatures together to force the Board to hold a special shareholders' meeting to discuss the question again, and this was arranged for 6th January. The Board elected Woollcombe as their new Chairman, and asked him, James Buller and Russell to prepare a report in response to Gill's pamphlet; this was considered on 2nd January and it was resolved (Gill dissenting !) to send copies to all shareholders. Sir A. Buller was the only other Director actively supporting Gill. So the arguments were thrown for the last time. Gill stressed the reductions achieved in coal consumption, adding that the coal could also be obtained more cheaply if shipped to Teignmouth and conveyed thence in S.D.R. trucks. He advocated fitting the 'weather cover' to the valve, and claimed that improvements to the

engines and valve costing only £6,000 would bring the Atmospheric costs down to 1s.3½d per train mile, which just happened to be ½d less than the G.W.R.'s charge for locomotive hire. The Board retorted that they could not realistically count on a cost of less than 2s per train mile in the immediate future. They claimed that the reduction in costs per train mile during 1848 was simply due to increasing train miles, the system having high overheads and low incremental costs. (This was quite untrue – there had been no significant increase in Atmospheric train miles after 23rd February). But their greatest argument was that Gill's attempt to argue the whole loss on costs per train mile was fallacious anyway, because locomotives could haul *heavier* trains than the Atmospheric. They pointed out that 3,140 train miles on average had been run in the three weeks prior to abandonment, and only 2,288 on average in the three weeks beginning 10th September, despite there being no diminution in the number of passengers. (This sounded impressive but was itself partly fallacious – the reduction in train miles was primarily due to the timetable having been cut by 548 miles per week as an economy measure, and the passenger trains were so light that the Atmospheric *could* handle them; only the *goods* had often had to be duplicated under the Atmospheric). The Board also made much of the point that a 20-mile stretch of Atmospheric was an inconvenience in the middle of a main line generally worked by locomotive power.

Gill achieved a certain amount of support on 6th January, but given that the block votes of the 'Associated Companies' were all against him, he would have had to secure an enormous majority amongst the ordinary shareholders to succeed. Predictably, he failed, and he then resigned from the Board. As for the other participants, Brunel's reputation was damaged, but he had plenty of other projects to worry about, and remained the S.D.R.'s Engineer. Samuda returned to London, giving up the Marine Parade house at Christmas. The S.D.R. made settlements with him, apparently without bad feeling. The Atmospheric was by no means Samuda's only business interest, but it must have been a bitter disappointment to him to be cut off on both the Croydon *and* the S.D.R. just when they seemed on the point of success. Woollcombe gained the chair as a reward for changing sides, and held it for 25 years; but nobody ever suggested that his actions had been guided by anything other than a desire to do what was best for the company.

Disposal (1849 to 1856)
Everything was left intact until after the January 1849 meeting. Then, on 16th January, the Board appointed James Buller and Derry as a Committee to oversee the disposal of Atmospheric property. At this stage there was a proviso that the Newton – Totnes pipe should be left in situ in case it should still be decided to test the Atmospheric as assistant power on the inclines,

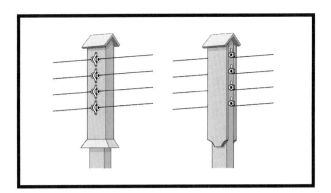

Telegraph Post Insulator Mountings
The S.D.R. telegraph posts were distinctive, although it was difficult to determine much detail from the original drawings. A standard post is shown on the left and a straining post on the right. Only the latter appears to be hollow.

but this proviso was dropped in May. No assistant power was ever provided on the inclines. The pipes had to be sold as scrap (although a few ended up as drainage pipes). There was at least no difficulty in this; between February and May most were sold, at around 55s per ton, mostly to Samuda, Hennet and South Wales foundries. A large number of 22" pipes were in fact still held by Hennet in Bridgwater, undelivered. By July there were few pipes left on the line; the Board asked Pearson to stock the remaining pipes at Dawlish and Newton. A large quantity was also dumped in a field at Torquay Junction and mortgaged. (Pearson's services had been retained to help in disposal. In 1850 he found a new job as B.&E.R. Loco Superintendent, but by the consent of the B.&E.R. he remained in charge of S.D.R. Atmospheric disposal until November 1852, when Margary was given responsibility). The valve was sold back to Samuda and the piston carriages were easily converted into ordinary coaching stock. The undelivered engines for west of Newton were sold back to their makers. The other engines all found buyers in the end, but only at very reduced prices. Brunel was asked in June 1849 to "draw up descriptions of all the Atmospheric engines and offer them for sale". But they were then mortgaged to the Devon & Cornwall Bank to raise much-needed capital. A first mortgage dated 29th June, for £21,550, covered the main engines, small engines and boilers at Exeter, Countess Wear, Turf, Starcross, Teignmouth, Newton and Dainton. A second dated 24th August, for £14,500, covered the main engines, small engines and boilers at Dawlish and Summer House, such equipment as had been installed at Totnes and the pipes at Torquay Junction. By permission of the Bank, four large engines and most of the small engines were sold in 1849 to 1852; but the majority of the equipment remained in the Engine Houses for over four years after the Atmospheric was abandoned. The mortgages were ended in November 1852 and the remaining large engines were all sold in 1853 (except that the purchaser of the Starcross engines defaulted , and they had to be re-sold in 1856).

The Engine Houses were obviously a difficult proposition (*Woolmer's* suggested that they be converted into asylums for the shareholders!) Somewhat optimistically, the Board asked in January 1849 "that an advertisement be prepared inviting tenders from persons to occupy the Engine Houses as Mills, Storehouses, etc". But nobody was going to be interested whilst the equipment was still in situ, so nothing further was heard of this idea until 1853. The remote Engine Houses – Countess Wear, Turf, Summer House and Dainton – were sold for their materials, demolished and the land sold back in the late 1850s, as also was Teignmouth, probably because it was felt to be in the way at this cramped station site. Starcross, Dawlish, Totnes and Torquay did find persons willing to rent them for industrial purposes (although Dawlish was demolished in 1873); and Exeter became in due course a railway gas production plant. Newton lasted for several decades as part of the works complex, before succumbing to expansion schemes. By the 1860s, therefore, there was little left of the Atmospheric; and today there is even less. The remaining Engine Houses at Starcross, Totnes (much altered) and Torquay (intact) are comparatively well known. Of the rest, one can see the back wall of Dawlish, part of the reservoir at Countess Wear and hardly-recognisable lumps of stone and reservoir remains at Summer House. Perhaps the most melancholy reminder of the Atmospheric, though, is the Turf site, where the reservoir is maintained in good order (and easily seen from the train) and the crumbling remains of the Engine House walls allow the layout of the buildings to be traced. The scene has hardly changed since 1848, and only the grazing cows and HSTs disrupt one's musings on what might have been.

Retrospect
Much has been said before about the various problems of the Atmospheric equipment on the S.D.R., and their role in the abandonment. But all of these problems *could* (at a cost) have been solved, *if* it had been thought desirable in overall terms to carry on with the Atmospheric. It is therefore more appropriate to concentrate on the wider factors that brought about the end of the system.

The Nature of the Atmospheric System. It was a complex *system* – if one got the details wrong, it was very expensive to alter. And on the Croydon and the S.D.R., mainly because Atmospheric power was still at an early stage of development, the engineers *did* get the details wrong (albeit that the equipment did just manage to work a fairly reliable service most of the time). By August 1848 Brunel had the knowledge to design a *far better* Atmospheric railway – bigger engines, bigger pumps, bigger pipes and a different design of valve – having much better economics. But it was beyond the financial capacity of a single railway company to fund such a reconstruction, and there was no Government money for experiments on improved transport systems. In contrast, locomotive designers could experiment

with different features at far lower costs. By the late 1840s locomotive design was already an established art, offering known operating capabilities and known operating costs. Indeed, locomotives were available on contract hire at fixed prices. The S.D.R. was not being unreasonable, from a railway company's viewpoint, in asking Samuda similarly to offer Atmospheric power on contract. The enormous *capital* costs of the Atmospheric – far greater than expected, again primarily because of the undeveloped state of the art – had put the S.D.R. in a financial position where the no-risk option of locomotive power on contract hire was the only option it could take. If they had carried on with the Atmospheric, they *might* have been able to reduce the working costs to an acceptable level. But it was *possible* that they might *not* have been able to, and that risk could not be afforded.

The Fatal Effects of Delay. The partly-unnecessary delays in getting the Atmospheric into operation, however sensible it may have seemed at the time to benefit from the Croydon's experiences, actually had fatal effects. The delays in storage suffered by the valve were probably the major cause of its difficulties. The delays in doing anything beyond Newton gave a fatal foot in the door to locomotive power, which was able to demonstrate that it *could* work the inclines. Had Brunel pressed ahead west of Newton in 1845, the whole Atmospheric would have acquired a greater inevitability, but as it was the anti-Atmospheric faction was able to argue that a 20-mile Atmospheric section in the middle of a locomotive line was an impracticability. The delays caused hostility in themselves, making people tired of the Atmospheric even before it came into use. And the unforgivable delays in installing the Telegraph made the working costs seem intolerable when they need only have been bad; if the Atmospheric Department had been able to run the service in January 1848 at the same cost as they were doing in August, things might have turned out very different.

The Mania and its Aftermath. At the end of the day, the real reason for the S.D.R. abandoning the Atmospheric in 1848 was simply that Atmospheric railways in general had gone out of favour. In part this was due to enthusiasm for the Atmospheric having reached its height in 1845 at the time of the 'Railway Mania' (many of the companies that collapsed had intended to be Atmospheric). The two things had somehow been associated, so that there was a reaction against the Atmospheric too when the bubble burst. If there had been a lot of other companies running and promoting Atmospheric lines in 1848, the S.D.R. would surely have been much more inspired to press on itself. As it was, the S.D.R. was left out on its own (apart from the Dalkey, which did not count for much). The unfortunate accident of the L.B.S.C.R. taking over the Croydon had robbed the infant Atmospheric of one of the two legs on which it was learning to stand, even before the S.D.R. began working. By the time it did begin, it its day had passed.

Reductions Achieved in Working Costs

Period	Working cost per train mile	Coal consumption per week
Month of January 1848	3s 2¼d	n/k
2 weeks commencing 3rd February	3s 1d	n/k
2 weeks commencing 17th February	2s 11¾d	n/k
2 weeks commencing 2nd March	2s 8d	304 tons
2 weeks commencing 16th March	2s 9d	280 tons
2 weeks commencing 30th March	3s 1½d	314 tons
2 weeks commencing 13th April	2s 1½d	236 tons
2 weeks commencing 27th April	2s 11½d	306 tons
2 weeks commencing 11th May	2s 2d	293 tons
2 weeks commencing 25th May	2s 7½d	284 tons
2 weeks commencing 8th June	2s 0½d	241 tons
2 weeks commencing 22nd June	1s 10d	264 tons
2 weeks commencing 6th July	2s 4½d	290 tons
2 weeks commencing 20th July	2s 3d	287 tons
2 weeks commencing 3rd August	2s 0d	214 tons
2 weeks commencing 17th August	1s 11d	208 tons
31st August to 9th September	1s 9½d	201 tons

Notes: Figures from Pearson's reports to the Board, quoted in Gill's pamphlet. The bad figures in May and July were due to the valve being in particulary bad condition then. The Telegraph was probably brought into use gradually, and the apparently spectacular reduction in coal consumption after 2nd August was probably due more to the weather changing and the valve accordingly improving.

Notes

1. These statements were made by Brunel to the Parliamentary Select Committee on Atmospheric railways in April 1845.

2. Before the Select Committee in April 1845, both Brunel and Samuda spoke of an expanding piston being intended, but Brunel never explained how this would have worked. Brunel also spoke of having a 'double pipe' (i.e. two pipes laid side-by-side between the rails) on the inclines, instead of a larger diameter pipe. The possibility of running trains *down* the inclines purely by gravity was also considered.

3. In fact there was probably collusion between Brunel, Guppy and Hennet. T.R. Guppy belonged to a leading Bristol business family, had known Brunel since around 1830 and had been heavily involved in the flotation of the G.W.R., of which he was a founder Director. In 1841-4 he built the 'Great Britain'. The 1870 Brunel biography says that the pipes were "undertaken by George Hennet, by the aid of a set of tools devised by T.R. Guppy". Guppy and Hennet must have known each other before 1844. Whilst Hennet certainly made *most* of the pipes, a *Flying Post* article refers to "the foundries at Bristol and Bridgwater" producing the pipes, suggesting that Guppy may have made some. Brunel's letterbooks in the late 1840s contain many references to a 'Hennet v Guppy dispute', and although they never actually specify what this was *about*, all the references are consistent with its being about the details of a closet agreement on the pipes. Brunel had to arbitrate in this dispute; by the time it was settled in 1849, Guppy had emigrated to Naples. There was also a contract for 2,600 tons of 15" pipes given to Tayleur & Sanderson of Warrington in November 1845.

4. The pipes were actually 10'6" long as cast, but included a 6 inch overlap where the next pipe was fitted in. Some contemporary illustrations (including some of the 15" pipes on the Exeter to Newton section) clearly show the pipes laid on *indented* transoms to reduce their height; in fact, as the 22" pipes laid west of Newton were 25" high including the 'valve' fittings, they at least *must* have all been laid on indented transoms in order to enable locomotives to run over them – some G.W.R. locos used on the S.D.R. had 3'6" diameter wheels – and one suspects that all the pipes were in fact on indented transoms.

5. These small engines were proposed from the start; Samuda refers to them in April 1845. They were *not* added to increase the available power as a result of the change from 13" to 15" pipes.

6. Exeter was of Pocombe Stone, Countess Wear is red in the watercolour, excavations at Turf revealed grey limestone with red quoins; Starcross is still there. It has been assumed that the red sandstone came from the Dawlish cliffs. This is quite credible, given that these Engine Houses were built at a time when cliff cutting was still in progress, whereas the later ones postdate the cliff work; but there is no direct evidence. Dawlish, Torquay and Totnes are still visibly limestone; Teignmouth and Summer House are stated to be limestone in the Auction Notices; Newton and Dainton are clearly grey in the 1848 watercolours.

7. Exeter had a well adjacent to the Engine House. Dawlish may have had an underground reservoir (it certainly did not have an open-air one).

8. The Starcross chimney has an internal staircase and small openings at intervals for light. None of the other chimneys had such openings, so we *assume* that they did not have internal staircases (no definite information is available).

9. It is known that Hennet built Newton; apart from this we only know that Hennet was paid £17,000 for building Engine Houses. As the total cost of the 11 locations was £48,000, this suggests that Hennet built four of them.

10. So Margary's diary says. If true, the locomotive was probably there to prevent the piston carriage running too fast. But when the Starcross – Dawlish tube was similarly cleared of water on 22nd March, Margary says that a locomotive towed the piston carriage (* See page 97).

11. Samuda's 10th May letter to the board implies that trains had already run to Dawlish by then, but a *Woolmer's Gazette* article speaks of the first test train to Dawlish on 25th May.

12. These are the timings given in the public timetables from October 1847 to March 1848.

13. 6 out of 10 down and 7 out of 10 up. Locomotive working was confined to evenings and early mornings.

14. MacDermot was led astray by this and others followed, until Hadfield set out a balanced picture.

15. It was *not* possible to turn the piston carriage on a turntable, because the angled plate connecting the carriage and the piston had to remain the same way round in both directions of travel in order to work in the hinged valve; hence the assumed need for two pistons. The pistons must have been movable in a vertical direction, because they were *lifted* over points during running by a device called a 'piston incline', of which again we know nothing except for the *Morning Herald* telling us that "by a very simple contrivance the piston is lifted over the crossing rails". This device clearly worked satisfactorily and was an improvement over the Croydon where the Atmospheric trains could not pass through points at speed.

16. Brunel told the Parliamentary Committee in April 1845 that the platforms would be made 'very long' to minimise this problem. Samuda, on the same occasion, said that the powered capstans intended by Brunel for the stations would be used to pull back trains that overshot. Neither of these things happened. It has been said that 'telescopic platform extensions' were provided at Starcross and Dawlish latterly, but contemporary evidence of this has not been found.

17. If, as would normally have been the case on the S.D.R., the next station was already being pumped for that train. If the next section was being pumped for a train coming the other way, the runaway train would quickly decelerate.

18. For a full description of these valves, see Sir Frederick Bramwell's talk to the Institution of Mechanical Engineers at Plymouth, 25th July 1899.

19. It is unclear whether this was ever done on the S.D.R. at all. Samuda, in April 1845, spoke of the possibility of having a shut-up valve halfway along each section, so that when one train passed it another train could follow more quickly, the Engine House in the *rear* exhausting that half section whilst the first train was still in the second half section. Although this was never done, it proves that pumping from the rear was regarded as *possible*.

20. The 20-minute claim seems a little incredible, given the slow speeds necessary through the three intermediate stations. Both runs may have been to / from St. Thomas (19¼ miles), rather than St. David's (20¼ miles).

21. On the same sort of spacings, *three* further Engine Houses would have been needed (Hemerdon, Plympton, Plymouth). This makes a total of *nine* Engine Houses west of Newton and this, plus a second pair of engines needed for Newton to enable it to pump three sections simultaneously, equates to the *ten* pairs of engines ordered.

22. On 6th June, Tripp, Rundle and Sir A. Buller (not to be confused with James Buller of the B.&E.R., another S.D.R. Director) were added to the Committee. The Committee's meetings were not minuted.

23. It is not stated exactly where this vital meeting, which effectively sounded the death knell for Atmospheric railways worldwide, was held; the Royal Hotel or the London Hotel are most likely.

24. Hadfield's footnote that "in fact locomotive working was brought forward and began on Wednesday 6th" is contradicted by all the newspaper reports and by a specific statement by Carr to the Board on the 12th.

Exeter Engine House

The top photograph is of Exeter Engine house (ref 3608) taken in 1916 from the opposite bank of the River Exe. By this time the roof had been replaced by a large water tank which served the locomotive depot beyond. This involved the insertion of substantial brick arches to accept the increased weight, as seen in the lower photograph (ref E0/814). Machinery was installed to produce gas for coach lighting and cooking, and included additional outbuildings and gasometers.

Paul Garnsworthy's 1997 painting was based on a photograph (ref 3609 from the same set), with the content backdated to show the building in atmospheric operation in the summer of 1848. The most striking difference is the illustration of the original patent tile roof over the engine room. To the right of the painting a piston carriage stands outside the S.D.R. carriage shed. In the background is the Bristol & Exeter Railway single sided station for down trains, there being a similar station for up trains just out of view. The B.&E.R. was worked by G.W.R. locomotives from its opening in 1844 until 1849, and one of the 'Fire Fly' class locomotives slumbers inside the engine shed to the left. The station and locomotive depot were replaced in 1862-1864, with further alterations in 1910-1912.

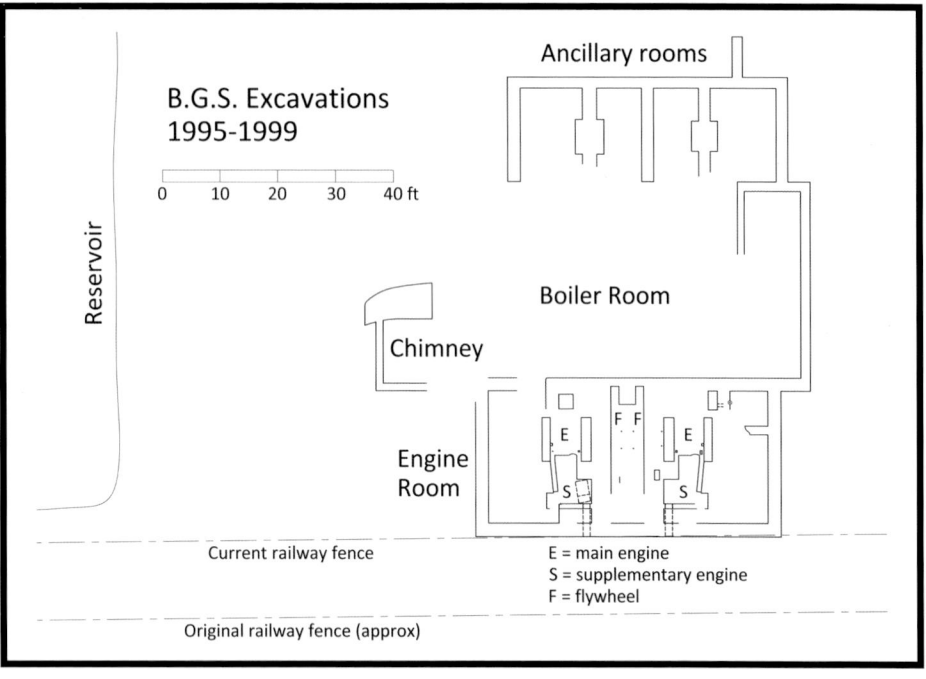

B.G.S. Excavations
1995-1999

0   10   20   30   40 ft

Reservoir

Ancillary rooms

Boiler Room

Chimney

Engine
Room

E = main engine
S = supplementary engine
F = flywheel

Current railway fence

Original railway fence (approx)

Turf Engine House

Paul Garnsworthy's painting of 2002 illustrates the two large 40hp Boulton & Watt vacuum pumping engines, with their impressive flywheels and long connecting rods. In the background are the two smaller 12hp engines used for secondary tasks, such as pumping water for the boilers and possibly maintaining the vacuum in the tubes once created.

The vacuum pumps were directly connected to the engine piston rods and were located in the pump room above this one. The steam pipes on the left of the picture were fed from the boiler room, whilst the S.D.R. railway line ran beyond the windows. To the east of the building was the large reservoir, which remains in place today.

The foundations of the building are still visible and the Broad Gauge Society made a series of archaeological investigations between 1995 and 1999. We uncovered walls of grey limestone with red conglomerate quoins. A number of the outbuildings of nearby Exewell Barton farm are of similar construction and may have re-used the materials.

The drawing records the structures which were uncovered, including the substantial threaded mounting rods which are apparent in the photograph of the flywheel pit. The other photograph shows the outbuildings, which may have continued in use after the main building came down in 1860.

Starcross

The Plymouth-based painter Nicholas Condy (1793-1857) included two watercolours of the atmospheric railway amongst his works, including this sketch of Starcross below.

The boiler house in the foreground is evidently in operation, with clouds of smoke from the chimney. The taller engine room has been built at right angles to the boiler room instead of the usual arrangement alongside, necessitated by the constricted nature of the site. The balcony of the Courtenay Arms is visible immediately beyond. In the distance the train shed is picked out in yellow ochre, enclosed on the town side but open towards the estuary.

Disc and crossbar signals can be seen beyond the station and near the harbour flag. In the foreground, in addition to the main traction pipe, there is also a starting pipe to the left, and a distribution pipe with valve to the right. This appears to have a connection to the telegraph system on the opposite side of the railway.

Painting reproduced from the Elton Collection by kind permission of The Ironbridge Gorge Museum Trust. Ref AE185.155

Langstone Cliff

William Spreat of Exeter (1816-1897) was a prolific publisher of lithographs, both from his own oil paintings and those based on paintings by others. A number based on Dawson's watercolours formed part of his range, including this view of Langstone Cliff above.

The original version by Dawson can be seen in the Sheet 10 South View on page 47. It was one of a number which Dawson re-worked as individual paintings in their own right, perhaps with lithography in mind from the outset. The intermediate painting was completed in 1848, and can be viewed by appointment at the Royal Albert Memorial Museum and Art Gallery, their reference 14/1929/4.

The tower of All Saints Church, Exmouth is prominent on the opposite bank of the estuary, but there is no development at all between the harbour and Orcombe Point beyond.

Lithograph reproduced by kind permission of The Newton Abbot Town and G.W.R. Museum. Photographed by Kate Green.

SOUTH DEVON RAILWAY.—Mr. Dawson, the talented surveyor, of Northernhay-place, has completed a series of water colour drawings of views on both sides of the line of this picturesque Railway from Exeter to Totnes. It is a very elaborate, faithful, and striking work, and we regret that a work so well calculated to do justice to a very picturesque portion of our fair and picturesque country, cannot be brought within the reach of her Majesty's multitudinous subjects, by popular publication. In addition to the views, Mr. Dawson's sketch book gives the technical details of the entire line, as far as he has illustrated its noble scenery.

The Dawson Watercolours

In 2013, a full 165 years after the appearance of this newspaper announcement, the Broad Gauge Society is delighted to be able to grant the wishes of the Western Times.

The Western Times, 5th August 1848, courtesy of the Devon Heritage Centre.

1 From the Exeter Railway Station to the Viaduct in St. Thomas

View South of the Line

Built on river meadows to the west of the city, the Bristol and Exeter Railway's Exeter terminus was opened on 1st May 1844. It was of typical single-sided arrangement, with separate arrival and departure stations, each marked by a decorative roof turret. The service was worked by the G.W.R. until 1st May 1849, and one of their locomotives has arrived with a train from Bristol. Painted green, with a brass clad haycock firebox, it is probably one of the Fire Fly class. Dawson has, not unreasonably, placed the engine between the stations for artistic purposes, whereas it would normally come to a stand out of sight nearer the river bridge. To the left of the view, behind trees marking the line of the River Exe, there is an imposing timber goods shed, with a disc and crossbar signal behind, and in the background the wooded hills of the Duryard Estate. Duryard is marked ∨ by Dawson, who uses a system of seagull groups to identify features of interest. A water tank stands in front of the arrival station, together with the timber-clad B.&E.R. engine shed. The South Devon Railway's Exeter presence is marked by the atmospheric railway engine house (∨) and by the timber bridge over the River Exe. The alluvial water meadows would produce lush grass for the grazing cattle to the left of the Exwick mill stream, and good hay crops for indoor and winter feed. The waggon drawn by three horses in tandem is being loaded by three labourers with pitch forks, whilst in the foreground workers with wooden hay rakes are drawing the hay into long rows or rollers, between which the waggon will move for loading. In the background the City of Exeter stands on the promontory behind its defensive walls, with the twin towers of the Cathedral (∨∨∨) prominent in the centre. Allhallows on the Walls Church (∨∨∨∨) can be seen to the right, and St. David's Church (∨∨) to the left, at the top of the hill leading from the station.

Longitudinal Section

The eight-span trussed-timber bridge over the River Exe formed the first engineering structure on the South Devon Railway. Built by George Hennet, it was complete in the late summer of 1845. It carried a single line of railway for most of its length, but due to the confined site of the station the pointwork extended onto the bridge, which was wider at the station end. Each span comprised a queen-post truss either side of the track, with a spine beam running centrally under the railway, upon which the cross-decking and ballast were laid. The trusses were designed to form a continuous structural member across all eight spans. A three-span stone bridge carries the railway over the Old Canal Road, today no more than a footpath, as the line rises on an embankment at 1 in 640 to cross Okehampton Road by a single stone arch.

Route Plan - 193¾ miles to 194½ miles

The twin station arrangement with its central turntable is shown clearly, together with the three-road B.&E.R. engine shed and S.D.R. engine house next to the river. On the opposite side of the running lines is the single-road S.D.R. piston carriage shed. There is an impressive group of goods sheds to the left side of the plan, several standing at right angles to the railway and served by waggon turntables. There is a toll gate across Cowley Bridge Road, and from the adjacent toll cottage a road leads down to the goods yard. This was soon extended over the railway and river to form Red Cow Crossing, an 1848 sketch of Exeter viewed from Exwick showing it. The Old Canal Road crosses the water meadows to pass under the railway, linking Exwick Mill to the City Basin. After passing across the flood plain the railway crosses Okehampton Road, and encounters the first buildings of St. Thomas.

View North of the Line

The 75 yard long bridge which carries the S.D.R. over the River Exe to reach the Exeter station of the B.&E.R. features prominently in this view. The queen-post truss layout was a development of traditional truss design; however, with the loads from the bridge deck bearing on the bottom string of the truss, the queen posts were actually tension members, and so were formed using iron tie rods. The house on the hill beyond is shown as Haccombe (∨). The S.D.R.'s Exeter Engine House (∨) stands out against the wooded hills of Exwick. It was built by Carpenter, starting in June 1845, and Boulton & Watt's engines were steamed for the first time in August 1846. The walls were of Pocombe stone, a fine-grained Permian basalt with individual stones varying widely in colour in the grey / red / liver / purple range. The boiler house was strengthened in the 1890s to support a large water tank for the locomotive depot, and stood until 1982. To its right, the artist, back in his studio, has confused the single track S.D.R. piston carriage shed on the near side of the railway, with the B.&E.R. engine shed on the far side. The compact down station, with its decorative turret, serves a long train shed, with a small toilet block at the left end. The matching up station is visible in the distance, to the right of the view. A long rake of brown-painted coaches stands in the down station; the locomotive, shown at the up end of the train, for artistic purpose, is probably one of G.W.R.'s Fire Fly class. In the station approach a four-wheel vehicle is being drawn at some speed by four horses. It is apparently an omnibus with three side windows and no roof accommodation.

Modern View – 01 South
G.S.

The Old Canal Road linked Exwick Mill, which was run by Thomas Shore during the atmospheric era, with the Exeter Canal. The three-span bridge still survives, having been widened on the up side in 1862, when the line was doubled. The headroom is very little more than a footpath, so the route has long since become limited under the bridge. Prior to completion of the Flood Relief Channel in 1977 the water meadows were prone to flooding and the bridge was provided with cutwaters as a precaution.

Modern View – 01 North
G.S.

The original single-sided station buildings at Exeter St. David's came under increasing pressure following the arrival of the Exeter and Crediton railway in 1851 and L.S.W.R. in 1862. The B.&E.R. completed a much improved new station around the old facilities in 1864. This boasted a magnificent overall roof, 132 feet wide and 363 feet long. A further rebuild in 1914 did away with this roof, but the front wall has survived, and is retained behind the modern station frontage of 1939, complete with G.W.R. 'shirt button' monogram.

From the Exeter Railway Station to the Viaduct in St. Thomas
View South of the Line.

1

Duryard · Exwick Mill Stream · Station and Engine House · Exwick Fields · St David's Church · Exeter Cathedral · Allhallows on the Walls

Section.

Horizontal Scale. Four Chains to One Inch

Vertical Scale. Eighty Feet to One Inch

Level of Rails

Plan.

Scale. Four Chains to One Inch

from Cowley Bridge · Exeter Railway Station · Engine House · Parish of St David · Exe · Parish of St Thomas the Apostle · to Exeter · River

River Exe · Haccombe · Railway Bridge · Engine House · Exeter Railway Station

From the Viaduct in St. Thomas to the Exeter Railway Station.
View North of the Line.

2 From the Station in St. Thomas to the Alphington Meadows

View South of the Line

The works from the west bank of the River Exe formed the start of contract No. 1, which was awarded to Carpenter & Chesterfield. This view is taken from track level on the 501 yard long stone-arched viaduct that traversed the district of St. Thomas. Exeter Cathedral (✓) is seen in the distance, and running from Exe Bridge to pass under the artist's position is Cowick Street, or St. Thomas's Street as it is named on the watercolours. A number of single-horse vehicles with driver only (no footman at rear) are probably station cabs on hire, or "growlers", that lasted from the 1840s into the twentieth century. The vehicle on the left with two horses in tandem is probably a waggon. The atmospheric pipe is well illustrated, although the row of fixing bolts for the continuous valve would actually have been on the opposite side, as indeed they are in the other view. The majority of the station platform was built as part of the viaduct in 1845, and the station opened in May 1846 without any buildings or covering. The train shed and street level buildings seen here were an afterthought, authorised in August 1846 and completed around April 1847. The train shed is interesting, with its arched opening at this end and rectangular opening at the other end. A secondary opening at the far end enables passengers to pass further down the platform, whilst at the near end there is only a small window above a covered flight of steps leading from the street 25 feet below. The 1847 booking office down at the lower level is not well drawn, and a generous use of artistic licence has raised it high enough to appear in the view. These buildings and the 1847 train shed were all removed in 1861, when the present station building and South Devon Railway offices were erected.

seen well in the foreground here, was built of timber, cantilevered out from the viaduct. The 25 feet height of the viaduct is under-emphasised in this view. The waiting passengers seem quite nonchalant about the drop, and it is obviously not possible to stand at the selected viewpoint. Oil lamps are provided for the platform, and an opening in the end screen allows access into the train shed. The stone parapet on the opposite side of the line includes regular refuge points, or telegraph pole access positions. There is a telegraph pole by the second one, and more beyond the station, but posts nearer the viewer have been omitted by the artist.

Longitudinal Section

The most impressive single engineering structure on the line, St. Thomas Viaduct begins with thirteen stone arches rising at 1 in 645 to cross Cowick St. by a wider stone arch and reach St. Thomas Station. From here the viaduct falls away at 1 in 181, a further forty-five arches leading finally to a larger arch over Alphington Road and onto a high embankment. Still falling gently at 1 in 278 and then 1 in 192, the embankment gradually reduces to more modest proportions, crossing a brook just before the end of the sheet (not the Alphington Brook which is actually on sheet 3). There was no pumping station at St. Thomas, and therefore no break in the tube. The trains had to be brought to a stand against the force of atmospheric pressure, and over-shoots were not uncommon. The arrangement of the viaduct with the station at the summit was possibly intended to assist in the stopping and re-starting of trains, but was mostly determined by the levels of the roads to be crossed.

Route Plan - 194¾ miles to 195⅜ miles

The area around St. Thomas Station is quite built up, and there are also buildings along Alphington Road. Elsewhere there are several orchards and market gardens. Creation of the high embankment has required considerable side cuttings, which have become flooded. The whole of each field would have been purchased, and the unused area offered back to adjacent landowners - at a price. Contract No. 1 was entirely on embankment, so this side cutting for material was inevitable. These side cuttings mark the site of the later 1867 City Basin Junction, and the 1903 Alphington Road Goods Yard and junction for the Teign Valley branch. Towards the end of the sheet, the line runs near the Exeter Canal, which it will follow across the flood plain. The original canal was constructed from 1564 onwards, and much improved from 1698. Further alterations and extensions were carried out between 1820 and 1830, so that by the time of the opening of the railway craft of 14 feet draught and up to 200 tons burthen could obtain access to the City Basin.

View North of the Line

The view commences with Addiscott's Nursery and the Cowick Fields (✓), both of which have been cut in half by the railway, although access was naturally available through the arches of the viaduct. St. Thomas's Church (✓) stands at the end of development along the road. First recorded in 1298, the present house dates from about 1800. The viaduct as built in 1845 was made wider than usual for seven arches, to accommodate the station platform, but this was only 175 feet in length and it was necessary to lengthen it at the south end in 1847. The extension,

Modern View – 02 South
G.S.

An appropriate van passes under the Cowick Street arch in the middle of Brunel's lengthy viaduct. This is the up side, added in 1861 when the line was doubled. This part of the widened viaduct, opposite the old station, across Cowick Street and on towards St. David's, was built wider than the remainder, allowing a generous up platform to be created. The buildings between the viaduct and the River Exe have been demolished and replaced, in connection with the building of the new Exe Bridges in 1969 and 1974.

Modern View – 02 North
G.S.

in connection with the viaduct widening in 1861, the temporary station at St. Thomas was replaced with a much grander affair. This incorporated the administrative offices of the South Devon Railway and an overall roof was provided for the widened station. The roof was removed in 1970, when the up side buildings were demolished. Note the granite nosing along most of the down side the platform edge. The 1861 building on this side remains in good condition, although no longer in railway usage.

2

From the Station in St. Thomas to the Alphington Meadows.

View South of the Line.

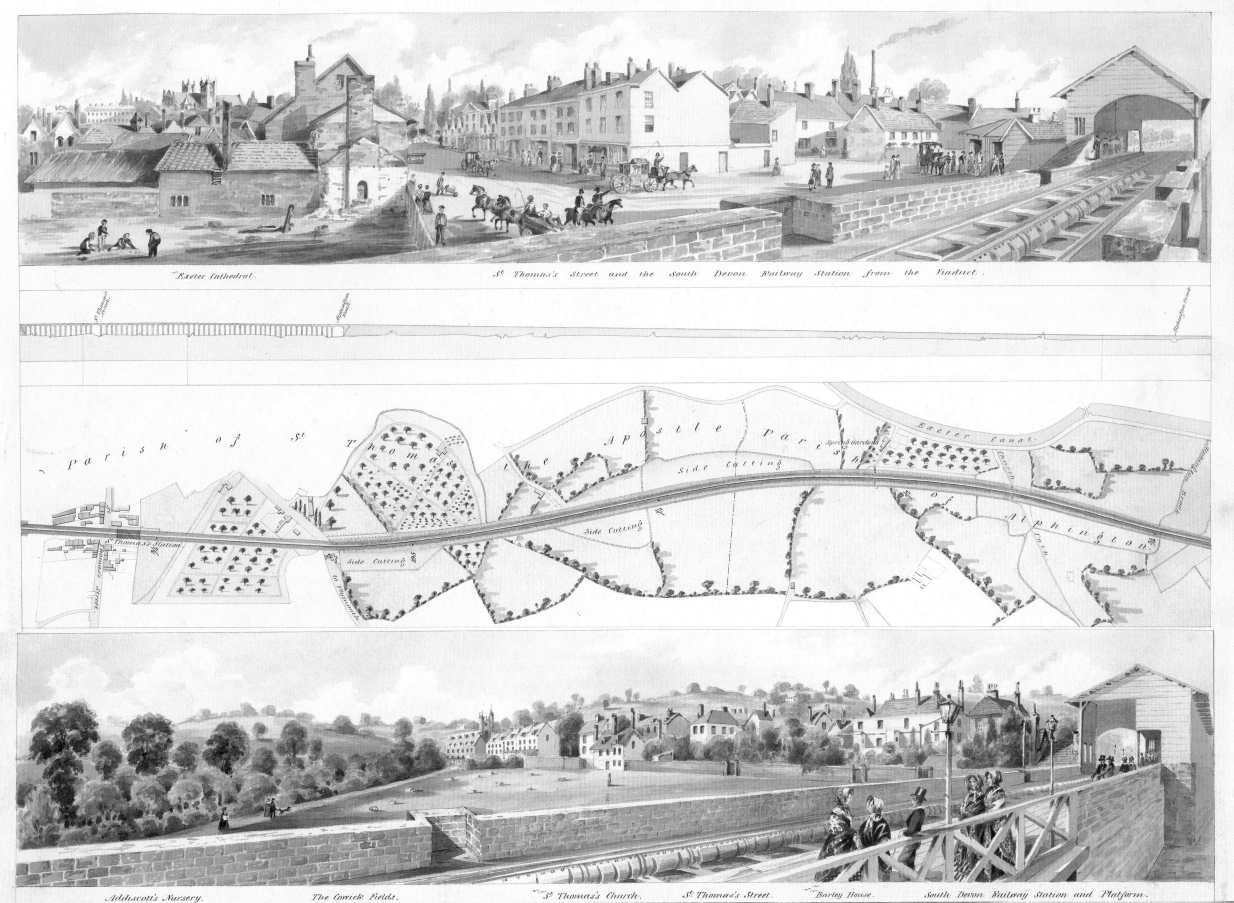

Exeter Cathedral.

St. Thomas's Street and the South Devon Railway Station from the Viaduct.

Parish of St. Thomas the Apostle Parish

Exeter Canal.

Spring Gardens

St. Thomas's Station

St. Thomas's Street

Side Cutting

Side Cutting

Side Cutting

of Alphington

Addiscott's Nursery.

The Cowick Fields.

St. Thomas's Church.

St. Thomas's Street.

Barley House.

South Devon Railway Station and Platform.

From the Alphington Meadows to the Station in St. Thomas.

View North of the Line.

3 From the Alphington Meadows to Countess Wear

View South of the Line

The view begins with the railway and a footpath both crossing the Alphin Brook on the skew. Behind, on the canal towpath, two horses are drawing a barque towards Double Locks (∿) and the sea, the position of the locks being marked by the 18th century inn. Thomas Perryman had been lock-keeper at Double Locks, being provided with a house, field and garden and employing one assistant. The job of lock-keeper carried with it the trade of innkeeper, the house being licensed, and having stabling and accommodation. Perryman had died in April 1841 and had been succeeded by his son. Beyond the River Exe, Countess Wear Chapel (∿∿) and the houses of Countess Wear (∿∿∿) are visible. The more common spelling Weir is incorrectly used on the drawings instead of the local Wear. Cattle graze on the water meadows beyond the railway, and cattle and sheep on the near side. The railway was fully fenced, despite the water filled ditches alongside the railway, but as on almost all of the views nothing has been shown by the artist. To the right the road to Countess Wear crosses the railway by a single-span sandstone arch, which hardly qualifies for the grandiose title of viaduct (∿∿∿) given on the drawing. This is an artificially shortened view; the Countess Wear road bridge was actually a mile from the artist's position, as shown on the plan on sheet 4. In the distance can be seen the hills of Woodbury Common.

Longitudinal Section

The least remarkable length of line on the railway, the trackbed runs more or less level on a shallow embankment raised just above the flood plain. Several drainage ditches have been interrupted by the earthworks, the isolated stretches being collected together by a new drain running alongside the embankment. Bridges within the embankment at intervals, such as the skew bridge for the Alphin Brook (incorrectly labelled as Alphington Brook), allowed water to cross under the railway and reach the main drainage ditch which ran beside the Exeter Canal as far as the Estuary at Turf. To the left Watery Lane crosses over the railway by a single arch bridge. This had been authorised and originally built as a level crossing, but in February 1848 Brunel was asked to make a bridge instead because of the difficulties of a level crossing under atmospheric working.

Route Plan - 196 miles to 196¾ miles

At the left-hand end of the plan the splendidly named Watery Lane passes over the railway and runs down to the canal bank, and a swing bridge leading to the far side and the River Exe beyond. Next, the Alphin Brook can be seen running diagonally under the railway in the direction of Double Locks. Another drainage ditch marks the boundary between the parishes of Alphington and Exminster. The complicated network of meadow drainage continues, all discharging into the collector ditch formed alongside the Exeter Canal, further progress toward the river being impeded by the canal banks, which were raised as part of the improvement works between 1820 and 1830. The embankment to the Estuary had been raised at the same time, following extensive flooding of the whole area in 1824.

View North of the Line

The Countess Wear Road crosses the line by a single-arch bridge (∿) to the left of the view, and continues on an embankment towards the main Exeter to Dawlish road in the distance. The railway runs across the water meadows on a low embankment, passing the cottage of the Reverend T. Melhuish, then Knoll Hill. (∿∿). Sheep are grazing on a small piece of the flood plain, isolated by drainage ditches. In the foreground runs the towpath of the Exeter Canal. A pair of heavy horses - Shires or Clydesdales - are harnessed in tandem for towing vessels on the canal. Note the single rope from the barge, and the whipple tree that spreads the line for a pair of chains to the iron harness of the horses' collars. There are mooring bollards on the bank, so the barge or small ship is probably waiting to pass through Double Locks, whilst the horses take a breather. The vessel is not moored to the bollards and is perhaps in the process of being manhandled into the lock. If this is indeed the case, over half a mile has been conveniently lost between the horses at Double Locks and Countess Wear Bridge.

Modern View – 03 North

P.R.G.

Following the disastrous floods of October and December 1960, Exeter's grand flood prevention project was implemented between 1965 and 1977. The village of Alphington had also suffered, and protection measures were included in the scheme, with the Alphin Brook being routed through a flood relief channel. This involved constructing a new railway bridge over the channel, which has sluices at this point. The channel continues between the railway and the Exeter Canal until it discharges onto the flood plain below Countess Weir.

Modern View – 03 South

P.R.G.

The Double Locks date from 1701 when the Exeter Canal was rebuilt to take ocean going ships up to 150 tons burthen. The name refers to the double width of the lock; at 75 feet wide by 350 feet long the pound acts as a passing place. The lock house of 1701 was remodelled in 1827 by James Green, to create the inn, hotel and stables apparent in Dawson's watercolour and still evident today. The towers of Exeter Cathedral and spire of St Leonard's Church are visible in the distance.

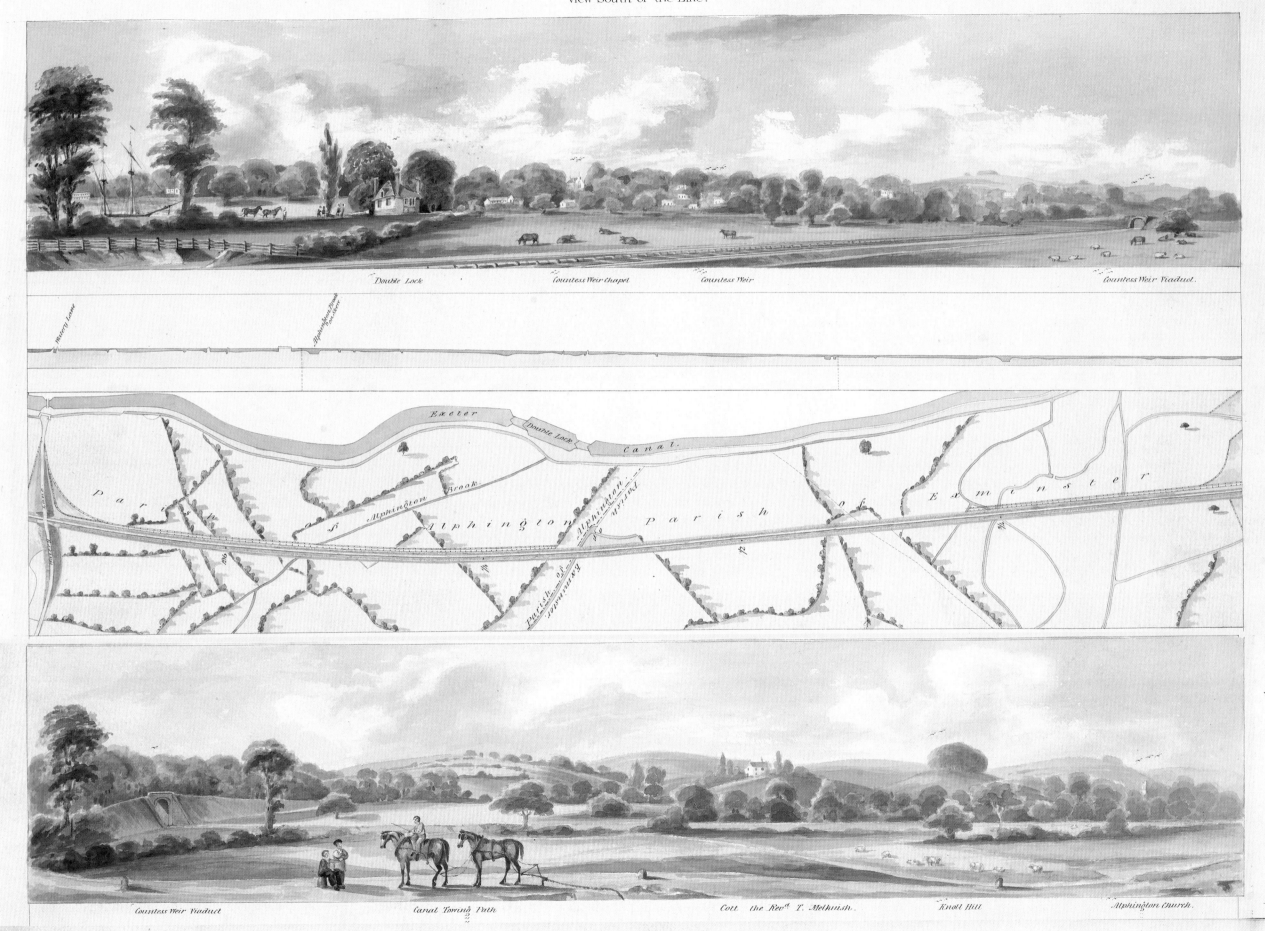

3

From the Alphington Meadows to Countess Weir.
View South of the Line.

Double Lock   Countess Weir Chapel   Countess Weir   Countess Weir Viaduct.

Exeter   Double Lock   Canal.

Parish   of   Alphington   Alphington   parish   of   Exminster

Countess Weir Viaduct   Canal Towing Path   Cott. the Rev.d T. Methuish.   Knoll Hill   Alphington Church.

From Countess Weir to the Alphington Meadows.
View North of the Line.

View North of the Line

The cutting face of Exminster Quarry (✓) is prominent in this view, the red sandstone being used locally in mediaeval times. The Devon County Lunatic Asylum (✓) forms an imposing feature on the heights above. This was of enlightened design, and comprised a series of wards radiating out from a central service block. It was built just before the railway in 1842-1845. The village of Exminster, which had a population 1,623 in 1851, is hidden by the trees. South Devon cattle, shown standing in the shade of a tree, are a breed known for 250 years. They are much larger and yellower in colour than the deep-red Devons, their milk being just as rich but of greater quantity. To the right of the view, which has been

Route Plan - 196 miles to 196¾ miles

The three road overbridges carrying Countess Wear Road, Lime Kiln Lane (shown as Trood's Viaduct on the View North of the Line) and Milbury Lane are clearly shown. Each has been diverted slightly from its former route, and the side cuttings formed in making their approach embankments have become flooded. The curved wooded area below the railway to the left of the third bridge is the Exminster Quarry. This dated from mediaeval times, its red sandstone being used for construction of

Longitudinal Section

The railway continues its level course across the flood plain on its shallow embankment. Engineering features are limited to single-arch stone overbridges. The first carries the road to Countess Wear, and the second Lime Kiln Lane which leads to the kilns shown in the view above. The line then passes alongside an old quarry, requiring a quarry pit to be

View South of the Line

The sheet begins with another view of the bridge carrying the Countess Wear road (✓) over the railway. The canal swing bridge is hidden from view, but the long river bridge (✓) of 1774 with three small arches to each side of its main span can be seen in the distance, with the houses of Countess Wear beyond. The Countess Wear Engine House (✓), the second on the line, is prominent in this view. It was built by Carpenter, starting in June 1845. The engines were constructed by Rennie, being steamed for the first time on 23rd February 1847. The two principal engines and two supplementary engines were housed in the tall engine house proper, the lower roofed building being the boiler house containing three boilers, each aligned with a large arched end door. The buildings are shown as constructed of red sandstone with Bath stone dressings, although this has yet to be proved by excavation.

---

foreshortened creating an artificially sharp curve to the railway, is the single-arch red sandstone overbridge carrying Lime Lane over the railway. In the view it is labelled as Trood's Viaduct (✓), Trood presumably being the owner or tenant of the line kilns. Trood House stood a mile or so inland from this point, so the line kilns were possibly associated with the house. As with most of these single-arch bridges, Dawson has seen fit to bestow on it the title of viaduct, which it hardly deserved. The atmospheric tube is shown in place on the railway, but the fencing and telegraph poles are not illustrated, as is the case with so many of these views.

churches between Exeter and Paignton, including Kenton and Paignton itself. Countess Wear Engine House is picked out in pink, together with its large reservoir, or "tank" as it is labelled on the plan. A new drainage ditch runs along the inland side of the new embankment, joining up the truncated ends of all the old ditches. It appears that only a limited number of culverts were cut through the embankment, rather than one for each of the old ditches.

Filled in before construction of the embankment. The last feature of note is a further overbridge carrying an occupation road known as Milbury Lane. A number of culverts were also obviously required, allowing drainage ditches to pass under the railway.

A preliminary investigation has however revealed a circular feature of about 21 feet diameter next to the engine house, perhaps connected with the water supply. A rake of four coal waggons stands in the siding, although the connection with the main line is not shown. Presumably there was a normal set of points, and a gap in the atmospheric tube with closure valves in the ends. There is a large open-air reservoir behind the waggons, to provide water for the boilers. A barque is again illustrated progressing down the Exeter Canal, although no draught horses have been shown. Prior to 1676 the Canal entered the River Exe at about this point, before it was extended towards the sea. The view finishes with lime kilns by the canal side, brought closer to the engine house to complete the composition.

Modern View – 04 North

G.S.

The Countess Wear swing bridge was completed in 1937 and replaced James Green's 8-feet wide cast iron swing bridge, which dated from the 1820s. Constructed of steel, it is 107 feet long, with a 20-foot wide carriageway and 5-foot pedestrian way. The northern bascule bridge (behind in the photo) was built in 1972, parallel to the swing bridge to form a duel carriageway. The lifting section is 57 feet long, with a 22-foot carriageway and 7-foot pedestrian way. The bridges are operated from a control room that looks similar to a bridge on a ship.

Modern View – 04 South

G.S.

Taken from Lime Kiln Bridge looking towards the road leading to Countess Wear, this shows the replacement of the bridge in Dawson's view. The railway was doubled along this stretch in 1862, a simple task involving a shallow embankment across the level meadows. It is also one of the very few lengths of straight track on the former South Devon Railway system. The site of the atmospheric railway Countess Wear engine house lay to the right of the picture.

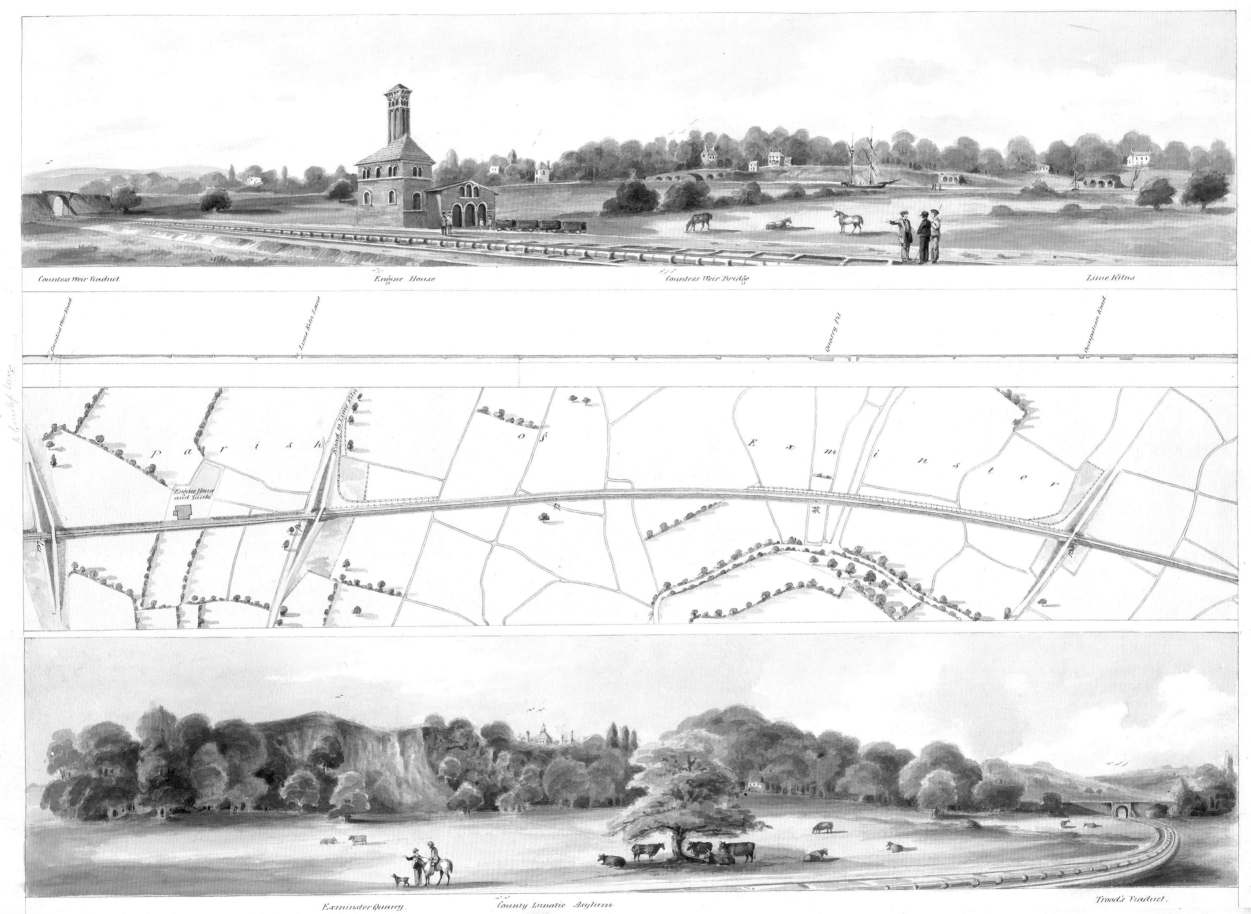

From Countess Weir to the Exminster Marshes.
View South of the Line.

4

Countess Weir Viaduct   Engine House   Countess Weir Bridge   Lime Kilns

Exminster Quarry   County Lunatic Asylum   Trood's Viaduct.

From the Exminster Marshes to Countess Weir.
View North of the Line.

5 The Exminster Marshes

View South of the Line

This is the first sheet to feature an atmospheric train, a covered piston carriage drawing a train of five coaches, all six vehicles being in brown livery. Behind the train is Exminster Viaduct (✓), also known as Milbury Lane Bridge, which is shown on the plan on sheet four. The Exminster Marshes, drained to form rich meadows and arable land, stretch out over a wide area here, to the Exeter Canal and River Exe in the distance. The Retreat of H. Hamilton Esq (✓✓) is featured on the far bank. The scene is taken from the top of the Topsham Road overbridge, the road leading

down to a swing bridge across the canal and a ferry across the Exe to the town of Topsham (✓✓✓), which can be seen in the distance. Exminster station was to be opened just to the right of this bridge in August 1852, after which the road became known as Station Road. Some cattle are standing on the truncated remains of the old road next to the new bridge. Beyond the hayrick standing next to the road, the River Exe (✓✓✓) begins to widen out into an estuary, at least when the tide is in as shown in the watercolour. At other times there are fairly extensive mud flats.

Longitudinal Section

The railway continues on the level across the marshes, raised clear of the flood plain on its shallow embankment. The majority of the drainage ditches crossing the route have been filled in by the embankment. The position of Topsham Road Bridge is indicated as "Occupation Road". A little further on there is a note reading "Cross Occupation Road", which almost certainly refers to a level crossing. Crossing an atmospheric

railway on the level must have been an interesting business. It is a pity that the apparatus did not catch the eye of the artist. Possibly they were among the last items to be constructed, and were not in place at the time of his visit. There is no actual evidence of active level crossings during the atmospheric period.

Route Plan - 198¾ miles to 199¾ miles

The marshes are so wide here that no feature beyond them appears on the strip plan. As elsewhere, there is a continuous drainage ditch on the inland side of the embankment, connecting the truncated ends of all the old ditches. Some of them were probably linked by culverts to the far side of the line. There is a particularly densely drained area near the centre of the sheet, the ditches with the trees along their banks being on the site of the future Exminster Station of 1852. The former route of Topsham Road is clearly shown, the new bridge being constructed just beside it. As elsewhere the side cuttings have filled with water. The

occupation road is illustrated in the centre of the plan, although nothing is shown of the actual level crossing. Other than at stations, a broad orange band has been painted along each side of the railway line. This has been done to emphasise the route of the railway, but does not prevent fine detail being shown adjacent to the line. To the right of the sheet we move from the Parish of Exminster into the Parish of Powderham. There is quite a high bank and a ditch forming the boundary, swallowed up by the new embankment.

View North of the Line

Apparently a hayrick is being built in the field - not unusual, particularly when the cattle are over-wintered there. The rick will be thatched with straw, by a farm worker having the necessary skills, using home produced straw when available. By far the greater part of hay and corn crops were still mown by hand - scythes being preferred for cutting grass and hooks (sickles) for corn. Gleaning was still widespread. Two waggons are hay-making, each with three horses in tandem. The nearer one is loading, and has a boy holding the leading horse, to control it when standing or walking. The far waggon is having its hay load pitched up onto the rick, behind which the 14th century St. Martin's Church, Exminster (✓) can be seen, together with its parsonage. The vehicle just moving off the bridge on the right, bringing a large load of hay from the meadows east

of the railway, appears to have but one pair of wheels. Although the need for four horses in tandem to draw it would suggest a "waggon" load, the large size of the wheels and body suggest a cart. Exminster Viaduct, or Milbury Lane Bridge as it is also known, appears to the right, the plan being shown on sheet four. Unlike the other bridges on this section, this was constructed with further segmental abutment arches either side of the main span. There are also arches in the piers. The abutment arches were walled up when the line was doubled in 1861, and a single iron main span was substituted, but the bridge remained known to local railwaymen as "Three Arch Bridge" into the days of British Railways.

Modern View – 05 North

G.S.

with the opening of Exminster station, Topsham Road was renamed Station Road. The railway was doubled in 1860, current concrete span dates from 1970. The right hand span was added in 1924 when the down platform loop was created. The left one followed in 1931 with the up loop, which required new steps down to the station, once carried on the projecting concrete brackets. The yellow sign indicates that this is a "legally protected environment site".

Modern View – 05 South

G.S.

Exminster was a large village of 1,177 inhabitants immediately prior to the coming of the railway, but surprisingly was not served by its own station when the line first opened. The S.D.R. was in a perilous financial state after the atmospheric debacle and the maintenance of the line was let out to George Hennet from 1849 to 1853. It was he who built and operated Exminster station, which opened in 1852. The booking office and waiting room were on the ground floor, with residential accommodation upstairs.

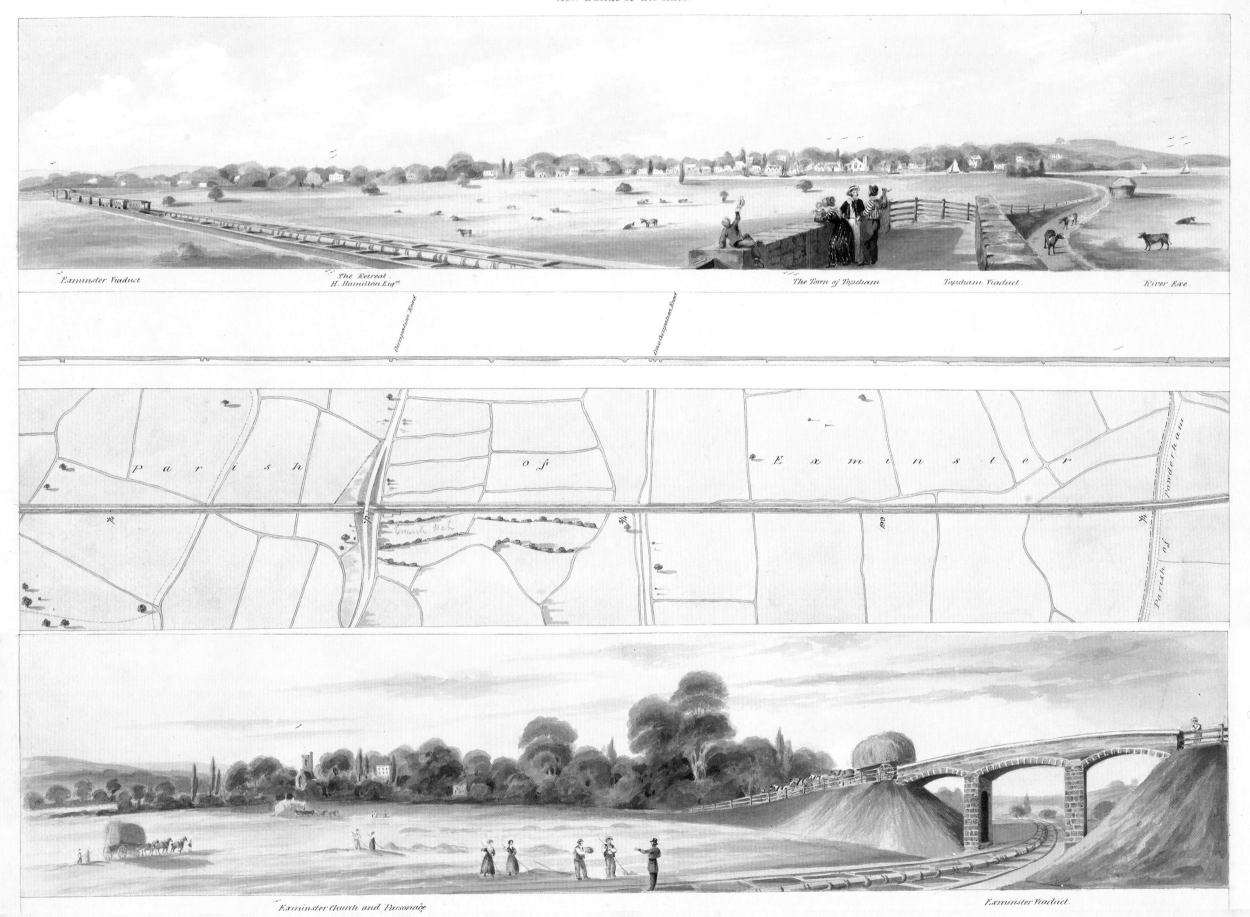

The Exminster Marshes.
View South of the Line.

5

Exminster Viaduct.   The Retreat. H. Hamilton Esq⁺ᵉ   The Town of Topsham.   Topsham Viaduct.   River Exe.

Occupation Road   Cross Occupation Road

Parish   of   Exminster   Townsham

Exminster Marsh   Parish of

Exminster Church and Parsonage   Exminster Viaduct.

The Exminster Marshes.
View North of the Line.

View North of the Line

This view is taken from the last section of sea wall forming Contract No. 2, which was let to John Waring. By the beautiful grounds of Powderham Park can be seen the 15th century St. Clement's Church, Powderham, and its parsonage, as shown on the plan view on sheet 7. The Church is built of red Breccia sandstone and is not grey as illustrated. Breccia is similar to conglomerate, but the largest fragments are angular and not water-worn. The Belvedere (v) in Powderham Park dates from 1773. The labourer to the right is sitting on the wall of the Powderham slipway, one of several provided under the line at the Earl of Devon's insistence, in order to maintain access to the water. The remaining part of the view looks along the stretch of line covered by sheet 6, with Turf Engine House (vv) in the distance, and telegraph posts erected beside the line.

Route Plan - 199¾ miles to 200½ miles

Turf Engine House is indicated in pink, with its coal siding to the right and reservoir to the left. The latter would have been constructed using conventional canal techniques of puddled clay lining. The feature on the opposite side of the line from the engine house is intriguing. Today both rectangular and semi-circular shapes form a depression below the general meadow level. Tithe maps of the era show a circular feature within the semi-circle and are labelled "reservoir" at this point. The "South" view shows pipework within a pit in a raised area of ground.

Possibly water from the embankment-side ditch was collected here before being pumped across to the engine house "tank". The occupation road on the left leads from Exminster, via the farm at Exwell Barton and the level crossing, to a lime kiln on the Estuary, and then Turf Lock at the entrance to the Canal. Along with animal manure and sea sand, lime was much used for fertiliser at this period, as well as in mortar for building purposes. The sea wall is clearly shown, with the railway joining it just before the end of the sheet.

Longitudinal Section

This final section of Contract No. 1 again consisted of simple civil engineering works in the form of a low-level embankment, before climbing briefly at 1 in 258 to reach the slightly higher level of the sea wall section of the line. Various ditches are shown as being filled by the embankment, and the only other feature of note is the occupation road crossing the line on the level. The policeman's duties presumably consisted of controlling this crossing, and perhaps operating valves external to the engine house. Whilst the down-side level crossing gate appears in the "South" view, the actual apparatus used at the crossing to enable vehicles to cross the pipe is unfortunately out of sight. There would have been a break in the tube, sealed by valves, opposite the engine house, separating one section of pipe from the next and allowing the installation of a waggon turntable to serve the coal siding. At the end of the sheet the embankment crosses the line of the old sea wall.

View South of the Line

The works appear newly constructed in this view, with no signs of plant life on the various excavations. The watercolours seem to have been completed in the studio, from sketches made on site - the soil in particular is lacking in colour. Turf House stands at the final entrance to the Exeter Canal, extended to this position in 1827. The lock-keeper cum innkeeper had been Nicholas Lewis, until he lost his job in February 1841 through being "incapacitated from performing the duties of his office". Two ships are moored within the pound prior to passing through the final lock into the Exe Estuary. On the far side of the estuary the high ground of Woodbury Common can be seen. The large reservoir or "tank" for the engine house has been newly excavated on the far side of the line from 150 yards nearer Exeter, following instructions from Brunel. There is some doubt over the walling materials used, which Dawson shows as red sandstone with Bath stone details. It is said that the stone was later re-used for Exwell Barton farmhouse, and the latter was indeed built around 1870 in red Heavitree stone, following a fire in the previous house. However, Broad Gauge Society excavations immediately below ground level have revealed walls of grey limestone with red sandstone quoins. Several outbuildings at Exwell Barton are constructed in this way, so it is possible that the story of second-hand stone should apply to them. The roof was clad in Italian tiling, stamped "Browne's Patent, Bridgwater" and glazed black on the outside. The building was substantially complete by December 1845, when the chimney was found to be out of true, and Brunel instructed Margary to build a buttress to stabilise it. Boulton and Watt were on site throughout 1846 installing the two 40 hp pumping engines and also two 12 hp supplementary engines. The engines were started for the first time on 4th February 1847, the first atmospheric train running on 25th February 1847. A coal waggon is seen standing on the siding beyond the engine house, at right angles to the railway line.

Modern View – 06 South   G.S.

The reservoir at Turf, approximately 130 feet long by 150 feet wide, is the best preserved of the former engine house ponds. In the background stands Turf Hotel, a timber framed building with slate elevations constructed in 1827 when the Exeter Canal was extended two miles to a point where craft of 12 feet draught could navigate at all tides. The Broad Gauge Society made four archaeological visits here between 1995 and 1998, when we were investigating the foundations of Turf engine house.

Modern View – 06 North   G.S.

St Clements church, Powderham was founded in 1259. The north aisle is the oldest part of the building and some of the original walls are still standing. The church was restored and rebuilt in the fifteenth century by Sir William Courtenay and his wife Margaret, who erected the nave and south aisle. They were buried in the church, though no trace of their tomb survives. Further renovation took place in the 1840s. The rectory was built by Henry Hugh Courtenay, who became the 13th Earl of Devon in 1891.

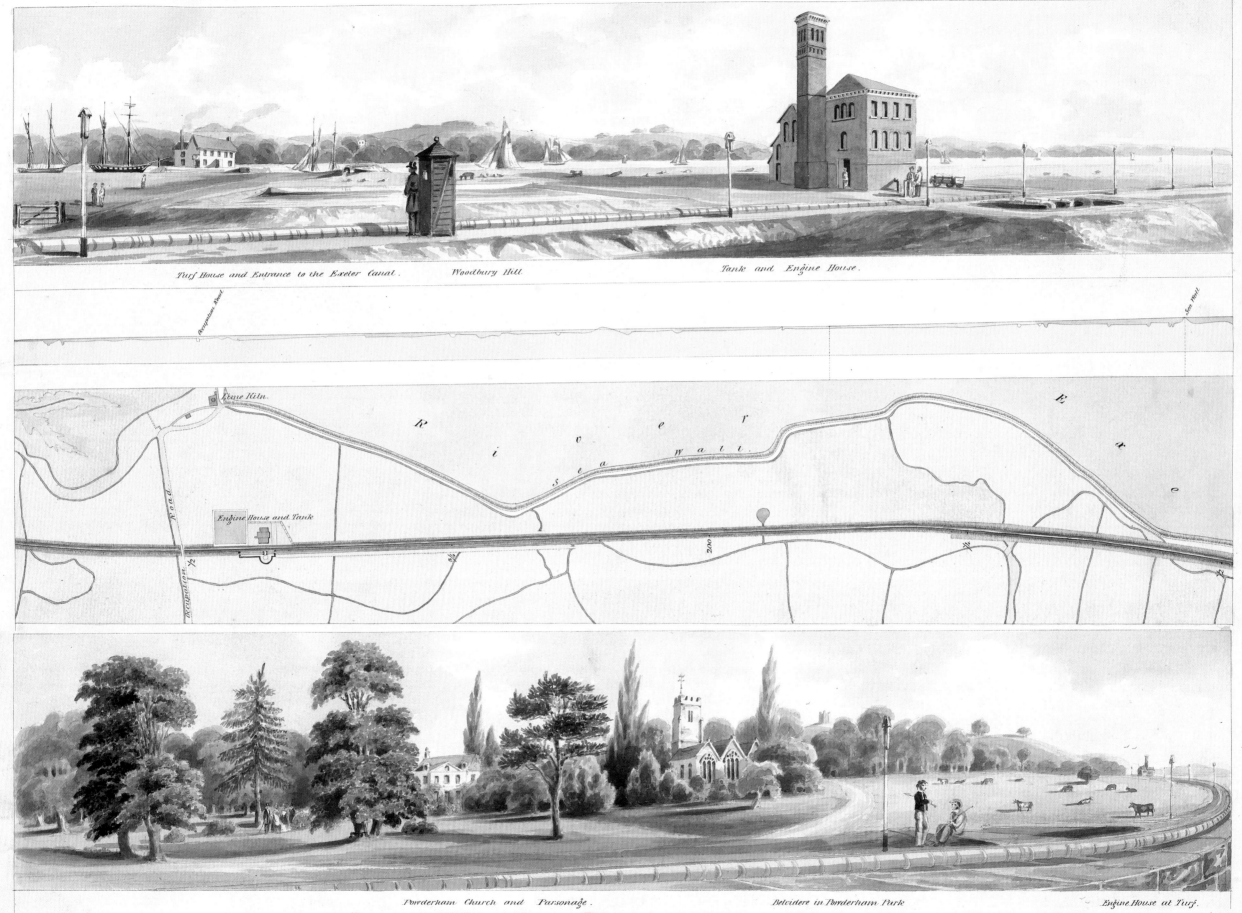

Turf House and Entrance to the Exeter Canal.   Woodbury Hill   Tank and Engine House.

Powderham Church and Parsonage.   Belvidere in Powderham Park   Engine House at Turf.

Powderham Marshes
View North of the Line

Modern View – 07 North   P.R.G.

The Manor of Powderham was mentioned in the Domesday Book and came into the Courtenay family in 1325. Construction of Powderham Castle was begun in 1391 under Sir Philip Courtenay, the third Earl of Devon. The Castle was much altered by lavish building works during the Georgian and Victorian periods. Following construction of the railway, the former shoreline has become an isolated pond within the Deer Park. The herd of fallow deer has been continuously maintained here since before 1723 and numbers around 600.

View North of the Line

This view is taken from the stretch of new river wall built out in the Exe Estuary. The perspective of the wall and railway leaves something to be desired, and quite why wet sand is shown right up to the top of the wall remains a mystery. It also seems an unlikely spot to leave a boat, although it does form a useful contribution to the artistic composition. The previous line of the river bank is clearly shown, although it is not possible to make out the old river wall, or the Powderham Road which ran behind it. The old wall was of inferior construction to the new railway wall, and may well have been used as a source of material for its replacement. In either case there is nothing very wall-like visible in the watercolour. The newly isolated area of mud flats waits to be filled in. Powderham Castle, home of the Earl of Devon, is well illustrated, together with its Park, which is well stocked with deer. Originally a fortified manor house of the 15th century, the Castle was largely rebuilt between 1770 and 1788. Further remodelling was carried out for the 10th Earl between 1835 and 1859. It seems surprising that the railway was able to pass so close to the Castle, but the Haldon Hills rising behind the trees demonstrate the attraction of a low coastal route.

Route Plan – 200¾ miles to 201½ miles

For most of this stretch the railway is carried on an embankment, with a new river wall constructed outside it. After passing Powderham Church and its rectory, the line runs inland to avoid the boat house with its landing stage. The pre-railway river wall and ditch remain intact on this stretch. Inland from the railway some of the beautiful planting of Powderham Deer Park is indicated. There then follows a stretch with the new embankment and river wall built out in the estuary. The old river wall, road and ditch follow their original course at this date, before the area is filled in and the road altered to follow the railway. The route passes from the Parish of Powderham to the Parish of Kenton, before crossing the River Kenn. The main channel of the Exe runs quite close to the railway on this stretch, as shown by the darker shade of blue, there being extensive mud flats on the Lympstone side.

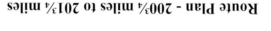

Longitudinal Section

The railway runs level on an embankment of varying height throughout this stretch, the highest embankment being required where the railway was built out beyond the high tide line on the estuary mud flats, whereas where the line passed inland of the boat house it was virtually at existing ground level. There is a bridge under the line to accommodate Powderham Slipway. The underbridge at the boat house shown in the view is marked "Road", and its adjacent footbridge as "Footbridge to Castle" allowing those arriving by boat to make their way to Powderham Castle. Two of the drainage ditches passing under the line are shown, and the Powderham Road at several points where the line runs alongside the railway. A bridge with two rectangular openings, presumably in timber, is shown crossing the River Kenn where it enters the Estuary.

View South of the Line

This view shows the section that formed the start of the works for Contract No. 2, which was let to John Waring. The timber footbridge over the railway only lasted until 1860, and is noteworthy by the fact that it is alongside an underbridge giving access to the same location. The low-lying road access to the boat house via the low under-line bridge may well have been prone to flooding, and as such warranted the extra expense of the footbridge. The underbridge appears to be constructed from limestone similar to that used for the Exe river wall, which came from Torbay. The permanent way seen from rail level depicts the atmospheric pipe standing high above the rails. On the other side of the Exe Estuary can be seen Nutwell Court (↗), home of Sir T. Drake, Bart., Woodbury Castle (↗↗), and the village of Lympstone (↗↗↗). The boat house, with its landing stage hidden beyond, is quite a substantial affair, converted from former salmon fishermen's cottages. A mast has been erected alongside, presumably used for signalling purposes, and possibly also used for training as it is still fitted with a spar. A pair of attractive topsail schooners are beating their way up the estuary.

Modern View – 07 South   P.R.G.

The limestone underbridge still gives access to the former salmon fishermen's cottages on Powderham Point. These are the three pitched roofs to the right of the bridge, which was widened in 1860 when the line was doubled. The Starcross Yacht Club was founded in 1772 and originally based at Starcross harbour. The trend away from stout clinker-built craft, designed to be left at moorings, towards modern lightweight dinghies resulted in a move to Powderham Point in 1957. The salmon fishermen's cottages now form part of the club's facilities.

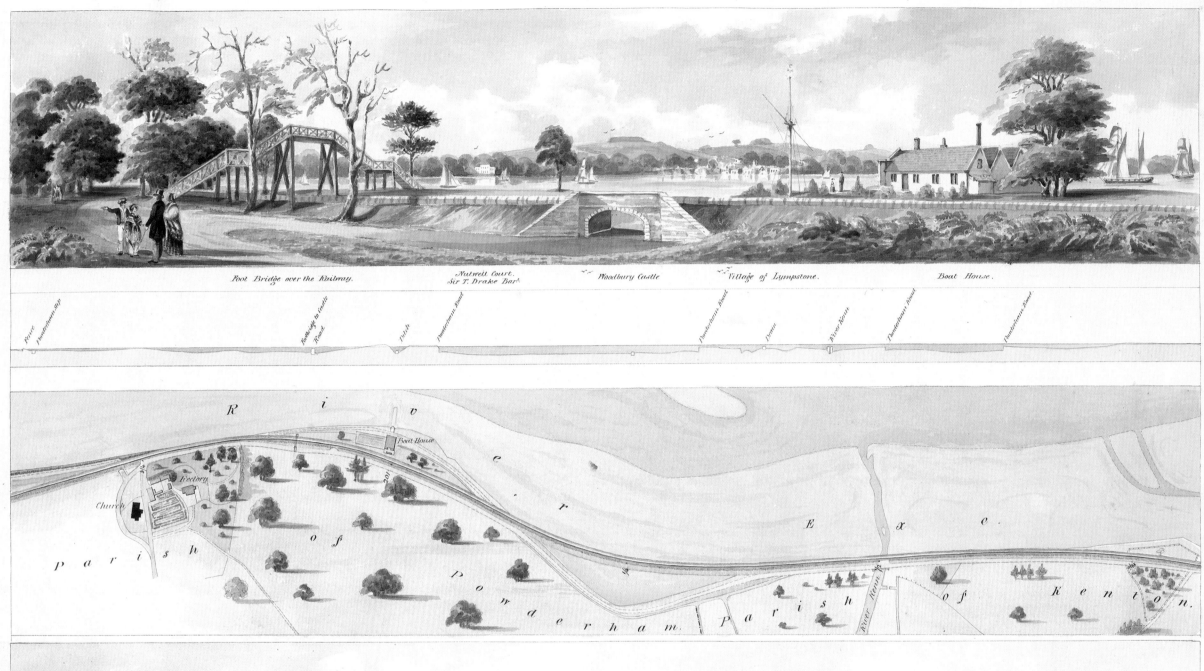

Foot Bridge over the Railway.   Nutwell Court.   Woodbury Castle.   Village of Lympstone.   Boat House.
               Sir T. Drake Bart.

Powderham Castle and Park
The Earl of Devon.

Powderham Park
View North of the Line.

8 From Powderham Park to Cockwood Lake

Modern View – 08 North

The Starcross engine house has served as a Wesleyan Methodist chapel from 1869 to 1958 and still stands as a testament to Brunel's immaculate attention to detail. The walls were constructed of red Breccia, said to have been recovered from tunnel excavation when building the railway. Exposure to the weather since 1846 has reduced the softer infill leaving the angular fragments exposed. The elegant profiles of the Bath stone corbels to the roof were based on sketches made by Brunel during his travels in Italy.

Modern View – 08 North   P.R.G.

Modern View – 08 South

Modern View – 08 South   P.R.G.

The sunken areas between the railway embankment and the old shoreline are still discernable around Starcross, this one in use as a car park. The embankment was widened inland from the estuary wall in 1874, to accommodate the new up line when this stretch of railway was doubled. In more recent years further infill has taken place, enabling the local portion of the Exe Estuary Cycle Trail to be opened in 2007. The engine house still dominates the village, even with its reduced tower.

View North of the Line

A splendid panorama of Starcross from the jetty, this time correctly located opposite the engine house ( ), although the space between the latter and the balconied Courtenay Arms Inn ( ) has been exaggerated. It is thought that stone excavated from the coastal tunnels was used for some of the engine houses, comprising Permian and Triassic red sandstone, Breccia and conglomerate. In some cases it provided contrasting quoins, whilst here at Starcross it formed the main building material. The window surrounds and other decorative features are in Bath stone, more elaborate than usual due to the proximity of the village and its influential residents. There is a disc and crossbar signal, with black policeman's cabin at the foot of the post, near the entrance to

the engine house siding indicated by the brown-painted coal waggons. A second disc and crossbar signal stands just before the typical South Devon train shed ( ), whilst a number of reddish-brown vehicles occupy the outer through track, to the right of the station. The timber pier was 270 feet long and built by the S.D.R. in 1846. A ferry service across the estuary to Exmouth, without its own railway until 1861, was let to James Pyne of Exmouth, who sub-let to a variety of boatmen. A small lugger and a large rowing boat, with smartly dressed passengers in the stern, are seen passing the breakwater, to enter the harbour. The passengers would be faced with a three hundred yard walk, using a foot crossing of the line by the Courtenay Arms, to reach the railway station.

Route Plan - 202 miles to 203 miles

The railway embankment and river wall swing away from the old shore line, creating a backwater with two long cross embankments, there being an arch through the embankment between them for Duntze's slipway. The nearby Exeleigh House is shown dark red. Starcross station consisted of an outer through line, with a loop serving a single platform, 280 feet long, on the landward side. The timber station was reached from the adjacent road by two sets of steps leading up to a veranda, from which a door opened into the booking hall. A 98 feet by 24 feet timber train shed covered part of the platform and the adjacent track. It

was open on the outer side, supported on eleven timber posts. Between the station and the engine house, the Courtenay Arms was retained in a rather cramped location, causing the engine house plan to be altered with the engine room turned at right angles to the railway. Opposite stands the quayside, breakwater and jetty, which is shown a little too far north. At the end of the village the railway again moves well away from the old shoreline, being joined by two cross-embankments, before passing on to Cockwood Viaduct.

The position of Starcross Quay is indicated, where the railway passed across the existing quay so that no new embankment was required. At the end of the sheet the first few of the twenty-eight spans of Cockwood Viaduct are nicely shown, typical timber trusses carried on piles driven through the mud to harder ground below.

Longitudinal Section

The line continues on the level on its embankment and river wall, built on the old foreshore, albeit only a few yards outside the old river bank through Starcross village. Powderham Road is indicated at the start, before the route swings away from it. Six different openings are shown through the embankment, one marked "Stream", one "Brook", and the remainder, unmarked, are slipways providing access to the waterside.

View South of the Line

This view gives a good illustration of how the line was built in the river bed, with masonry outer wall and tipped embankment behind. The permanent way, atmospheric piping and masonry facing are well defined. The tubes are in 10 feet lengths, each with three large stiffening flanges. A supporting foot is bolted down to the transomme just short of each jointing socket. The fixing bolts for the continuous valve would be on the opposite side only, but Dawson shows them everywhere when the tube is close to the viewer. The telegraph poles and insulator mounting blocks are also well illustrated. The labourers in the pit between the new embankment and the old shore line are possibly removing weed, or strengthening one of the cross embankments appearing on the plan. The tide was meant to flow into these backwaters by means of culverts

through the embankments, but in practice they became clogged with mud and weed, the evil smell leading to numerous complaints from the likes of Sir John Duntze, Bart., of Exeleigh House shown on the right. Taking the Powderham Road above the old river bank is a pony phaeton, enjoying popularity again in the 1840s after its introduction in the late 1700s. With its mudguards, low body and step irons only a few inches above ground level it was well suited to ladies with flowing dresses. A child is perched on the rumble seat at the rear. A brig is making its way out to sea, and there is a small steam vessel beyond it. Beyond Starcross village ( ) and its engine house, the Warren ( ) stretches most of the way across the estuary in the direction of Exmouth ( ), which can also be seen.

From Powderham Park to Cockwood Lake.
View South of the Line.

8

Exmouth.   The Warren   Starcross Engine House and Village of Starcross   Exe Leigh House   Sir John Duntze Bart.

Jetty   Starcross Engine House.   Courtenay Arms Inn   Jetty   Village of Starcross   Station

From Cockwood Lake to Powderham Park
View North of the Line.

9 From Cockwood Lake to the Warren

View South of the Line

The crossing of Cockwood Lake (✓✓) was originally to be by walled embankment as elsewhere in the Estuary, with a 50 foot timber underbridge across the harbour entrance channel. However, deep mud and estuary deposits proved to be poor foundation for earthworks, and the design was changed to a continuous timber viaduct with 28 spans covering 187 yards. A longer main span over the navigable channel included wrought iron sides. The view does not feature this, and consequently has one span too many at 29. The structure comprised a continuous-span queen-post truss design bearing on timber piles which were driven to some 30 feet in depth. The development of a continuous-span design was supported by full-scale tests at Bristol by Brunel's assistant, Bell, and was clearly "state of the art" scientific investigation and analysis, laying a basis to the theory of structures and structural design. The continuous-span viaduct with queen-truss sides and spine beam under the line of track supported cross-decking upon which the ballast was laid. The permanent way was formed using Barlow rail bearing onto the ballast, providing an allowance for movement between the structure and the permanent way. The design loading for the structure was that of empirically based static loads, with the consideration of sway and motion from train movements being in their infancy. The waggon on the left drawn by a pair of horses in tandem strongly suggests a Devon type, even to a blue body and pinkish red wheels - the traditional Devon colours. The waggon sides are higher by the rear wheels. This makes it a hoop-rave waggon, although sometimes they were called "cock-rave" (i.e. sticking up like a cockerel's tail) or "ship" waggons, as their rear was reminiscent of an sailing ship's poop deck. The waggon may turn left towards Starcross or continue through the arch, another of those required by Lord Devon, onto the beach. The cross-embankment shown on plan 8 between the arch and the viaduct is not illustrated, and was probably not actually constructed. To the right a second similar waggon follows the Cockwood Harbour wall, crossing the bridge over the stream to approach the hamlet of Cockwood. Beyond this some large ships are moored in the shelter of the Warren (✓✓✓), and on the far side of the Estuary is the town of Exmouth (✓).

Longitudinal Section

The section begins with the last four spans of Cockwood Viaduct, although unfortunately sheets 8 and 9 do not give complete coverage between them. The embankment continues on the level along the foreshore, before rising gently at 1 in 409 on approaching the Warren.

Route Plan - 203¾ miles to 204 miles

The sheet begins with the second half of Cockwood Lake, the main channel being picked out in a darker blue. As before, the railway embankment and river wall are built outside the former shoreline, and are linked back by a series of six short cross-embankments. The pair opposite Eastdon House form Eales' Dock, and the Shutterton Brook was actually diverted to exit through the dock into the estuary, not as shown on the plan. Arches through the embankment between pairs of these give access to possible landing points for small boats. The hamlet of Cockwood is shown, the ruins of Cockwood House in its ornamental park, the hamlet of Eastdon (to give the current spelling), Eastdon House, and the toll house for the Starcross and Warren Turnpike. The railway embankment continues across Shutterton Lake, crossing the creek channel by a single-arched bridge with large wing walls, to emerge onto the Warren.

Two small slipway arches are shown through the embankment, but a third appears to have been overlooked. A single larger arch is shown carrying the railway over the Shutterton Brook, although not in its final position as finally constructed.

The cross-embankments seen here, leading back to the old bank near Eastdon House, are erroneously omitted from the Route Plan, which only shows a bridge over the creek. The space between them, wider than appears here, became known as Eales' Dock after F. Eales Esq., the owner of Eastdon House (✓✓✓). The bridge under the railway at the end of this dock also allowed egress for water from the Shutterton Lake Stream, which had been diverted alongside the railway to avoid the construction of an extra bridge. Further to the right, the village of Eastdon can be seen, behind the first telegraph pole. South Devon cattle are grazing by the wreck of an old boat, next to Shutterton Lake, whilst to the right a number of small craft are sailing in the Exe Estuary.

View North of the Line

For a few hundred yards north of the Warren, where the route was well sheltered, there was no masonry wall. Instead there was a stone-faced embankment as shown here. On the skyline can be seen the obelisk at Mamhead (✓), erected in 1743 by Thomas Ball as a navigation aid, whilst on the former shore line below there is an old salt works (✓✓).

The house reflected in the water of Shutterton Lake is the toll house for the Earl of Devon's "Starcross and Warren Turnpike". With tolls of £3 per annum, the road can have seen little use, other than those employed by the estate. In the distance above the toll house can be seen the Haldon Belvedere (✓✓✓), built about 1780 for Sir Robert Palk in memory of his friend Stringer Lawrence, former Governor of Madras.

Cockwood Harbour retains much of its character from Victorian times and includes three listed buildings. The Anchor Inn dates from the early 19th century, as does Rock Cottage, whilst The Thatches is 18th century. The timber viaduct shown in Dawson's illustration was duplicated by a second viaduct to serve the up line in 1874. These were both replaced by a stone-faced embankment in 1898, which included a three-span bridge at the south end and a smaller bridge at the north end.

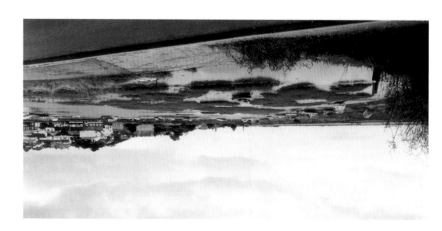

Modern View – 09 South

P.R.G.

The space between the railway and the original shoreline has gradually been reclaimed for farming use over the years, but some stretches of water remain. Here at Eales' Dock boats still moor between the railway and the estuary bank. The diverted Shutterton Lake Stream runs out to the estuary which run between the railway and the dock. The bridge over the dock entrance was widened in 1874 to accept a second running line.

Modern View – 09 North

P.R.G.

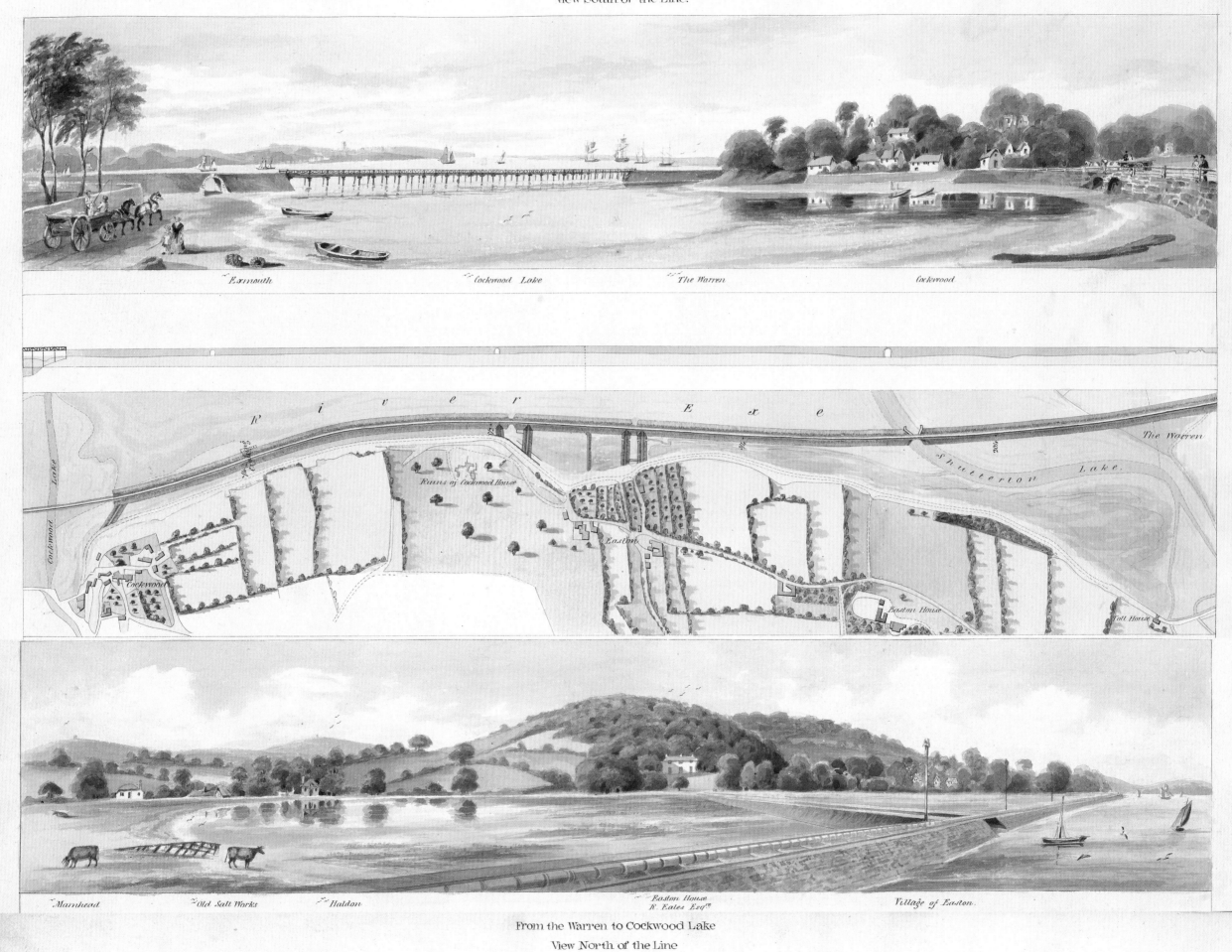

Exmouth   Cockwood Lake   The Warren   Cockwood

River Exe

The Warren

Shutterton Lake.

Cockwood Lake

Cockwood

Ruins of Cockwood House

Easton

Easton House

Toll House

Mamhead   Old Salt Works   Haldon   Easton House R. Eales Esqr   Village of Easton.

From the Warren to Cockwood Lake
View North of the Line

View South of the Line

The panoramic view across the Warren shows the sea wall embankment in the foreground and the Langstone Cliff cutting, then much narrower than it is today, to the right, the red sandstone being well illustrated. The main part of the view is taken from the heights of Mount Pleasant, which still provides the best viewpoint in the area. However the view of Langstone Rock is taken from a lower level, and it is necessary to cross over the railway before the natural arch in the rock can really be seen.

The sandspit that forms the Warren provides a natural defence against the ravages of the sea, and offers further protection to the river wall sections towards Starcross. However, from the Warren westwards the sea wall takes a stronger and structurally more significant role as far as Dawlish, where the first section of Contract No. 2 finished. To the left, a number of waggons are taking the track from the Exmouth Ferry (/), although the ferry crossing to the Exmouth had become less significant since the construction of Starcross Pier in 1846. Exmouth (///) can be seen clearly beyond the channel of the Exe, which then follows the far coastline for some two miles before reaching the open sea. Between this and the Warren, in the area marked "Estuary of the Exe" extensive sand banks are exposed at low tide, and the steam ship illustrated should be firmly aground! The cliffs beyond Exmouth at Orcombe Point and Straight Point can be seen, but some artistic licence has been allowed to reveal Otterton Point (///) beyond. It should be invisible from this viewpoint. The Royal Albert Memorial Museum, Exeter holds another watercolour of this view, reference 17/1929/4, which is signed and dated by Dawson in 1848. The latter is of more conventional proportions (20" x 11") which reduces the distortion in the position of the underbridge, but is otherwise quite similar. It shows the telegraph posts alongside the railway, and a different selection of local characters and shipping. It also indicates more clearly the parapet wall between the railway and the footpath at the Langstone end of the view.

Longitudinal Section

Having climbed slightly to cross the Warren, the railway embankment drops gently at 1 in 320 and 1 in 377 to reach sea wall level. There is an underbridge through the embankment, also seen in the view, which allows the ferry road to pass through. The bridge is shown on section, plan and view, approximately 100 yards north of its actual position. At the end of the Warren the old defensive bank is cut through, following which the embankment is much deeper as it crosses the beach. A deep but short cutting through the sandstone of Langstone Cliff follows, before the embankment resumes, following the shore line along Langstone Sand.

Route Plan - 204¾ miles to 205 miles

The embankment is shown crossing the Warren, with an underbridge where the Exmouth Ferry track passes through. At the end of the Warren, the embankment, now protected by a sea wall, cuts off the sandy bay whilst curving sharply to cut through the cliffs at Langstone Point. It then runs along the back of the beach at Langstone Sands. Whilst sheltered from the prevailing winds, it is however exposed to any gales blowing from a south-easterly direction. The area inland from the railway features the hamlet at Mount Pleasant, which is built on higher ground around the road leading to Dawlish, followed by Langstone House with its extensive landscaped grounds.

This is the first stretch of line open to the sea.

View North of the Line

With the sea lashing against the wall adjacent to Langstone Cliff, the concerns of many lay observers during the construction of the railway may be understood. On a number of occasions, persistent easterly storms during construction prevented limestone shipped from Torbay from reaching the sea wall construction sites, and deliveries by road had to be substituted. The report on the inspection of the line by Major General Pasley makes much reference to the sea defences, and considers them satisfactory. Clearly there was a dilemma of perceived risk between cliff fall if the line was pushed back landward, and storm over-topping if the line was moved seaward. Further to James Walker's report, much of this length of sea wall included a high level footpath, on the seaward side of the track. The footway is not well depicted by Dawson here though. Behind Langstone Cliff, Langstone House is seen set within its walled grounds. Further to the right is the hamlet at Mount Pleasant, and on the skyline is the monument at Mamhead. It can be seen how the former Langstone Cove has effectively been destroyed by the railway. The waggon to the right lacks the rear hoop-rake (sheet 9 south view) and therefore falls into the category known as box waggons - in this case a Devon Buckrowe. Two masts for navigational and storm warning purposes are seen, one beyond the waggon and the other on the cliffs near Mount Pleasant.

Modern View – 10 North

P.R.G.

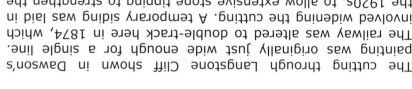

Facilities for holiday makers, including camping coaches from 1935, have transformed the area since Victorian times.

The Mount Pleasant Inn was already in existence in 1756 and is still recognisable when compared with Dawson's illustration. It has been extended several times during the intervening years, but still enjoys magnificent views over Dawlish Warren. There was no station at the Warren in broad gauge days, but a halt was eventually opened in 1905 and a full station in 1912.

Modern View – 10 South

P.R.G.

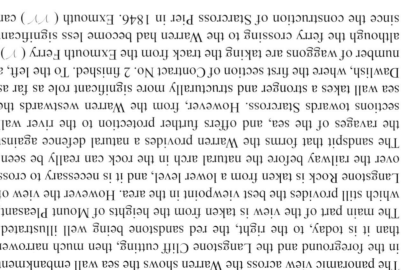

The cutting through Langstone Cliff shown in Dawson's painting was originally just wide enough for a single line. The railway was altered to double-track here in 1874, which involved widening the cutting. A temporary siding was laid in the 1920s, to allow extensive stone tipping to strengthen the cutting. As a consequence a large part of Langstone Cliff sea defences has been removed over the years. The Warren has also been extensively strengthened, to avoid the need for heavy works to the estuary wall beyond.

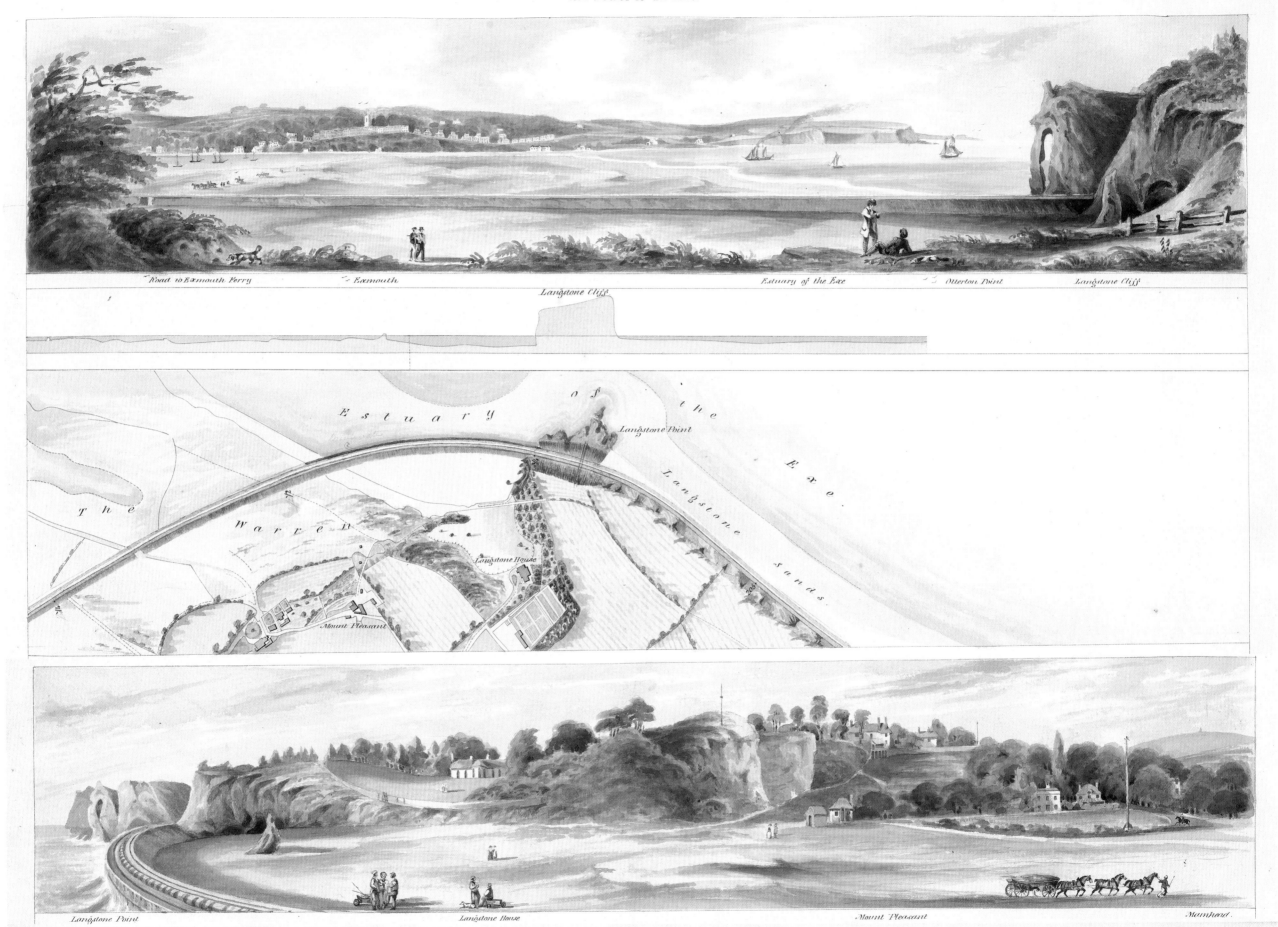

Across the Warren to Langstone Sands.
View South of the Line.

Road to Exmouth Ferry   Exmouth   Langstone Cliff   Estuary of the Exe   Otterton Point   Langstone Cliff

Estuary of the Exe

Langstone Point

The Warren

Langstone Sands

Langstone House

Mount Pleasant

Langstone Point   Langstone House   Mount Pleasant   Mainhead

From Langstone Sands across the Warren.
View North of the Line.

11 From Langstone Sands to the Kennaway Tunnel
Dawlish

View South of the Line

A Dawlish resident's view, looking across the railway out to sea, with Boat Cove and the eastern portal of Kennaway Tunnel to the right. This formed the start of the Tunnel Contract let to George Hay Findlater of Dawlish, although John Waring carried out some work, probably lengths of sea wall. The route originally planned would have taken the track over Boat Cove and required fewer tunnels beyond. This scene shows a much earlier state of affairs than in most views. The site sketches must have been drawn around February 1846, when tracklaying was in progress, although like other views it has been painted as a summer scene. The sea wall, which was very low on this stretch, is complete, and the baulks and transomes have been laid towards the tunnel. Further transomes are being fitted to the left, and surveyors are checking the levels of those just installed. The laying of the atmospheric pipe has not yet commenced here. The Kennaway Tunnel portal is similar in design to the others, with segmented semi-circular arch and large key stone, but this one was built on the skew to suit the rock formation above. The sea has eroded away the softer parts of the red sandstone leaving strangely-shaped remains known as Cowhole Rock and Old Maid Rock. The Boat Cove breakwater, with its blind stone arches, is seen jutting out to the left of them, to shelter small fishing boats pulled up onto the beach. There is only one boat in at the moment, but there is a great variety of shipping out to sea, including a two-masted ship at anchor. Being only 205 yards long, it is possible to see right through Kennaway Tunnel.

Longitudinal Section

The railway continues on its embankment and sea wall along this stretch. Its level progress is interrupted only by a short rise to cross Colonnade Viaduct, dropping away immediately afterwards to regain the general level. The short gradients were very steep originally at 1 in 30, but were much eased in later years, particularly after 1928 when the viaduct was finally replaced. Other than at the viaduct, the line had been kept low by agreement, to avoid spoiling views from the houses opposite. The viaduct was finished in stone, in keeping with its location, and had nine spans totaling 120 feet. As well as road and pedestrian access to the sea front, it also passes over a brook known as Dawlish Water, the latter being boarded over beyond the viaduct in order to continue the low-level walkway.

Route Plan - 205¾ miles to 206¾ miles

One of the straighter sections of line, the embankment and sea wall followed the old front. Groynes (actually stone breakwaters) were put in to protect the beach. Boat Cove with its breakwater can be seen at the right-hand end of the plan. Sea Lawn House belonging to Mr. Powell is seen in the middle, in its landscaped grounds. Near the first groyne is the coastguard station, or "Preventive Station" as it is labeled. The atmospheric railway Dawlish Engine House is shown next, followed by the railway station, very convenient for the town of Dawlish which occupies the remainder of the sheet. The station had a single platform on a loop line inland of the main line, and there was also a coal siding for the engine house. There were no goods facilities here during the atmospheric era, goods services not commencing until May 1849.

View North of the Line

The railway alignment in front of Dawlish was much influenced by the James Walker Report, which led to the Dawlish Agreement, giving limitations to the track elevation, and ensuring access and slipway provisions, together with footbridges and fixings to the sea wall for fishermen. The view from the breakwater begins with Boat Cove and the eastern face of Kennaway Tunnel ( ), followed by the houses on the Teignmouth Road ( ) and Marine Parade. Some of the town's numerous fishing boats are pulled up onto Dawlish Beach, and there are also three bathing machines. Behind the central boat can be seen the Colonnade Viaduct. Built by Roach and Pidditch, at 120 feet long, it was one of the more stylish structures on the South Devon Railway, and reflected the pedigree of the Dawlish environment. With nine spans, not all illustrated here, the access height of eight feet under the iron bridge was a compromise between the limitations to the track elevation and access to the beach for waggons and bathing machines. The colonnade columns of granite are to the classical Doric Order giving detailed aesthetics to the structure, while the use of iron I beams offers a slim elegance to the deck of the bridge. Behind stands the timber station building, with its 98 feet train shed over part of the 300 feet long single platform and its loop line, the main line passing to seaward. Dawlish Engine House stands to the right, built of grey limestone with red sandstone quoins. This was served by a single coal siding. Construction started in January 1846, and the engines supplied by Maudslay were first started on 11th February 1847. Beyond this is the coastguard station with its unusual arched footbridge over the railway, then Sea Lawn House ("Mr. Powell's Villa") which had such an influence on the sea wall. To placate Mr. Powell the S.D.R. had to end the high-level footway from the Warren just short of Sea Lawn, with only a low-level footway at the base of the wall, unusable at high tide, from there into Dawlish.

Modern View – 11 South

P.R.G.

Kennaway Tunnel was widened in 1905, to permit the final stretch of the line to be doubled. The new sea wall and King's Walk had already been opened in 1902. Unaccountably this length of wall was built without the normal wave deflector capping. As a result large quantities of water are thrown over the line in bad weather. A footbridge had been added in 1879 to permit access from the extended Marine Parade to the shoreline. This was replaced by the current simple concrete footbridge in 1965.

Modern View – 11 North

P.R.G.

The classical Colonnade Viaduct was replaced in 1928 by the current 3-span steel girder bridge. The original timber station subsequently burnt down in 1873, following lengthy negotiations regarding the layout of the new station, which eventually opened in 1875. The atmospheric railway engine house also came down as part of this redevelopment. The ridge and furrow platform canopies were replaced by simple flat ones in 1961. The beach in the foreground has been depleted by altered wave action since the re-alignment of the sea wall in 1902.

From Langstone Sands to the Kennaway Tunnel Dawlish.
View South of the Line

11

The Kennaway Tunnel.

Dawlish Brook.

Breakwater

English Channel

Terrace Walk

Groyne

Groyne

Breakwater

Preventive Station

Engine House

Station.

Eastern Face of the Kennaway Tunnel.

Houses on the Teignmouth Road.

Dawlish Beach

Engine House and Station

M.r Powell's Villa.

Langstone

From the Kennaway Tunnel Dawlish to Langstone Sands
View North of the Line.

12 From the Kennaway Tunnel to the Parson Tunnel Dawlish

View South of the Line

This vista typifies the South Devon tunnels synonymous with the line. The tunnel entrances were each adorned with an imposing 22 feet high by 20 feet wide monumental Roman arch with four feet wide facing stones and a prominent key stone. The tunnels had bell-mouth entrance sections and so the tunnel section proper was reduced to the normal structure gauge requirement of 16 feet width. The sea wall here on the eastern approach to Parson's Tunnel was only built in winter 1846/47, replacing an original "wall" of loose stones that was destroyed in the storm of October 1846. This would seem to give an 1847/48 date to the view, yet the artist has omitted the atmospheric pipe. The track here was constantly being damaged by cliff falls and shifted its exact alignment, so it is no surprise to see additional transommes by the track side. Workmen are busy cutting back the cliff faces above the line. This activity continued intermittently during the early years of the railway, before a degree of confidence in the stability of the cliffs built up. Two policemen are also present to supervise operation and ensure security.

The 352 yards long Parson's Tunnel passes through the sandstone of Hole Head (///), with the famous Parson and Clerk rock formation. Berry Head (//), ten miles away beyond Tor Bay, is visible in the distance, and out to sea is the Ore Stone (/).

Longitudinal Section

A rather more spectacular section than usual appears here. The line may remain reasonably level, but very heavy civil engineering works had been required to achieve this. The sheet starts with a shallow climb at 1 in 339 through the 200 yard Kennaway Tunnel. Continuing on an embankment at the same gradient the railway quickly enters Coryton Tunnel, 234 yards long. With the climb stiffening a little to 1 in 172, the Philot Tunnel of only 51 yards is followed by a short length of embankment at the same gradient, and the Clerk's Tunnel of 57 yards.

After a level stretch the descent begins at 1 in 367 into Parson's tunnel, 352 yards long, easing to 1 in 712 before emerging from this extraordinary stretch of railway engineering. Other than the two named after rock formations, the tunnels were named after the landowners, Mark Kennaway, Jane Coryton and the Reverend Charles Phllot. The lengths given are those from the watercolour, and vary slightly from later official railway statistics.

Route Plan - 206½ miles to 207¾ miles

At the start of the sheet the railway emerges from Kennaway Tunnel to cross Crane Cove, more usually known as Coryton's Cove, with its twin breakwaters and overlooked by Cliffs Cottage. Sweeping S curves take the railway through Coryton Tunnel behind the Horse Rocks to cross what is shown as Philot Cove or Horse Cove, more usually known as Shell Cove. It then curves to the left again to plunge through Philot Tunnel and Clerk's Tunnel in quick succession. Above Shell Cove is the property known as Clevelands. A longer open stretch then sees the railway curving right again following the cliff face and passing Breeches Rock before, still curving sharply, passing through Parson's Tunnel, the longest of the group, through Hole Head with its well known Parson and Clerk rock.

View North of the Line

The view is from the east end of Coryton Beach - although nobody could actually stand, or survive in a boat, at this point if waves of such ferocity were rolling in. Beginning with Hole Head (/\), and followed by Phllot or Horse Cove (//), the railway emerges from the east face of Coryton Tunnel, below Cliffs Cottage (///) the home of Miss Coryton. In front of the east face of Coryton Beach (vvv) the two short breakwaters are seen. The sea wall on Coryton Beach is in reality well protected, and has never been damaged by sea action. The arch under the line gave private access to the beach, and may be the escape route for the admiring figures, who are otherwise in danger of being cut off. Artistic licence has crept in, in showing the western portal of Kennaway Tunnel, which is actually invisible from this spot, or at best fully side-on. At the right are a low breakwater (not shown on the plan) and the Cowhole and Old Maid rocks. Another version of this view is held by the Royal Albert Memorial Museum, Exeter, reference 14/1929/3. Dawson has signed and dated it 1848, and it shows a steam-hauled train emerging from Coryton Tunnel, on a much calmer day. The proportions and details were altered to suit the 20" x 11" format. In particular the underbridge is shown much closer to Kennaway tunnel, the stepped walls each side of the tunnel mouth are shown more clearly, and the view to the right is curtailed, short of the Cowhole and Old Maid rocks. Comparison of the two views provides a good indication of the accuracy of the views in general, with individual details being quite reliable, but distances between them adjusted, and bushes and figures added as required, to suit the composition.

Modern View – 12 South

P.R.G.

Perhaps not the most obvious spot to construct a railway! The Horse Rocks are seen centrally, linked together by a short section of breakwater. In the distance the sea wall curves around the bend to Parson's Tunnel, cut through Hole Head. The Ore Stone is visible on the horizon, situated off Hope's Nose in Torquay, The rock formations have been subject to change over the intervening years, and a cliff fall in 2007 has left the luxury home on the headland above Coryton Tunnel close to the edge.

Modern View – 12 North

P.R.G.

The stretch of sea wall behind Coryton beach is well protected by its breakwater. The rock formation really is as fascinating as shown by Dawson, with alternating layers of Permian breccia and softer Aeolian sandstone. Where once only the isolated Cliffs Cottage occupied the headland, there is now intrusive housing development. This stretch of track was doubled in 1905 and Coryton Tunnel was rebuilt to an asymmetrical cross-section with a plain portal and flying arch to the wing wall. These rebuilt tunnel mouths are certainly an ugly collection.

12

From the Kennaway Tunnel to the Parson Tunnel Dawlish.
View South of the Line.

The Ore Stone   The Berry Head   Hole Head   East Face of the Parson Tunnel.

Kennaway Tunnel 200 Yards   Coryton Tunnel 234 Yards   Phillot Tunnel 51 Yards   Clerk Tunnel 51 Yards   Parson Tunnel 552 Yards.

ENGLISH CHANNEL

Hole Head   Breeches Rock   Breakwater   Kennaway Tunnel   Crane Cove   Coryton Tunnel   Phillot Horse Cave   Phillot   Clerk Tunnel   Parson Tunnel   Cliff Cottage   Clevelands

Hole Head   Phillot or Horse Cave   East Face of the Coryton Tunnel   Cliff Cottage (Miss Coryton)   Crane Cove   West Face of the Kennaway Tunnel.

From the Parson Tunnel to the Kennaway Tunnel Dawlish.
View North of the Line.

13 From the Parson Tunnel Dawlish to the Teignmouth Tunnel

View South of the Line

To the south, the view of Teignmouth, its foreshore and East Teignmouth Tunnel offer a vision of civil engineering in harmony with its surroundings that has featured as the backdrop to so many locomotive studies since. The East Teignmouth Tunnel marked the start of Contract No. 3 which was awarded to Samuel Garratt, and took the line through to Hackney at the head of the Teign Estuary. The railway is fully illustrated, with the atmospheric tube fitted, telegraph posts in place, and a fine disc and crossbar signal, complete with policeman's box and two policemen. South Devon Railway signals have previously been reported as painted black and white, but this one is shown in red like those of the other broad gauge companies. The tunnel portal was of the usual style, not particularly well captured in this view. The first houses of Teignmouth and St. Michael's Church were obviously drawn at comparatively close range, but in using the sketch as part of a larger work, with a more distant viewpoint, Dawson has not felt the need to adjust the perspective accordingly. Dawson's system of using groups of seagulls to locate features of interest reaches its climax with this sheet. We are offered The Ore Stone (✓) off Torquay about six miles away, Hope's Nose (✓✓✓) the headland at Torquay, Anstey's Cove (✓✓✓), the Marble Quarries (✓✓✓) at Oddicombe which supplied much of the limestone for the railway, the village of Babbacombe (✓✓✓✓✓), and finally the hamlet at Watcombe (✓✓✓✓✓) around four miles distant. Closer at hand, The Ness at Shaldon stands on the opposite side of the Teign Estuary, with a ship entering the narrow channel from the sea. The small lighthouse standing on the Den was erected by order of the Teignmouth Harbour Commissioners in 1844-45. It showed a red light which vessels entering the Teign had to keep in line with another small light at the corner of a house behind it. There were no other navigation aids once in the Estuary however, right up until 1922 when buoys were provided to mark the channel. Further out to sea is a small paddle steamer, while on the beach seine netting is in progress. The beach is indeed a hive of activity, with donkeys bearing pannier baskets waiting to carry away the fish, several bathing machines, and well-dressed sightseers. The gentleman with the stick who is looking towards us would have a very similar view to the drawing of Spray Point featuring later in the book.

Longitudinal Section

The sheet should start with Smugglers' Lane Viaduct, just outside the western portal of Parson's Tunnel, a three-arch stone structure which was to be lost in the storm of February 1855, but the space has unfortunately been left blank. The line undulates rather on this stretch, perhaps because there was already a lot of fallen rock in the Spray Point area to form a foundation. After first falling gently at 1 in 279, the railway runs briefly on the level, before climbing at 1 in 182 to the high point at the breakwater. Beyond this, the line falls away again at 1 in 173, before running on the level through East Teignmouth Tunnel which appears to the right.

Route Plan - 207¾ miles to 208¾ miles

To the left Smugglers' Lane leads down to the seashore, although the Smugglers' Lane Viaduct is not picked out. The railway on its sea wall at the foot of the cliffs is well shown, with the famous terrace walk on the seaward side. The large breakwater at Spray Point is clearly shown, with secondary breakwaters to each side, all designed to prevent the full force of the sea from undermining the wall. This strategy was to prove not entirely successful. Above the cliffs the neatly-hedged field pattern runs right up to the cliff edge, passing from the Parish of Dawlish to the Parish of East Teignmouth. Large parts of the cliff, marked '1st Wares' and '2nd Wares', have either fallen or been brought down to provide material for the embankments.

View North of the Line

The rough seas sweeping against the breakwaters give an indication of the forces of nature that John Waring needed to overcome in this section of Contract No. 2, stretching from East Teignmouth Tunnel mouth (208m 56c) to Smugglers' Lane (207m 47c). With Spray Point to the foreground (an existing rock fall built in by the sea wall), the construction of the wall again followed the James Walker Report, and included a footpath along the top of the sea wall in front of the railway. A dividing wall separated the public from the railway, and also provided additional protection against spray depositing excess water on the trackbed. Here again the limestone was shipped from Torbay, and clearly the difficulties in off-loading during strong easterly winds are self-apparent. Some sightseers have come to watch the seas pounding against the breakwater (✓), with its secondary walls and slipway. A piston carriage with five coach train is running along the sea wall beyond, near Smugglers' Lane Viaduct (✓✓✓), and beyond that is the western portal of Parson's Tunnel, which cuts through Hole Head (✓✓✓). The Parson and Clerk Rock and the Shag Rock are well shown at the headland. A lugger is making its way into Teignmouth before the weather worsens.

Modern View – 13 South

P.R.G.

The opening out of Teignmouth East Tunnel in 1884 has given us one of the classic railway views. The wrought iron lattice girders for the replacement Eastcliff Bridge were fabricated at Swindon works. Through the bridge can be seen the former Congregational Church (now United Reformed Church) which was completed in 1883. The tower of St Michael the Archangel Church, completed in 1889, is visible above the buildings to the left of the bridge. Teignmouth Pier, completed in 1867, can be seen in the distance with The Ness behind it.

Modern View – 13 North

P.R.G.

The village of Holcombe dates back over a thousand years, but has greatly expanded since Dawson's time, encroaching into the cut-back cliff face, rockfall netting and catch fence demonstrate the continuing effort required to keep this picturesque stretch of railway operational. Hole Head is formed of Teignmouth Breccia, with the Parson and Clerk rock looking out to sea.

From the Parson Tunnel Dawlish to the Teignmouth Tunnel
View South of the Line.

13

The Ore Stone.   Hope's Nose.   Anstey's Cove.   Marble Quarries.   Babbacombe.   Watcombe.   The Ness.   Teignmouth Light House and Den.   East Teignmouth Church.   East Face of Teignmouth Tunnel.

Smuggters Cove   Breakwater   Breakwater   Breakwater   Terrace   Walk
Terrace   Walk
1st Wanes   2nd Wanes
Parish   of   Dawlish   Parish of   East   Teignmouth

Breakwater   Smuggler's Lane   Hole Head.

From the Teignmouth Tunnel to the Parson Tunnel Dawlish
View North of the Line

14 From the East Teignmouth Tunnel to the Teignmouth Gas Works

Modern View – 14 South
P.R.G.

The original Shaldon Bridge, which had opened on 8th June 1827, was rebuilt between 1927 and 1931. It was bought by Devon County Council in 1948, after which the tolls were abolished and the gates removed. The Old Toll House still stands however, and is now a Grade II listed building. The faceted eastern end of the building gives good views of traffic approaching the bridge, but the side wall facing the road embankment does not appear to have ever had the windows shown in the watercolour.

Modern View – 14 North
P.R.G.

To the right of the current Shaldon Bridge, further modified between 1998 and 2002, the semi-circular arch still pierces the stonework to link the foreshore on either side. A similar but larger arch serving the railway was doubled in 1865. West Teignmouth has expanded considerably in the intervening years, with buildings covering the hillside inland from the bridge. The stone buttresses to the railway retaining wall mark the location of the well known 1935 publicity shot of King William IV heading the new Centenary stock.

View South of the Line

This view across the railway and the Teign Estuary is almost that which William Mackworth Praed, a noted objector to the railway, would have experienced from his properties. The Albert Memorial Museum, Exeter has another Dawson watercolour of this scene, reference 14/1929/2. It is taken from a slightly different viewpoint, but is fairly similar in content. Shaldon Toll Bridge demonstrates the existence of multi-span viaduct structures using timber "fans" before the railways made such prominent use of the concept under Brunel's direction. The first main span of the bridge, between the stone approach and the stone pier, formed a drawbridge over the main channel of the River Teign. A new arch has been put into the bridge approach to allow the railway to pass through. Waiting at the toll house gate is a carriage drawn by two horses. It is low-slung, lacking a rear seat or "rumble", and most closely resembles a "droshky" - a vehicle of Russian origin and seating two facing forwards. The view is taken from the turnpike road approaching the bridge, with what appears to be the gate post of Bitton House to the left, and the lower road sweeping up to the toll house from below. Bitton Brook has been channeled and culverted to pass through the railway embankment. On the far shore can be seen The Ness, the village of Shaldon, and upstream of the bridge the hamlet of Ringmore.

Longitudinal Section

The section reflects the great difficulty in bringing the railway through Teignmouth. The East Teignmouth Tunnel of 320 yards passed under Dawlish Road and Myrtle Hill, bringing the railway to the station site, which required filling over the culverted Brimley Brook. On leaving West Teignmouth Station by crossing under Shute Hill, the railway entered Teignmouth Tunnel, which passed under Brewery Lane, Fore Street, Park Street, Saxe Street and Chapel Street. A brief open stretch was followed by a very short tunnel under Parson Street, another open stretch, and a final short tunnel under Mulberry Street and Willow Street, before running in a last length of cutting as far as the Old Quay Inn. Other than the first hundred yards of East Teignmouth Tunnel, which was bored, all of these tunnels were constructed as cuttings, arched over afterwards. In later years they were to be opened out. After this the railway runs on a length of low river wall, passing "Mr Praed's Wall" which appears to be a retaining structure for the gardens above, and through the approach stonework to Shaldon Toll Bridge to reach West Teignmouth Works. Beginning on the level through East Teignmouth Tunnel and the station site, the line begins to descend at 1 in 144 in West Teignmouth Tunnel, then undulates to suit the street pattern, first falling at 1 in 381, level again, then rising at 1 in 230, before running on the level along the river wall.

Route Plan - 208¾ miles to 209¾ miles

The station was built on land belonging to Samuel Langley, comprising the gardens, orchards and meadows of a house known as Shute Hill. Originally the station had a single platform with a train shed over this and two of the three tracks. Waggon turntables gave access to two goods sidings, in addition to a coal siding for the Engine House on the northern side of the line, with a reservoir behind it. At the western end of the site there was a locomotive turntable, connected to a two-road building perhaps used for stabling engines at first and then piston carriages, prior to the extension of operation to Newton. The piston carriages had no need of the turntable, as they always faced the same way relative to the tube, and had conductor's boxes at both ends. At the end of the town the buildings standing almost at right angles to the railway are warehouses on the Old Quay, operated by William Rendle. The water has not been coloured in on the towward side of the buildings, where a second quay wall was later to be built. There was no rail connection at this stage. Sadly, this was done in 1849 to enable the redundant atmospheric pipes to be shipped away. Beyond the town are Westcliff House and Bitton House, both owned by Mr. Praed, who actually lived in Westcliff House when in Teignmouth. Westcliff House still exists but, rather confusingly, is now called Bitton House. The railway then passes Shaldon Bridge and follows the Teign Estuary upstream.

View North of the Line

A marvellous panorama from the back beach in Teignmouth, even if little can be seen of the railway. In the distance to the left is the Teignmouth Gas works (∧∧∧), behind the trusses of Shaldon Bridge (∧∧). The latter was erected in 1826-27 under Roger Hopkins, engineer, at a cost of £19,000, and was 1,671 feet in length. It had thirty-four spans of iron and wood, and a drawbridge over the deepest part of the channel, to allow vessels to pass. Following a partial collapse in 1838, extensive repairs were carried out, and the bridge was re-opened in 1840. Below its toll house can be seen the new arch formed for the railway. The stretch of the S.D.R. in this view runs on a low river wall, the freshly cut limestone of which shows up as a pale strip across the view (∧∧∧∧). Two culverts can be seen piercing the wall. The upper parts of this strip would appear to be the retaining wall within Mr. Praed's grounds, and Bitton House (∧∧) and West Cliff House look out over the water from the far side. The buildings of West Teignmouth are shown, together with the warehouses on the Old Quay, and further to the right is St. James' Church, West Teignmouth, rebuilt about 1820 except for the medieval tower, with the New Quay at right foreground.

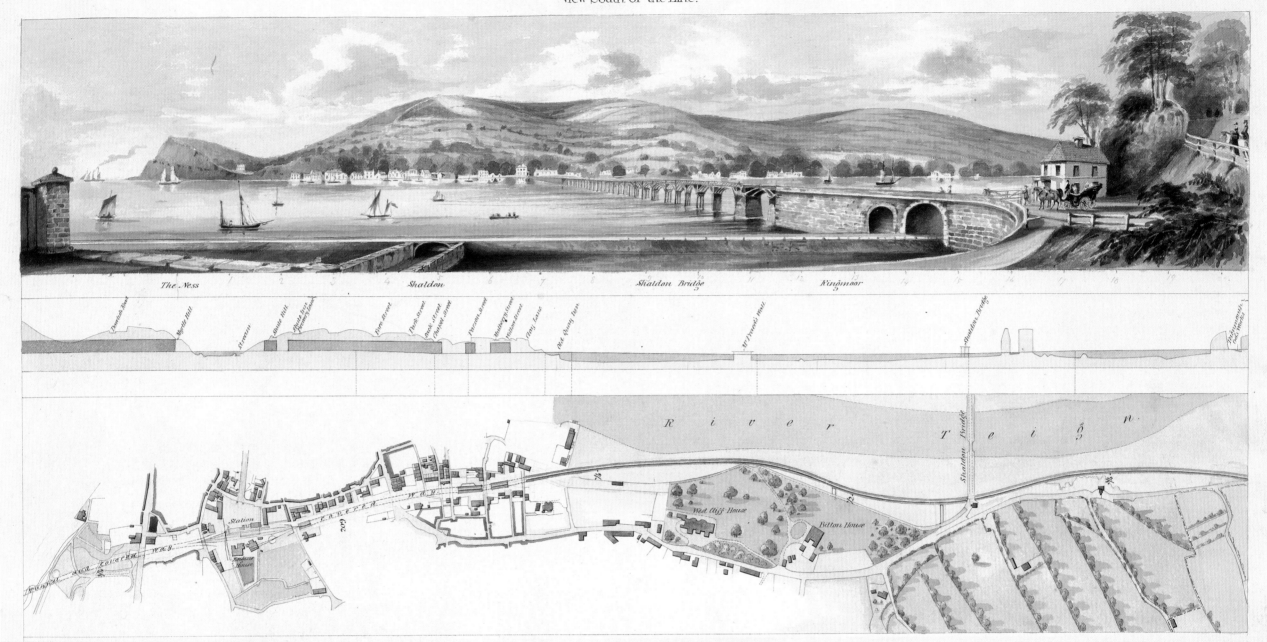

The Ness   Shaldon   Shaldon Bridge   Kingmoor

R i v e r   T e i g n.

West Cliff House   Bitton House

Station

Gas Works   Shaldon Bridge and Toll House   Bitton House   Line of the Railway   West Teignmouth   West Teignmouth Church.

From the Teignmouth Gas Works to the East Teignmouth Tunnel

View North of the Line

Modern View – 15 North

P.R.G.

Although Teignmouth Gas works has been demolished, one of the walls has been left standing, providing a link with the site's history. Doubling of the railway line brought it very close to the public road, requiring a retaining wall to be constructed. The masonry bridge giving access to the Gas Works was replaced with a steel one of wider span. There is noticeably more tree cover to The Ness and the hills behind Shaldon than there was in Dawson's time.

Modern View – 15 South

P.R.G.

Flow Cottage is a much grander affair these days, as several extensions have more than doubled its original size. It now boasts a first floor balcony above a rebuilt veranda, whilst the dormer window suggests that it has also received a loft conversion. Boasting superb views over the Teign estuary, courtesy of its unique location, it must have become an extremely valuable property. Despite this, its humble origins are still apparent, and the gable end and front windows of Templer's Cottage remain evident among the modern additions.

View South of the Line

The gentle curving line of the railway up the north bank of the Teign Estuary is a mix of stone-faced embankments built in the river bed and short cuttings through rolling headlands, there being little need for protective measures along this section of the line. The Flow Lane underbridge access to Templer's Cottage is hidden by bushes in this view. The cottage, later known as "Flow Cottage" does not look much older than the railway, with ornate barge boards and a slate roof. It also has a slate roofed veranda, with climbers growing up the posts. Set by the Estuary half a mile away from the village of Bishopsteignton, the cottage must have been a tranquil location before the railway arrived to disturb the peace. It still stands today, although much altered. The front half of a piston carriage is illustrated, receiving an "All Right" signal from the policeman, although he should really be holding his arm out towards the line, not away from it. There are thought to have been four piston carriages used on the Exeter to Newton line. Looking through later register entries for potential ex-piston carriages there are a number of 27 feet long six-wheeled vans which would fit the bill. However none of these are identical in all details or from the same manufacturer. The fact that the vehicle is different in style from that shown in the chapter on piston carriages should not therefore be taken as an indication that one or the other is incorrect. The chassis and general layout were probably all similar, but this vehicle has an outside-framed timber body, painted brown all over. The conductor's box has an open entrance, here mistakenly shown on the front instead of the side. It is followed by a second class compartment with glazed panels either side of the door droplight. A lamp is shared between the second class compartment and the third class cum van which follows. Behind the carriage are the hills of Little Haldon, and on the far side of the Estuary are those of Combeinteignhead.

Longitudinal Section

This stretch of line is constructed on an embankment built on the mud flats, the parts which look like cuttings on the section representing sloped back cliffs on the landward side. The former river bank is cut through at a point marked "Slocombe". The isolated piece of estuary bed which follows, between the embankment and the former river bank, was later known by the very similar name of Salcombe Pit, when it was used for dumping tunnel excavation spoil in the 1880s. The embankment then crosses an old river wall, presumably connected with the saltings, before rising briefly at 1 in 182 to cross Flow Lane. The railway passes on the level through a short shallow cutting before regaining an embankment built on the Estuary flats.

Route Plan - 210 miles to 211 miles

From sheet 15 onwards less effort is put into detailing and colouring the plans. Possibly the days of the Atmospheric were numbered, and Dawson was running out of time. At the joint between sheets 14 and 15, situated between the estuary and the railway is Teignmouth Gas Works. It had been established on its riverside site in 1840, the selected location enabling coal to be delivered by lighters. The appearance of a railway alongside the works came about entirely by accident, and it was not until the twentieth century that a rail connection was put in. Alternate lengths of headland cutting and embankment on the estuary shore follow.

as the railway passes through the Parish of Bishopsteignton. Towards the end of the sheet the railway crosses the triangular Flow Point promontory where there are saltings, before crossing Flow Lane and passing Templer's Cottage, which is not labeled. The Templer family, owners of Stover House, were responsible for construction of the Stover canal in 1792, the Haytor Granite Tramway in 1820, together with the quarries themselves and the New Quay at Teignmouth, also in 1820. This cottage must have been one of the family's smaller properties. In 1829 however, the estate had been sold to the Duke of Somerset.

View North of the Line

From this point just before the Teignmouth Gas Works, and continuing as far as the Old Quay, the line was bounded by a stone-faced river wall, this being similar in design to that of the Exe river wall. The promontory has been cut back to allow the railway to pass, leaving a rather precarious looking cliff, with tree roots hanging over the edge. Three workmen, armed with one spade and one pickaxe are on site ready to remedy the situation, once the policeman can get them back to work! The Gas Works forms an interesting little group of buildings, in limestone and brick, with its chimney, and an access arch from the Newton to Teignmouth road, sloping down away from the viewer beyond the buildings. Coal for gas making was delivered by lighters. Gas was presumably supplied to Teignmouth by a pipeline buried underground. In the background is the Shaldon Toll Bridge, crossing the Teign Estuary to the village of Shaldon on the south bank. The triangular-shaped headland that side of the river mouth is The Ness.

Templar's Cottage.

River Teign

Parish of Bishop's Teignton

Teignmouth Gas Works   Shaldon Bridge   Shaldon.

Bishop's Teignton to the Teignmouth Gas Works

View North of the Line.

16 Through Bishop's Teignton to King's Teignton

View South of the Line

The route certainly did not want for varied and attractive scenery, as this fine view demonstrates. No wonder the Revd. Commyns built his summer house here to take advantage of the beautiful setting. The summer house was built of limestone, and was slightly wider than illustrated. On the opposite bank of the Teign Estuary is the hamlet and landing point at Coombe Cellars (√), whilst the distant hill is at Haccombe (√√). In the distance beyond Commyns' summer house (√√√) stands the seventh engine house, which, in the absence of any other features of note, received the name Summer House. The name Wear or Ware after the nearby farm had been used before construction, but this was abandoned due to possible confusion with Countess Wear. Construction of the engine house began in summer 1846, and the engines built by Maudslay were first started in Autumn 1847. Unfortunately these distant views are the only ones which we have. The sale notice for 3rd September 1855 for the Teignmouth and Summer House buildings and chimneys tells us much about the variety of building stone used in their construction:- limestone for most of all main walls, Bath stone cornices, moulded storey bands and turret windows, slate for steps and risers and also granite for the same. York stone landings and Italian tile roofing. The railway is finished, complete with electric telegraph, but the watercolours have an endless supply of workmen resting from slightly vague and unspecified toil. Behind the railway lies Lindridge Hill, in the direction of Kingsteignton.

Longitudinal Section

The railway runs on the level throughout this stretch, beginning with a length of embankment built below the high tide line in the Teign Estuary. It then passes through a deep cutting through an outcrop of red conglomerate in an area of Devonian slate and valley gravel. A further short length of embankment buries an old length of river wall, followed by another cutting, another length of embankment, and the length of shallow cutting which practically converts the site of Commyns' summer house into an island. After this there is a long stretch of embankment out in the estuary, followed by a long shallow cutting through the next headland, the location of Summer House Engine House. Towards the end of the sheet the railway begins to climb gently at 1 in 270 prior to heading inland.

Route Plan - 211¾ miles to 212½ miles

As the railway sweeps in from its embankment in the estuary it passes through a deep sandstone cutting known as Red Rock. A footpath from Bishopsteignton passes across the cutting on a high bridge. Dropping down Luxton's Steps to the river side, a ferry could be taken across the estuary to the Ferry Boat Inn at Coombe Cellars. The railway cuts through two small headlands in quick succession, and on the second a small piece of pink indicates Commyns' summer house. This is followed by a long stretch of embankment out in the estuary. In this area away from dense habitation these cut off segments of former estuary developed into marshlands rich in wildlife. The River Teign follows a number of channels within the wide expanse of the Estuary, one of them passing close to the railway embankment on this stretch. As the railway comes inland again it passes through a long shallow cutting, leaving the Parish of Bishopsteignton and passing into that of Kingsteignton. Summer House Engine House is shown in pink on this headland, with the engine house proper parallel to the railway with its chimney at the western end. The boiler house stands at right angles pointing out towards the water, and the reservoir or "tank" occupies a triangle between the railway, engine house and a bank to the estuary, later washed away after the abandonment of atmospheric traction.

View North of the Line

To the left, the railway passes in a cutting through the second of a group of three small headlands. South Devon cattle graze on the following flood plain, with the village of Bishopsteignton in the background. Farms in this area were generally of moderate size between 50 and 250 acres, and farming was mixed. A tenant farmer might carry out several different operations, including dairy farming, breeding or fattening beef cattle, sheep and pigs, or growing corn and cider. Two-horse ploughs were universal, and light carts and waggons. Beside the workmen adjusting the line and level of the trackwork baulks, the stone-faced embankment is shown, keeping the high tide at bay, whilst on the other side of the track is more trapped water, which was to become marshland. Beyond the very closely-supervised workers a high timber footbridge crosses from one side of the steep cutting to the other at Red Rock, giving access to Luxton's Steps, leading down to the water-side, for the ferry to Coombe Cellars. The South Devon Railway board agreed to have this bridge constructed in 1846, after receiving requests from local inhabitants, although Brunel was instructed to make it "as inexpensive as possible".

Modern View – 16 North
P.R.G.

By following the footpath across the fields from Bishopsteignton (to use the modern spelling), it is still possible to cross over the railway by means of a foot bridge at Red Rock, in the position where Dawson shows it. However, when the railway was doubled in 1865, further rock needed to be cut away and the replacement bridge had to be replaced with a wider one. From Luxton's Steps still lead down to the foreshore, about 70 stone steps in total.

Modern View – 16 South
P.R.G.

Standing on an outcrop of red conglomerate in the Teign estuary, it is still possible to enjoy the same view which Revd. Commyns obtained from his summer house which used to be located here. Parts of the walls remain in situ and demonstrate that the building was actually octagonal in plan. The railway runs on a low embankment built on the foreshore, towards the green patch on the promontory in the distance. This marks the site of the atmospheric pumping station which was given the name Summer House.

Coombe Cellars. Haccombe. Commyns' Summer House. Engine House. Electric Telegraph.

River Teign

Parish of Bishop's Teignton

Engine House and Tank

Bishop's Teignton.

From King's Teignton through Bishop's Teignton
View North of the Line.

17 Through the Parish of King's Teignton

Modern View – 17 North
P.R.G.

This small pound at the head of the Teign estuary marks the spot where the Hackney Stream enters the Hackney Channel, and crosses over the Channel just to the left of this view. To the right the Channel turns away from the railway and quickly reaches the site of the lock which used to control the entrance to the Hackney Canal. These days the route of the Canal is cut off by Newton Abbot Racecourse.

Modern View – 17 South
P.R.G.

The heyday of Hackney Clay Cellars has long since passed. Lord Clifford, the owner of Ugbrooke House and the surrounding ball clay workings, used to send clay here by pack horses for loading into barges and subsequent transhipment into coasters at Teignmouth. Due to the large tidal range this was an inefficient process and the opening of the Hackney Canal in 1843 effectively brought activity at the clay cellars to an end. Nevertheless some stone structures remain, nestling under the modern A380 road viaduct.

View North of the Line

To the north we see the entrance to the Hackney Canal (again labelled as "Newton Canal"), opened just before the railway on 17th March 1843. It was only five furlongs long, and had a tide lock at its entrance 108ft 3in long by 14ft wide, and with 3ft 9in on the cill, which would pen two barges at once. A wharf, basin and clay cellar were constructed at its terminus in Kingsteignton. The main user was Lord Clifford, owner of Ugbrooke House and of most of the ball clay excavations on the north side of the Teign, especially around Chudleigh Kingston, Preston and Kingsteignton. The tide lock is well shown, and in the distance the uplands of Dartmoor (   ), with Haytor (   ) visible on the skyline.

The Hackney Stream enters the channel through sluice gates in the centre of the picture, and cattle and sheep graze on the river meadows beyond. In the distance can be seen Kingsteignton Church (   ). In the foreground, the railway runs onto the trussed-timber bridge to cross the Hackney Channel. The termination of the queen-post truss is seen on the top member, giving what must be assumed to be improved weather resistance to the timber. Also a mitred coping is the bridge has the top string of the truss member resting on the stone end-wall and not tied to the bottom member.

Route Plan – 212½ miles to 213½ miles

Leaving the cutting beyond the engine house, a final stretch of embankment built on the estuary mud flats aligns the railway to pass inland of the Hackney Clay Cellars, and the nearly L shaped building which is the Passage House Inn. Before the channels were dredged it was possible to cross the Teign Estuary here by ford at low tide, to reach Netherton on the southern bank. The channel leading to the Hackney Canal was dredged right alongside the Clay Cellars, shown in a darker shade of blue, although little loading of clay here took place with the canal open for traffic. The quayside around the Passage House Inn (which was built around 1761) was also dredged, and trade here must have been good, with craft waiting to pass into the canal or stopping for a break after emerging. On leaving the cutting the railway continues through the parish of Kingsteignton, crossing over the channel cut to link the River Teign with the pound at the entrance to the Hackney Canal (shown here as "Newton Canal"). The first lock on the Canal is shown just inland from the bridge. The railway embankment blocks off an old creek course, the line running straight for once in the direction of Newton. The former main course of the Teign above the line is shown and to the left of this the final section of the estuary.

Longitudinal Section

This stretch begins in cutting just after Summer House Engine House, rising at 1 in 600 onto an embankment in the estuary. A single-arch underbridge links this isolated area of water to the remainder. The railway passes inland for the final time, running on the level for a while, then climbing again at 1 in 284, running in a deep cutting crossed by the road to the Hackney Clay Cellars, and also by a footpath on a flying bridge. The railway then emerges onto an embankment above the valley floor, crossing the Hackney Canal entrance by a typical trussed-timber bridge and running on the level towards Newton. Towards the end of the sheet there is a single-arch bridge over a stream.

View South of the Line

From the head of the Teign Estuary, this view looks down the Teign, with Hackney Clay Cellars (   ) to the left of the scene. These had been the shipping point for the highly plastic Bovey "ball clay" or "pipe clay" prior to the coming of the canals, but were now little used. The ruins still stand today, most built in limestone but the nearest cellar being rendered sandstone. This is the start of the "Newton Deviation" sanctioned under the S.D.R. (Amendment and Branches) Act 1846 following a deputation from Newton. The original route of the line would have passed further away from the town, although in the event the realignment only brought the station some 150 yards closer. Beyond Hackney Clay Cellars can be seen the chimney of Summer House Engine House (   ). Some five miles away in the distance, the town of Teignmouth and the headland of The Ness (   ) mark the opening to the English Channel. On the opposite bank from the engine house, Coombe Cellars (   ) can be seen again, and nearer at hand is Netherton Point. The waters of the Teign take several meandering courses through its estuary, just visible here, the southern channel next to the high ground beyond the mud flats was dredged by the Teignmouth Harbour Commissioners following an Act obtained in 1836. This provided better navigation upstream to the entrance of the Stover Canal, which had been built in 1792. To the left of the scene the northern channel of the Teign was also dredged to provide access to the Hackney Canal, opened in 1843 to provide a new line of transport to a wharf near the centre of the village of Kingsteignton. Between the two, next to the Teign proper, duck shooting is in progress.

Through the Parish of King's Teignton.
View South of the Line.

17

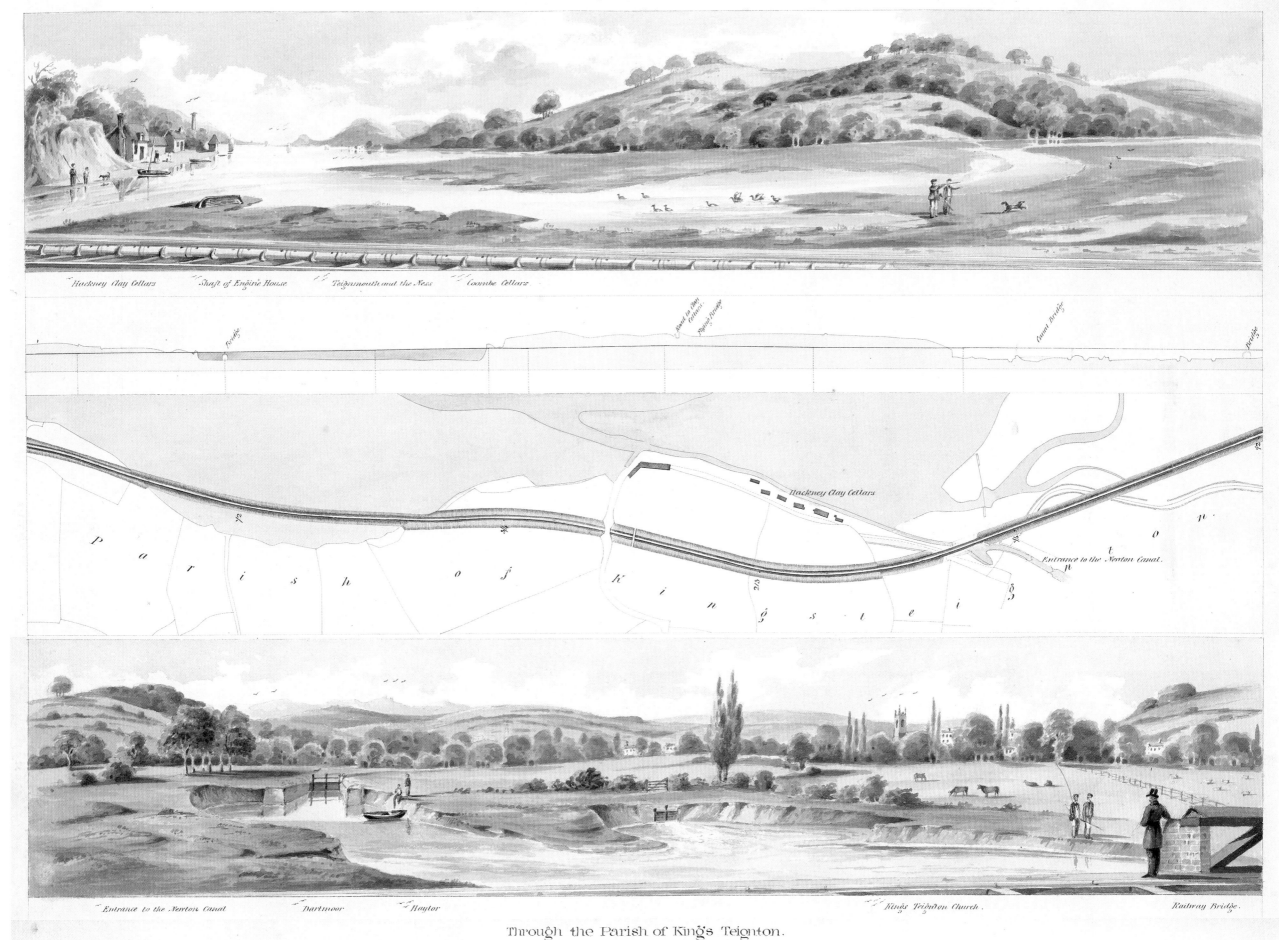

Hackney Clay Cellars   Shaft of Engine House   Teignmouth and the Ness   Coombe Cellars

Bridge   Road to Bay Cellars   Wigan Bridge   Canal Bridge   Bridge

Hackney Clay Cellars

Entrance to the Newton Canal.

P a r i s h   o f   K i n g s t e i g

Entrance to the Newton Canal   Dartmoor   Haytor   King's Teignton Church.   Railway Bridge.

Through the Parish of King's Teignton.
View North of the Line.

View North of the Line

The River Teign Bridge forms the focal point in this scene. The view of the side truss in the first span shows the use of iron tie members as queen posts, this being a prudent use of materials, as the posts were members in tension and required no compressive capability. The two timber gantry frames would seem to be temporary works, used for lifting. The strengthening of structures along the line was known to be in hand at the time of the illustrations, and was required to meet the demands of heavier locomotives. It is evident from the view that a triangular truss (with an iron king post) is being erected over one of the mid spans, to be tied into the north side continuous truss. Such a triangular-trussed bridge design was later used by Brunel to cross the Thames at Culham. A policeman is giving an "All Right" signal to the atmospheric train leaving Newton, with five or six carriages behind the piston carriage. The policeman's uniform is green, with red collar and red vertical stripes on jacket and trousers. The Newton Engine House and Station (✓✓) are shown behind the train, with a two-horse waggon standing at the New Quay (✓). A pair of barges are being poled downstream after passing under the bridge, there is another barge at the Quay, a boat sailing upstream and a rowing boat above the bridge. Round the curve of the Whitelake Channel, two barges are coming towards the river, and a sailing barge is passing the other way near Ferry House (✓✓✓). Behind this the turnpike road from Teignmouth to Newton crosses the Teign Valley on a long stone viaduct.

Route Plan - 213¾ miles to 214¼ miles

The River Teign passes under the railway to the left of the plan, the river still being navigable at this point. A little way upstream from the bridge the Whitelake Channel (marked by the parish boundary line) diverges from the river. Originally a drainage leat, it was enlarged in 1792 to provide access to the Stover Canal. The latter, built for James Templer, ran to Teignbridge near the clay works at Fishwick, then to Teigngrace and to Ventiford Basin where clay cellars were built. There were five locks on the system, each with 15 feet wide gates, the shallowest cills being 4 feet 3 inches deep. From Ventiford to Haytor, the Haytor Granite Tramway was built in 1820, to bring building stone down to the Canal. A road from New Quay on the Teign is shown curving round the "tank", and passing under the railway by the engine house. As at Countess Wear and Turf, there is an unidentified circular feature about 21 feet in diameter, possibly a sump from which water was drawn for the reservoir. The station site is shown in some detail, a relatively modest complex when compared with the extensive development in the years to come. Beyond the station the roads to Forde House and Torquay cross the line, but a third has been terminated by the railway cutting.

Longitudinal Section

The railway approaches the station on a high embankment above the valley floor, crossing the River Teign by a five-span timber bridge. All five spans are shown as the standard size on the section, prior to modification as shown in the North View. The road from the New Quay to Newton pierces the last part of the embankment with a single-arched bridge. After passing the Newton Engine House, the line enters a shallow cutting to reach Newton Station. Building work on the Engine House started in the autumn of 1846, and the engines constructed by G. & S. Rennie were first run in August 1847. On leaving Newton the cutting becomes deeper, and overbridges carry an access road to Forde House and the main Newton to Torquay road across the line. The railway continues in cutting, beginning to rise to 1 in 259.

View South of the Line

To the left is the engine house "tank" or reservoir, with a one-horse cart taking the road from the New Quay to pass under the railway into the town. The Newton Engine House stands beyond the road at the lower level, with a two-arch bridge linking it to the railway embankment. Possibly this carried a coal siding, served by a waggon turntable on the embankment, but these arrangements are not shown. Behind the engine house there is a large timber-clad shed, which was later incorporated into the railway works. With a turntable on the plan, it may well be the original engine shed. In the distance are the separate up and down stations, with train sheds over the platforms and loops off the running line. There is a two-road timber goods shed to the right, with a piston carriage and an open waggon inside. Atmospheric pipework is shown on the line leading to the station, and secondary starting tubes to each side. Newton Station marked the limit of the 15 inch diameter tube, and two surplus lengths stand to the right. A policeman has emerged from his cabin, and is ready to operate the point capstan at the entrance to the goods shed. Both the capstan target and the disc on the signal in the distance are painted in the usual S.D.R. colours of white ring and black disc. There is another tall disc and crossbar signal (for down trains) by the workmen to the right, painted black at low level and white above. There appears to be a lamp at low level, and above this the footholds run up the post to the signal itself which is out of the picture. The houses beyond stand on the newly built road into Newton, known as Queen Street.

Modern View – 18 North

G.S.

The S.D.R. commenced a piecemeal widening of their approaches to Newton being amongst the first to be tackled. Additional spans for the River Teign Bridge were brought into use in 1865, when the line from Teignmouth was doubled. At the end of the Broad Gauge the bridge was rebuilt, with steel girders carried on stone piers. As well as the two running lines, this also carried a headshunt for down refuge lines. This also became a running line when Hackney Sidings opened in 1911.

Modern View – 18 South

G.S.

The original repair shop at Newton was constructed in wood on stone foundations. The new locomotive factory was under construction as the Broad Gauge came to an end, opening in 1893. Built from local stone, it followed the layout of its predecessor, with locomotive bays accessed by a traverser running the length of the building. The new building was erected to the north of the old one, leaving room for an improved engine shed. It was initially 245ft x 140ft, being extended in brickwork by 65ft in 1924.

From the Parish of King's Teignton to the Newton Station in Wolborough
View South of the Line.

18

Tank   and   Engine   House   The Newton Station   Road to Newton.

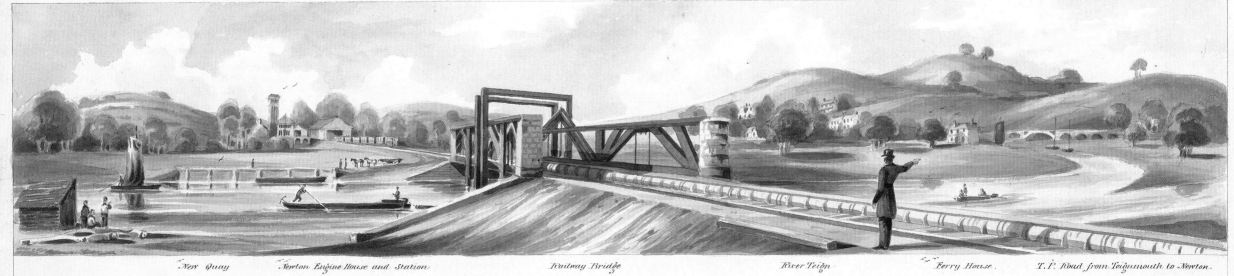

New Quay   Newton Engine House and Station   Railway Bridge   River Teign   Ferry House.   T.P. Road from Teignmouth to Newton.

Through the Newton Station to the River Teign.
View North of the Line.

19 From the Newton Station to the Parish of Abbot's Kerswell

View North of the Line

This view shows the site of Aller Junction, although it was really only to be a point of divergence in its early years, as the two railways ran separately back into Newton. As the main line railway embankment rounds the corner from the left, it crosses the Aller Brook by a single small arch, and runs on the level to the overbridge adjacent to the building in the centre of the plan, although the plan does not show the bridge. Surveyors are busy setting out the line of the Torquay Railway, their marker posts smartly identified by red pennants. This must therefore be an earlier sketch than 19 South, probably the winter of 1846/47. It is in fact painted up as a winter scene, the only one in the whole set. The policeman's cabin for this length of line will need to be relocated when the civil engineering work starts in earnest, but it can hardly be said to have much of a view of the railway in any case!

The Torquay Railway was to be opened for passengers on December 18th 1848 and for goods on October 6th 1849. It too was intended to be operated on the atmospheric system, and an engine house was constructed at Long Park from the summer of 1847. Engines for it were fabricated by Boulton and Watt, but were never installed, as atmospheric working was abandoned in September 1848 prior to the branch opening. Like the main line, the Torquay Railway was operated by Great Western locomotives until contractors took over in 1851. The first train was headed by the G.W.R. 2-4-0 Taurus, a Leo class goods built by Rothwell & Co, Bolton, in July 1841.

Route Plan - 214¼ miles to 215¾ miles

The cutting from Newton ends just after the start of the sheet, as the railway passes over Keyberry Road adjacent to Keyberry Mills. The mill leat, known as Forde Leat, also flows under the railway to link up with the Aller Brook. Both leat and brook run right across the sheet, re-joining the Aller Brook. The railway crosses the Aller Brook twice. On leaving the Parish of Wolborough, the line runs close to the Torquay Road in the Parish of Combeinteignhead. The trackbed of the Torquay Railway is shown in place, with embankments and cuttings well advanced, although bridges await construction. The building in the centre of plan appears to be connected with the gateway on the opposite side of the line on the Torquay Road, although the bridge has not been indicated. After passing the site of Aller Junction the line turns into the Parish of Abbotskerswell to re-cross the Aller Brook.

Longitudinal Section

As the sheet starts, the line passes out of the cutting shown in the View South of the Line onto an embankment crossing the small valley of the Aller Brook. There are single arches through the embankment for Keyberry Road, the leat for Keyberry Mills and the Aller Brook. Climbing gently through this stretch, the railway then levels out to run along the valley side to Aller Junction. The overbridge shown on the View North of the Line is not repeated on the section, but is noted on the plan. At the end of the sheet the railway runs on embankment once more, dropping gently at 1 in 502 to re-cross the Aller Brook although the bridge is not shown on the section.

View South of the Line

Works are shown in progress here in connection with the construction of the Torquay branch. The stone bridge carrying the Torquay Road (✓✓) over the line (seen in plan view on sheet 18) still only has one arch, but from the bridge towards Aller Junction the cutting is being widened to accept a second track to take the Torquay trains. The Newton to Totnes line had been opened on July 20th 1847, the first train being drawn by G.W.R. 2-4-0 Pisces, a Leo class goods built by Rothwell & Co, Bolton, in July 1842, and 7 foot single Pegasus, a Fire Fly class built by Naysmyth, Gaskell & Co, Manchester in December 1842. Goods traffic had commenced on December 6th 1847. Although the larger 22" diameter tubes used west of Newton are in place, the line was never to be operated under atmospheric traction. The Newton to Torquay line was to be opened on December 18th 1848. The works are in their early stages and this must therefore represent an 1847 sketch. Quite why the horses should be hauling track baulks at this stage is difficult to say. There is a disc and crossbar signal for up trains beyond the bridge, with the disc painted red rather than the usual S.D.R. black and white. However, the same signal is painted white and black in the View South on sheet 18.

Two carriages are taking the turnpike road to Torquay, with a pair of gate posts beside the road, at the entrance of the driveway leading to Forde House (✓✓) which was built in 1550. At the time of the sketch it was occupied by Henry Cartwright Esq. The turnpike toll House can be seen beside the road in front of the carriages. On the near side of the line are South Devon sheep, an old local breed, large with much lean mutton, large head and black spotted ears (the nearest one shows this). They were hardy, doing well on arable land or pasture, and producing long wool. The fleece weight of 15 lbs was three times the average for the country.

Modern View – 19 North

G.S.

The line from Newton to Totnes opened in 1847 as single track. A second line was added alongside in 1848 for trains on the Torquay branch which diverged at Aller. Additional rails were laid for ¼ mile west of Newton in 1852 and the main line was doubled through to Totnes in 1855, when a new junction was provided at Aller. The fourth track was brought into operation in May 1876, when the farm access bridge was replaced with the current two arch stone structure. Photos of the conversion were taken from it.

Modern View – 19 South

R.S.

Dawson shows the railway bridge over Keyberry Road on his plan, but does not provide an illustration. Like many on the line, it is a simple arched bridge in grey limestone, which can still be appreciated from the up side of the railway. A modern housing estate has surrounded Keyberry Mill. The trackbed was progressively widened on the down side, eventually totalling four tracks serving both the main line and the Torquay branch. The extended side of the bridge away from the photo is built of steel girders.

From the Newton Station to the Parish of Abbots Kerswell.
View South of the Line

19

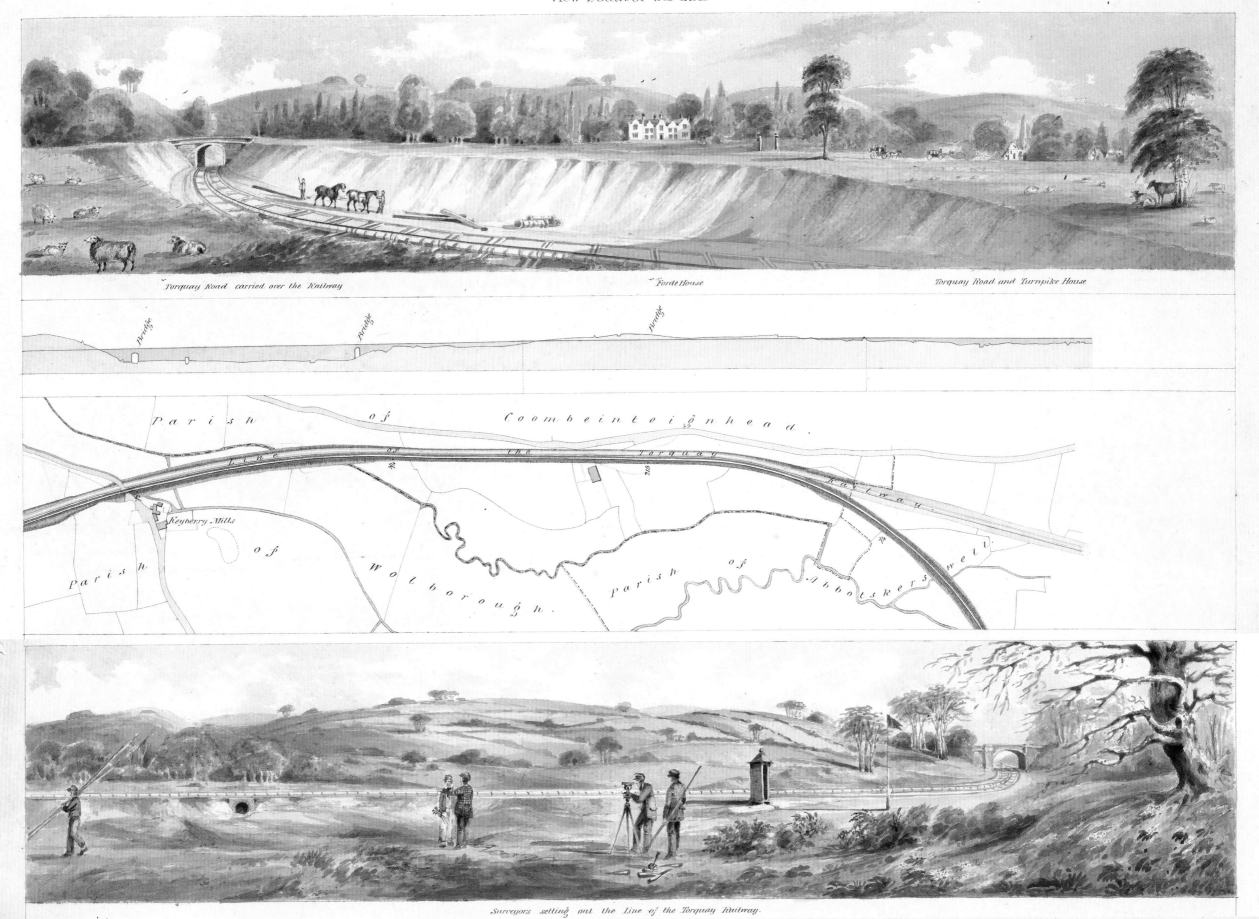

Torquay Road carried over the Railway

Forde House

Torquay Road and Turnpike House

Surveyors setting out the Line of the Torquay Railway.

From the Parish of Abbot's Kerswell to the Newton Station.
View North of the Line.

20 Through the Parishes of Abbot's Kerswell and King's Kerswell

View North of the Line

The valley of Stoneycombe, passing through an area of Devonian limestone uplands is prominent on the central horizon. Dawson has shown an atmospheric train emerging from the valley, running downhill to pass out onto the embankment above the valley of the Compton Brook. In the spring and early summer of 1848, with the railway in use for locomotive-hauled trains, the atmospheric pipes in place, and the installation of engines in Dainton and Totnes engine houses nearing completion, this probably seemed a reasonable proposition. However, with the decision to abandon atmospheric traction in September 1848 when the Newton to Totnes system was not quite completed, atmospheric trains never actually ran west of Newton, and so Dawson ended up with a piece of artistic fantasy. The engineering of the route sought to balance the amount of excavated cut with the filling required for the embankments necessary as the line followed the falling contours. The train will soon be crossing the limestone underbridge at the Maddacombe Cross, the parapets of which are local in the foreground. The road approach to the bridge is dry-walled in limestone, and appears to include a stock compound to the left. To the right is a shepherd is taking his flock along the road, and has stopped to talk to a rider on horseback. Cattle and sheep graze in the fields on the valley floor.

Route Plan - 215½ miles to 216½ miles

Running through the Parish of Abbotskerswell on an embankment, the railway frequently curves to maintain a reasonably even gradient. It follows the Compton Brook upstream away from the River Teign throughout this stretch, passing over a brook, then under the Abbotskerswell to Kingskerswell road, which crosses the railway on Langford Bridge. A short cutting brings the railway out of the Parish of Abbotskerswell into the Parish of Kingskerswell. Passing close to the Compton Brook on a ledge formed in the hillside, as shown in the View South of the Line, a meander of the brook has been filled in, avoiding two unnecessary bridges, and the brook has been diverted to run at the foot of the railway embankment. A wide curve takes the railway up the valley side, passing over the lanes from Maddacombe to Kingskerswell and Compton in quick succession, before crossing the Compton Brook for the last time, on a high embankment, to tackle the remaining mile and a quarter of the steep climb to Dainton.

Longitudinal Section

After a final gentle drop on an embankment at 1 in 247, the long climb towards Dainton begins in earnest. The first stretch rises at 1 in 98 with fairly light earthworks of embankment and cutting alternating. Following an underbridge for a brook, the overbridge at Langford Bridge carries the Abbotskerswell to Kingskerswell road over the railway. After a long shallow embankment and a shorter deeper cutting, the railway runs on a high embankment, filling in two crossings of the diverted Compton Brook. After the second the gradient stiffens considerably to 1 in 57, passing through cutting again and out onto another embankment, before crossing over a local parish road on a single arch. The gradient then eases to 1 in 71 as, still on an embankment, another single-arch underbridge carries the line over the Maddacombe to Compton Road.

View South of the Line

Whilst the design of the Exeter to Newton line involved heavy engineering works and regular maintenance in order to provide a level route suitable for early locomotives, but did in fact operate under atmospheric traction in 1847-48, the converse was true of the Newton to Plymouth line. Designed with heavy gradients suitable for atmospheric traction, and with correspondingly light engineering requirements, it has always been locomotive operated. In this view the route of the line takes on the start of its steady climb towards Dainton tunnel. This is the first of the four "planes" that delineate the route across the southern edge of Dartmoor to Plymouth, rising from Newton to Dainton Tunnel, then falling down to Totnes, rising out of Totnes on Rattery incline towards Marley Tunnel, and finally falling towards Plymouth down Hemerdon bank. The line here passes through an area of Devonian limestone, the thin soil supporting only heather and gorse. On the left are the woods of Compton Vale with pheasant shooting in progress. After passing under the line by a stone arched bridge to our left, a lane winds up the valley to Compton Mill and Compton Castle. Ahead of us the railway is built on a ledge in the hillside as it passes into the limestone quarrying area towards Stoneycombe. The main quarry entrance was later formed where the figures are standing in the lane. The permanent way is complete, with the atmospheric tube in place, never to be used. A lonely policeman stands at the corner, with no fence to protect him from tumbling down the embankment, into the valley below.

Modern View – 20 North

P.R.G.

The modern countryside is much more heavily wooded than in Victorian times and there has also been extensive limestone quarrying here since 1851. The S.D.R. allowed George Hennet to build a siding and extract stone from the company's land north of Stoney Combe, and an aptly named Mr. Stone was granted permission at the same time to do likewise on the south side. As a result of the quarrying, the current view from Maddacombe Cross bridge, looking up the 1 in 71 gradient towards Stoneycombe, is rather less dramatic than that painted by Dawson. The quarry buildings are visible in the distance.

Modern View – 20 South

P.R.G.

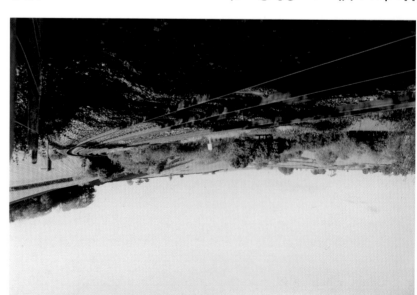

Maddacombe Cross bridge, shown at the right hand end of the plan, still stands and is a single arch limestone structure typical of the line. This is the view from the bridge looking back down the 1 in 71 and 1 in 57 gradients towards Newton Abbot. This represents the last of the rolling farmland before the tougher climb through the limestone outcrops to come. Conversely, Dawson's view shows the continuing ascent into Stoneycombe, corresponding with the plan on sheet 21.

Through the Parishes of Abbots Kerswell and King's Kerswell.

View South of the Line.

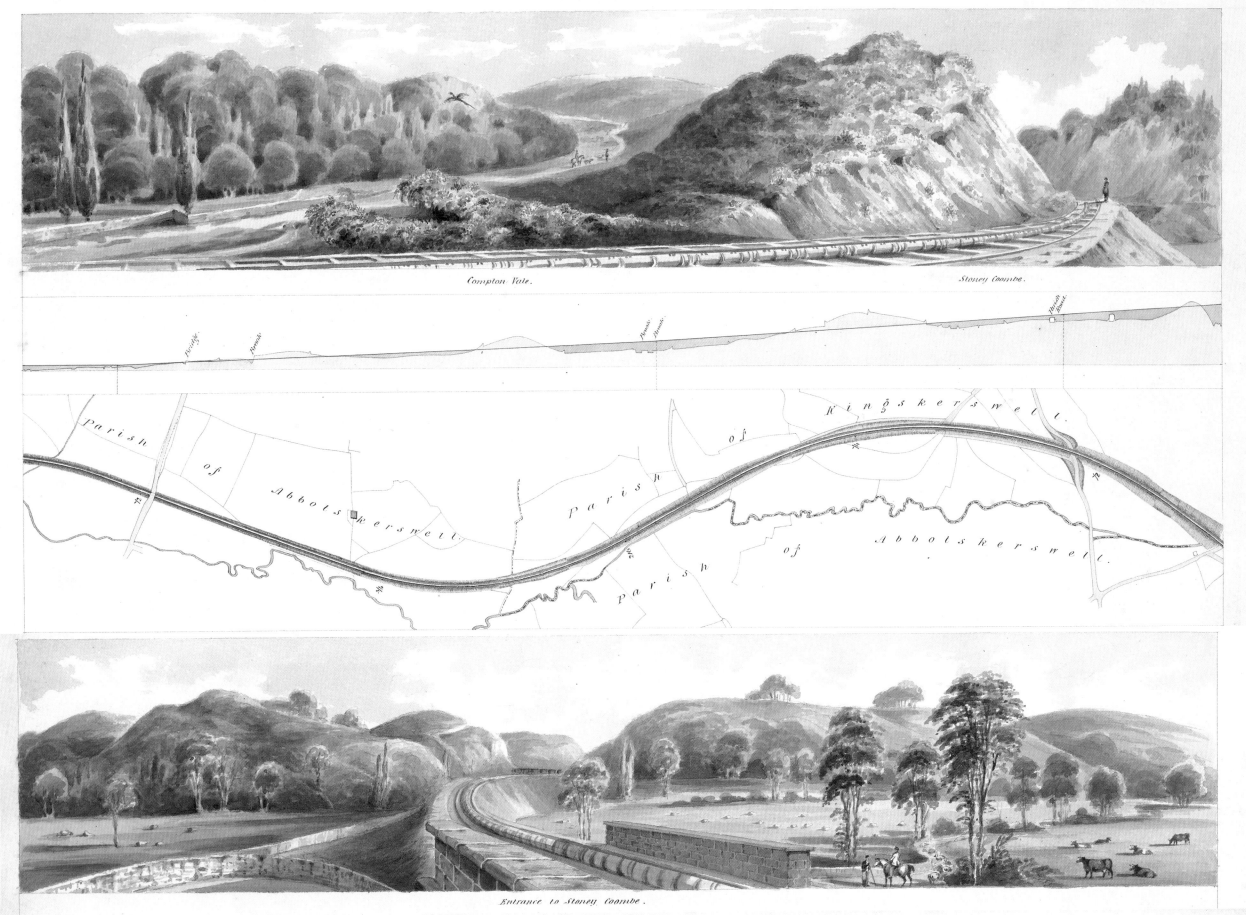

Compton Vale.

Stoney Coombe.

Entrance to Stoney Coombe.

Through the Parishes of King's Kerswell and Abbot's Kerswell.

View North of the Line.

21 Through the Parish of Ipplepen to the Dainton Tunnel

View South of the Line

Looking back to the east, the cutting through Stoneycombe visibly demonstrates the hard labour necessary to form the route of the railway through the southern Dartmoor terrain of Devonian limestone, slate and shale. The near completion of the atmospheric system between Newton and Totnes is apparent, with the permanent way in place, atmospheric tubing laid and the electric telegraph posts raised, with weathered pitched tops to the wooden insulator mounting blocks. A stone wall prevents sheep from falling down onto the cutting onto the railway. To the south of the line, navvies are seen breaking rock for use on the works, within the Stoneycombe Quarry. With pickaxes, shovels and wheelbarrows this was slow and back-breaking work. A dog is guarding the workmen's lunch rations, the principal ingredient of which is contained in a barrel! In later years the quarry was to expand to cover a large area, on both sides of the railway. The area above the cutting to the right however, grew heavily wooded, bringing quite a different atmosphere to the scene.

Longitudinal Section

The final gruelling stretch of the climb to Dainton is readily apparent on this drawing. Extensive cutting has provided an equal amount of material for the embankments shown on sheet 20. The final mile of the incline involved gradients of 1 in 46, 1 in 56, 1 in 41, 1 in 49, a maximum of 1 in 36 which must have been extremely taxing for early locomotives, and then easing to 1 in 84 and 1 in 190 through the tunnel to the summit. There is a footpath which crosses the line early on, whilst in the final length of embankment two single-arch bridges cross an occupation road and a parish road. The railway then enters a deep limestone cutting before gaining the 264 yards length of Dainton Tunnel, and the relief of the falling gradients beyond.

Route Plan - 216¾ miles to 217¾ miles

The railway continues to curve repeatedly as it climbs through the Parish of Ipplepen, the only straight stretch of line being in the tunnel itself. The main area of Stoneycombe Quarry occupied the space marked by the letters i, s and h of the word Parish shown on the plan, but, with this being early days, there is nothing yet worth illustrating on the drawing, it would appear. The access road running alongside the railway was eventually to be cut away by quarrying work, and substituted by a replacement further from the line. An occupation road known as Swallow Lane passes under the railway as it begins the steepest part of the climb. A parish road then also crosses under the line, connecting a few farms on Dainton Hill to the village of Dainton, which is illustrated at the bottom of the drawing. The railway enters a deep cutting before passing through Dainton Tunnel. Above the tunnel, a local road from Ipplepen to Compton and Marldon climbs over the summit near the eastern portal, although not quite so close as shown here.

View North of the Line

The village of Dainton nestles below the embankment just to the north of the railway, as the track drops at 1 in 36, the steepest gradient anywhere on the South Devon (other than the immediate approaches to Colonnade Viaduct at Dawlish), falling away from the eastern portal of Dainton Tunnel. The distance between tunnel mouth and village has been compressed a little here to obtain the desired artistic composition. In fact the cutting from the tunnel extends for about 200 yards before reaching the nearest houses of Dainton village. Again Brunel has added grandeur to the location with a monumental Roman-arched portal, similar in design to the coastal tunnels built earlier. The feeling of solidity given by the heavily-segmented arch and prominent keystone was possibly also intended to reassure nervous prospective passengers, unused to the novel experience of travelling below ground but Dainton was not a much frequented location. Unlike the other structures on the line, Dainton Tunnel was built large enough to accept two Broad Gauge tracks. As the watercolour shows, only one was laid initially, located in the position of the later Up line. In contrast to the opposite view, Dawson has not shown any telegraph poles alongside the line. The houses in the village are mostly built of cob, earth mixed with straw and then lime washed, and with thatched roofs with generous eaves overhangs, to keep the cob dry to prevent it losing its durability. One or two of the buildings appear to be of stone construction. In the field on the right, a farm worker is driving a pair of horses, probably engaged in ploughing. On the railway, workmen are resting from trimming back the cutting side, possibly to obtain material rather than improve the profile, as there is already generous clearance to the railway. Their wheelbarrow appears to be in need of re-wheeling if it is to be of any further use. In the distance the weather seems pleasant enough over the southern slopes of Dartmoor, but the west wind is blowing and rain could be coming from the denser clouds beyond the tunnel.

Modern View – 21 South   P.R.G.

At the left hand edge of the plan this limestone bridge carries the railway over Bickley Road, which can be seen in Dawson's view on sheet 20. On the up side, the original stone arch is topped by an embankment. When the track was doubled in 1855, new stonework was built on the down side and built all the way up to track level, as shown here. As the lane climbs to the left, the space between it and the railway climbs up by the extensive workings of Stoneycombe Quarry.

Modern View – 21 North   P.R.G.

Dainton village lies mostly to the north of the railway, although a few outlying farm buildings are located south of the line. Access to these is gained by a track running through this arched stone bridge. The 1855 doubling involved widening the railway on the south side, where today the trackbed is carried on steel girders. The farm track does not run as far as it used to, as its former route was destroyed by the extractions made at Stoneycombe Quarry.

Stoney Coombe.

Foot Path.

Crompton Road

Parish Road

Dainton Tunnel.

P a r i s h   o f   I p p l e p e n.

Smallow Lane

Dainton.

Dainton Tunnel

East face of the Dainton Tunnel.

Village of Dainton.

Through the Dainton Tunnel and Parish of Ipplepen.

View North of the Line.

22 From the Dainton Tunnel through the Parish of Ipplepen

View South of the Line

Dawson shows the single running line and atmospheric tube following the north wall of Dainton Tunnel, with space left alongside for a future down line. The connection to the engine house coal siding is just outside the tunnel mouth, but nothing is shown of the pointwork in the view, which has the atmospheric pipe continuing without a break. Dainton Engine House is positioned at the summit of the two inclines falling away to Newton in the east and Totnes in the west. The second batch of engine houses, Dainton, Totnes and Torquay were built to a new design to suit much improved machinery. Dainton was commenced in May 1847, and was built of local limestone. The chimney again took the form of a campanile, like the earlier engine houses, but the boilers and engines were all housed in three low-roofed bays with overhanging verges and Roman-arched windows. The earlier houses had contained two vertical beam engines of 40 horsepower and two supplementary beam engines of 12 horsepower,

totalling 104 hp and requiring tall buildings. To meet the demands of the 22 inch diameter pipe used west of Newton, Dainton Engine House contained two massively constructed 68 horsepower horizontal engines totalling 136 horsepower, driving large flywheels, and solidly mounted on the engine house floor. In view of the reported lack of power of the earlier engines, it is interesting that the horsepower at Dainton had only been increased by a factor of 1.3, compared with a 2.1 increase in area of the tube. The siding incorporating coal drops is assumed to be level, emphasising the steep gradient here. The coal waggons have narrow wooden bodies with "flying buttress" side stanchions, and are painted a reddish brown. The six-wheel waggon between the four-wheel opens may be loaded with atmospheric pipes, and the nearest unloaded six-wheeler had perhaps brought rails or timbers. The labourers appear to be breaking rock in order to extend the siding.

Longitudinal Section

The railway drops away from the summit at the western portal of Dainton Tunnel, briefly at 1 in 130, then very steeply at 1 in 37, followed by lengths at 1 in 43, 1 in 38, 1 in 65, 1 in 55 and 1 in 105. The upper reaches are in cutting, crossed by two road overbridges. The middle stretch is carried on a high embankment, crossing an occupation road, a brook and a parish road by underbridges. Passing through a rock outcrop in cutting and over a short embankment, the final stretch continues in a shallow cutting as far as the overbridge carrying the turnpike road from Newton to Totnes.

Route Plan - 218 miles to 219 miles

The sheet begins with the engine house tank, more irregular in shape than usual due to the lie of the land, and at a higher level than the engine house floor. The Dainton Engine House is shown next in pink, with the chimney behind its central boiler house, and engine rooms proper to either side. An occupation track crosses the railway by an overbridge, followed soon after by the local road from Ipplepen to Wrigwell Hill and Marldon, the houses of High Wrigwell and Lower Wrigwell being located either side of the railway. The track crosses a small stream several times, the stream being partly diverted into ditches alongside the railway, which are not coloured. A small lane follows the railway, crossing from one side to the other by an underbridge and linking up with the parish road from Ipplepen to Combeshacre. Rounding another long curve, the line passes into cutting again, and is crossed by an overbridge carrying the Newton to Totnes turnpike road.

View North of the Line

The scene depicts the final steep climb towards Dainton in the distance, whilst Dawson shows an imagined atmospheric train descending towards us. There appears to be differential settlement between the embankment and Combeshacre Bridge beyond, giving the bridge structure a humped appearance. Work appears to be in hand to remedy this, and with a line fitted with atmospheric tubing, accurate alignment of the permanent way is even more critical than usual. The embankment takes the railway towards the slope of Wrigwell Hill, which is prominent to the right. To the left of the railway, some of the houses of Ipplepen are just visible amongst the trees, with the hill fort at Denbury on the skyline, the artist once again shifting position to bring it in to the scene. It would otherwise be at the edge of the page, to the left of the tree. To the right of the picture, the fallow field is being worked. Note the team on the edge of the brown, darker area. The posture of the pair of animals would suggest oxen, and the implement they are drawing a harrow, used to prepare a seed bed, by breaking the furrows to produce a tilth fine enough for seed sowing. The harrow's frame is likely to be of oak or elm, with tines of iron. Oxen were to be used in England until the early 1900s. In this county the breed of cattle would be Devons, which were originally bred as plough oxen. The man at the rear guides the harrow by the two handles, and the other will lead if necessary or use a goad when required. The smartly turned out horse and rider in the lane below, with faithful hound following obediently, have perhaps come from nearby Combeshacre House.

Modern View – 22 North

The historic route of Combeshacre Lane was altered to create two sharp approach bends, so that it could pass through the new railway embankment at right angles. As elsewhere on the widening took place on the down side in 1855. Stone abutments were built to accept a girder bridge, the current girders being of steel. Part of the southern face of the original arch is still visible below them.

P.R.G.

Modern View – 22 South

Although following the general styling of the coastal tunnels, the semi-circular arched portals of Dainton were less heavily rusticated, reflecting the isolated location. The generous dimensions of these bell-mouths reduced to standard dimensions further within the 291 yard long bore. The second line through the tunnel was added in 1855. The gradient descends at 1 in 37 here and the railway soon drops below the level of the overgrown Engine House site to the right.

P.R.G.

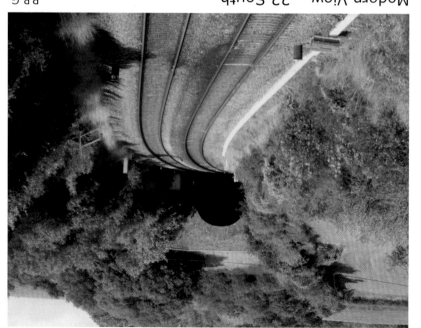

From the Dainton Tunnel through the Parish of Ipplepen.
View South of the Line

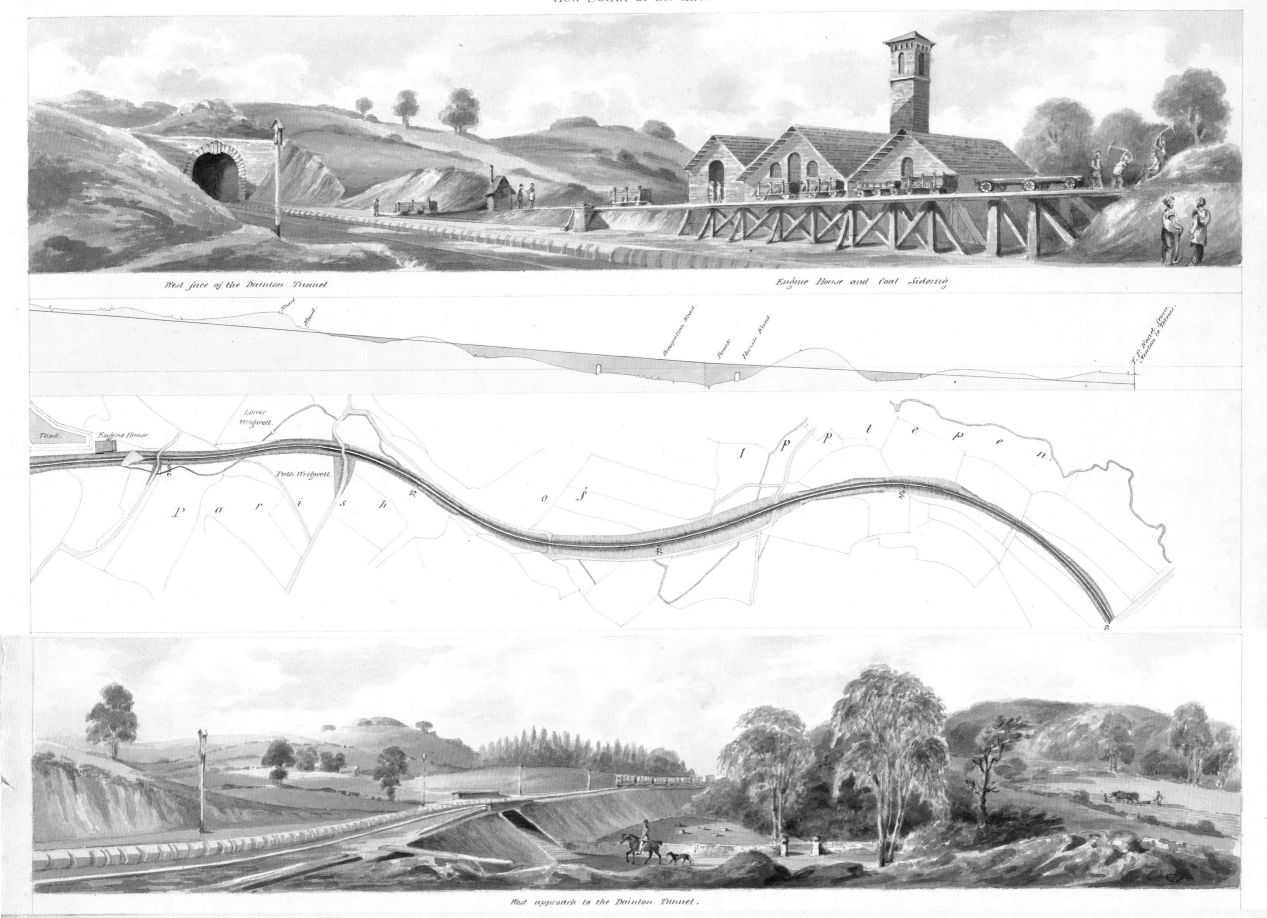

West face of the Dainton Tunnel

Engine House and Coal Sideing

Through the Parish of Ipplepen to the Dainton Tunnel.
View North of the Line.

West approach to the Dainton Tunnel.

23 Through the Parish of Ipplepen to Little Hempstone

View South of the Line

This view is actually looking north-east, and shows a larger area north of the line than south of it. The parapet of the limestone underbridge is for the parish road from Broadhempston to Marldon, and is known as Fishacre Bridge after the nearby Fishacre Barton. The flying arch in the distance is called Hardup Bridge, and leads back towards Ipplepen. It is really half a mile away, but some judicial compression has been applied to aid the artistic composition, although this does leave the horses with a much steeper climb! The two horses in tandem are drawing a cart, much favoured over waggons in the hillier parts of Devon. Note the blue body and pinkish red wheels. There is a conspicuous post and wire fence between the railway and the road, giving way to a stone wall in the distance. Railway fences are rarely shown in the watercolours, but this one has obviously caught Dawson's attention. Telegraph poles have been shown, although they are probably misplaced. In all other views they are shown on the up side of the line, not the down side as here. To the left, the Littlehempston Brook flows down to join the River Hems behind the viewer, a tributary of the River Dart, which it will join at Totnes. It is quite a good-sized stream, and worth a little fishing. Sheep are grazing on the valley floor.

Longitudinal Section

The descent from Dainton towards the Dart Valley continues more gently now, first at 1 in 76 on a low embankment, passing through a short cutting, and then easing to 1 in 260 on a long embankment with a bridge over the Littlehempston Brook, which runs alongside the line here. The railway continues through a cutting crossed by a parish road on Hardup Bridge. Level ground is regained as the line follows the Brook.

Route Plan - 219¾ miles to 220 miles

Beginning at the overbridge for the Newton to Totnes turnpike road, the railway continues to curve repeatedly to follow the valley contours through the Parish of Ipplepen. It then crosses the Littlehempston Brook on an embankment incorporating an arched bridge over the brook. The latter has been diverted to the north of the railway, following the foot of the embankment before regaining its former meandering course. Beyond the brook the railway enters the Parish of Littlehempston. Various farm buildings are shown to the south of the line. To the north of the line a mill stream is drawn off from the brook, feeding the mill pond for Ford Mill which is shown alongside the railway. Two parish roads from the south have been joined by a new wide length beside the railway, as also shown in the view south of the line. However, the underbridge from the middle of this new length to link up with the old road by the mill is not clearly shown, and the apparent overbridge at the end of the sheet should not be illustrated. It would appear to represent the former road alignment, which had actually been stopped off.

and another road (or more likely field access track) crosses the railway, although is not shown on the plan. The railway begins to drop again at the end of the sheet, falling at 1 in 86. The former routes of two parish roads have been blocked up, and replaced by Fishacre Bridge under the line, which is shown in the View South of the line, but does not appear correctly on the plan.

View North of the Line

The Ford Mill and Farm, and the mill stream fed by the Littlehempston Brook, are illustrated next to Fishacre Bridge under the railway. A policeman stands with his back to the bridge parapet, giving an "All Right" signal to an oncoming train. A piston carriage is shown at the head of the train, although atmospheric power was never actually brought into operation on the Totnes to Newton line. Telegraph poles are shown on the up side of the line. The mill is lime-washed and has a slate roof and brick chimneys. Further to the right, the farm house and outbuildings would appear to be Fishacre Barton, although notes on the views, like colour on the plans, are rather sparse on the higher-numbered sheets. From the range of hills beyond, there would be a good view back into the Dart Valley. A shepherd and his sheepdog are preparing to round up sheep in the field by the mill stream. There is no bridge parapet shown here again, with the trees and limestone cutting used from a viewpoint slightly further along the line. In reality the road runs briefly adjacent to the line at rail level here, before diving away to the left and then curving sharply to the right to pass through Fishacre Bridge. Treatment of the atmospheric pipes varies through the sheets, but those illustrated here are fairly accurate, with three stiffening flanges between the jointing sockets of each ten-foot length of pipe.

Modern View – 23 North

P.R.G.

The original stone arch of Fishacre Bridge can still be seen on the up side of the railway. Brickwork has been added to raise the rail level at some time, where the stone parapet used to be, and there are steel railings above this. When the line was doubled in 1855, stone abutments were constructed on the down side with girders spanning between them. The current girders are of steel. The driveway to Ford Mill marks the original route of the lane, before it was diverted to pass under the railway.

Modern View – 23 South

P.R.G.

The impressive flying arch at Hardup Bridge had a very short life. Opened with the railway in 1847, it needed to be replaced just eight years later when in 1855 the Newton to Totnes stretch of the South Devon Railway was doubled. This involved widening the cutting on the down side and constructing new stone abutments to carry cross girders over the railway. Although these may have been of timber or iron, the current girders are of steel.

Through the Parish of Ipplepen to Little Hempstone.
View South of the Line.

23

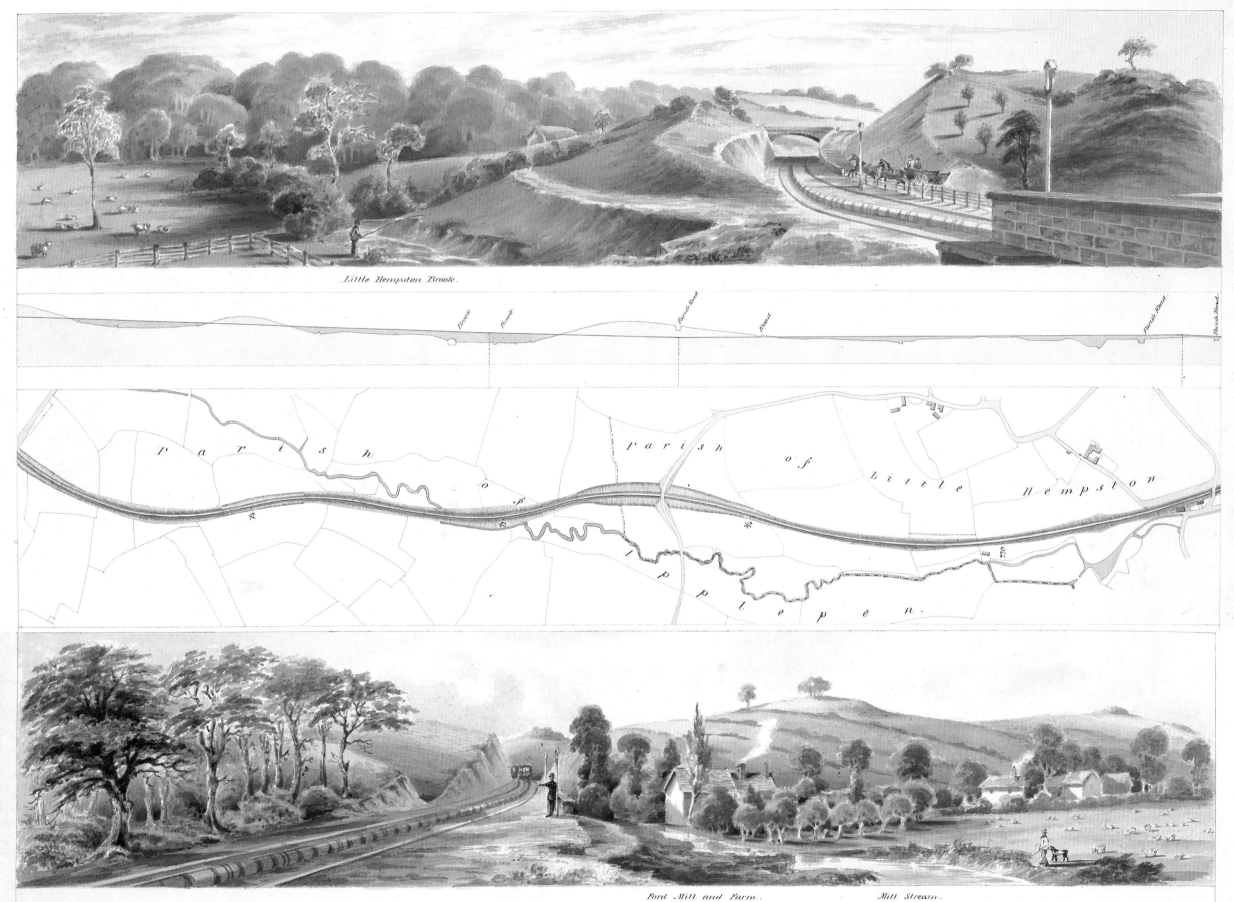

Little Hempston Brook.

Ford Mill and Farm.   Mill Stream.

From Little Hempstone through the Parish of Ipplepen
View North of the Line

24 Parish of Little Hempstone

Modern View – 24 North

P.R.G.

The arrival of steam locomotives caused several fires in the thatched roofs at Littlehempston. The S.D.R. stationed a policeman here to watch the houses, and offered to whitewash the thatch of several buildings or replace it with slate. The parish boasts a staggering total of nineteen listed buildings and structures, two of which are grade I. The church of St John the Baptist had received new windows not long before Dawson painted it, but otherwise remains much as when rebuilt in 1439. The other notable survival is the old manor house, built around a courtyard just twenty feet square. This dates from the late 14th century and was used as a parsonage from the mid 15th century until 1921.

Modern View – 24 South

P.R.G.

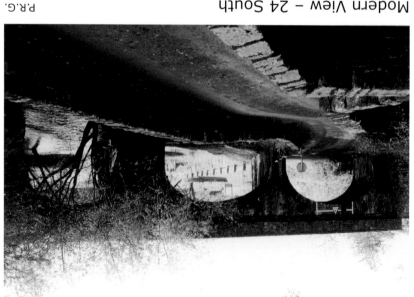

The scene approaching Littlehempston is very picturesque. Like several in this area, the parish road is flanked with stone walls as it nears and then crosses over the River Hems. The original line of the river viaduct is carried on an impressive three-arch stone viaduct. The two outer spans pass over the road and the river, whilst a wider central span above the river bank effectively links together what would otherwise have been two separate underbridges. The later down line is carried on steel girders on stone piers.

View South of the Line

Local children idling on the parapet are chatting to two of the workers carrying pickaxes, who may have been trimming back the cutting face to the right. The setting would appear to be the bridge over the River Hems shown on the plan on sheet 25 beyond the 221½ mile post. The River Hems can be seen flowing away to the south, before turning back towards the railway. The flying arch in the distance carries an occupation road into the area cut off by the meander of the river. A waggon of the box type, a Devon Buckrowe in traditional Devonian colours of blue body with pinkish red wheels, is making for the bridge, drawn by two horses in tandem. A fisherman is trying his luck in the river, whilst above the trees on the river bank runs the Newton to Totnes turnpike road (\\). The turnpike gate house (\\) can be seen in the centre of the picture, with smoke coming from the chimney. Hidden from view by the hill to the left is Coombe Park, and not far away stands Gatcombe House. The railway appears complete, other than the usual omission of fencing and telegraph poles by the artist. The 22 inch diameter of the atmospheric pipes used west of Newton has also been underestimated.

Longitudinal Section

The descent towards the Dart Valley continues more steadily, although fairly heavy earthworks are still required. Beginning at 1 in 227, the line follows the valley side, before steepening to 1 in 120 and passing through a cutting, to avoid following a meander of the River Hems. The two roads indicated would appear to show the original positions of the lanes, before they were combined to pass through Tallyho Bridge, adjacent to that over the River Hems, through a deep embankment crossing the river valley. A little further on, two parish roads are also shown in their original positions, as the railway passes through another cutting to avoid following a meander of the river. Carried on a new stone retaining wall, the lanes were combined to cross the cutting at Bycellar Bridge. A short deep embankment follows, as the railway re-crosses the River Hems by a single arch. The descent continues at 1 in 205, 1 in 78, 1 in 153 and 1 in 118 as the railway follows the river. In Littlehempston a three arch limestone viaduct carries the railway over a parish road and the River Hems. The Gatcombe Brook is also indicated where it joins the river next to the bridge. At the end of the sheet the river is crossed a fourth time by a further arch through the same embankment.

Route Plan - 220¾ miles to 221¼ miles

The railway continues to curve repeatedly as it follows the Littlehempston Brook past the hamlet of Hemsford. There appears to be a man-made loop in the watercourse where it crosses the Staverton to Marldon road. The course of the River Hems should be shown approaching from the bottom of the plan and meeting the brook at this point, just downstream next to the River Hems. There are two separate limestone bridges for two parish roads have been joined and diverted to pass under the railway road and river, the former being Tallyho Bridge. A little further on, a sharp bend in the Hemsford to Littlehempston road has been straightened to follow the edge of the railway cutting, a flying arch called Bycellar Bridge crossing to the other side to reach clay cellars by the river. There is another short cutting as the railway re-crosses the river, which it then follows into the village of Littlehempston. The railway passes through the village on an embankment and short viaduct, the first arch crossing the road from Staverton to the turnpike, and the third arch accommodating the River Hems. The overbridge shown on the plan is not correct. The Gatcombe Brook approaches from the top of the plan to join the River Hems next to the viaduct. The buildings of the village of Littlehempston are shown in pink, with its church in black. The River Hems is crossed once again at the end of the sheet.

View North of the Line

The village of Littlehempston straddles the River Hems, and the railway takes the same route as the river, cutting the village in two as it makes numerous river crossings. The illustration gives the impression of double transommes supporting the ends of the pipes either side of the joint, although surviving castings only have supporting feet on the eastern, socket side of the joint. Particularly in a location such as this, the absence of fencing must be artistic licence. The farm building is delightful, much modified over the centuries, with a strange arrangement of chimneys. The cart on the right, of typical Devonian colouring, rests with its shaft ends on the ground. Caring farmers would never allow this out of doors, since the damp will encourage the shafts to rot, or a careless step from a one-ton shire horse could break a shaft. In fact, out of use, the cart should be put in the cart shed and the shafts lifted skywards until the cart rests on the ends of the long side timbers or "soles". The pigs in the yard, from their markings, would appear to be Saddlebacks. The building with low pitch slate roof and creeper to the left hand bay is the former manor house, which became the parsonage when the village church was built in the 1470s. Unfortunately the view does not include the picturesque arrangement of railway viaduct and road bridge over the River Hems, to the right of the farm.

Turnpike Road from Newton to Totnes

Turnpike Gate House

Village of Little Hempston.

Church

Church and Village of Little Hempston.

Through Little Hempstone.
View North of the Line.

Modern View – 25 South
G.S.

The length of railway from Newton to Totnes was the first part of the S.D.R. to be widened and the River Dart bridge was duplicated on the down side as early as 1855. Following the end of the Broad Gauge, the timber bridge was replaced with new steel girders on stone piers. In more recent years, welded steel spans have been introduced.

Modern View – 25 North
G.S.

The lower height of the pumping house at Totnes was because it was designed to accommodate horizontal engines, although some machinery was installed by 1848, along with the larger 22" pipes laid from Newton to Totnes, none of it was put into working order. From 1959 the Unigate dairy complex buildings formed part of the Engine House complex until closure in 2007, and then lay disused for a number of years although it was re-roofed in 2012. The Engine House chimney was demolished between the wars.

View South of the Line

The River Hems flows in from the left to join the River Dart beyond the three men puzzling over a drawing. Beyond this runs the Newton to Totnes turnpike road, with the stone quarries (\/\/) at Mockwood behind. The Dart flows off to the right, with the 17th century tower of St. Mary's Church, Berry Pomeroy (\/\/) visible in the distance. Beyond the river meadows, with sheep and cattle grazing, can be seen the 15th century tower of St. Mary's Church, Totnes, several houses in the town, and the keep of Totnes Castle, built soon after the Norman conquest. The River Dart bridge is consistent in design with the other trussed viaducts built by George Hennet elsewhere on the line. A three span structure, the perspective on the northern elevation appears misleading to the eye. The simple concept of the design is most clearly expressed by the southern elevation. The effective use of both timber

Longitudinal Section

The final approach to Totnes is very evenly graded along the valley floor, dropping at only 1 in 254 and then running on the level across the bridge and into the station. Beginning in cutting, a short embankment takes the railway over the River Hems by a single-arch bridge. A cutting avoiding a long meander is crossed by the flying-arch occupation bridge

Route Plan - 221½ miles to 222½ miles

Once again there is not a single stretch of straight railway line on this length of the plan. The railway follows the River Hems, with the S bends of the latter evened out to a more easy flowing series of bends on the railway, a compromise between sharpest permissible curvature of the line and desired limitation to the necessary earthworks. As a result, the railway has to cross the River Hems three more times before reaching the River Dart. The only other intermediate structure is the flying arch over the cutting, giving access from the farm at Grattons to the meadows

View North of the Line

Looking up the Dart, the distant weir looks to be in full flow, providing good fishing for the man on the promontory below. Meanwhile, works are still in progress with the laying of atmospheric pipes. Whilst supervisors and policemen discuss the issues of the day, a small gang are making preparations for positioning of pipe sections. Due to the use of 22 inch diameter pipes between Totnes and Newton, transommes similar in section to the baulks had to be used, with scalloped cut-outs for the pipes to sit into. The pipes are underestimated, being actually ten feet long, with three large-diameter flanges, and a mounting foot next to the socket. As can be seen, the sockets are at the western end, which means

and iron, utilising the respective qualities of each material, is apparent, giving an efficient and economic design. Telegraph posts are illustrated, and beyond the bridge a disc and crossbar signal stands at the approach to Totnes Station. Behind the signal is the large timber goods shed (which survived until the end of goods traffic), then (not accurately drawn and out of position) the up and down platform train sheds and, finally, Totnes Engine House. This is similar in style to Dainton, built of limestone, with red conglomerate dressing and clay Italian-tiled roofs. Building work commenced in the summer of 1847, and horizontal engines of the new design built by Boulton and Watt were largely installed, but unfortunately were never brought into operation. By the summer of 1848 the sun was setting (in the south in this view!) over the atmospheric railway.

shown in the View South of the Line on sheet 24, before the railway re-crosses the river by another arch through an embankment. After a final short cutting the railway runs on a long shallow embankment, crossing the River Hems one last time to reach the banks of the River Dart, where the section comes to an abrupt halt without illustrating the bridge.

cut off by the meander of the river. Towards the end of the sheet the farm buildings at Hampstead are shown, and finally the bridge over the River Dart, after which the plan is immediately discontinued. The book of watercolours is labeled Volume One, but with the abandonment of atmospheric working in September 1848 a second volume was never required. It is a pity that Totnes itself and the short Totnes Quay branch were not covered however.

that the continuous valve will be fixed on the southern side, through bolt mountings which are just visible. Little work appears to remain, but time is fast running out for atmospheric pipe laying, the decision to abandon atmospheric working taking effect on September 9th 1848. As with the other timber bridges, the top member is weathered and rests on a stone pier. Telegraph poles are shown in place alongside the railway, with weathered tops to the insulator mounting blocks. Cattle graze in the river meadows, and behind the workmen a pair of horses are drawing a plough. It is likely that the plough has an oak body with iron attachments including share, coulter and mouldboard for turning the furrow.

From Little Hempstone to Totnes.
View South of the Line.

25

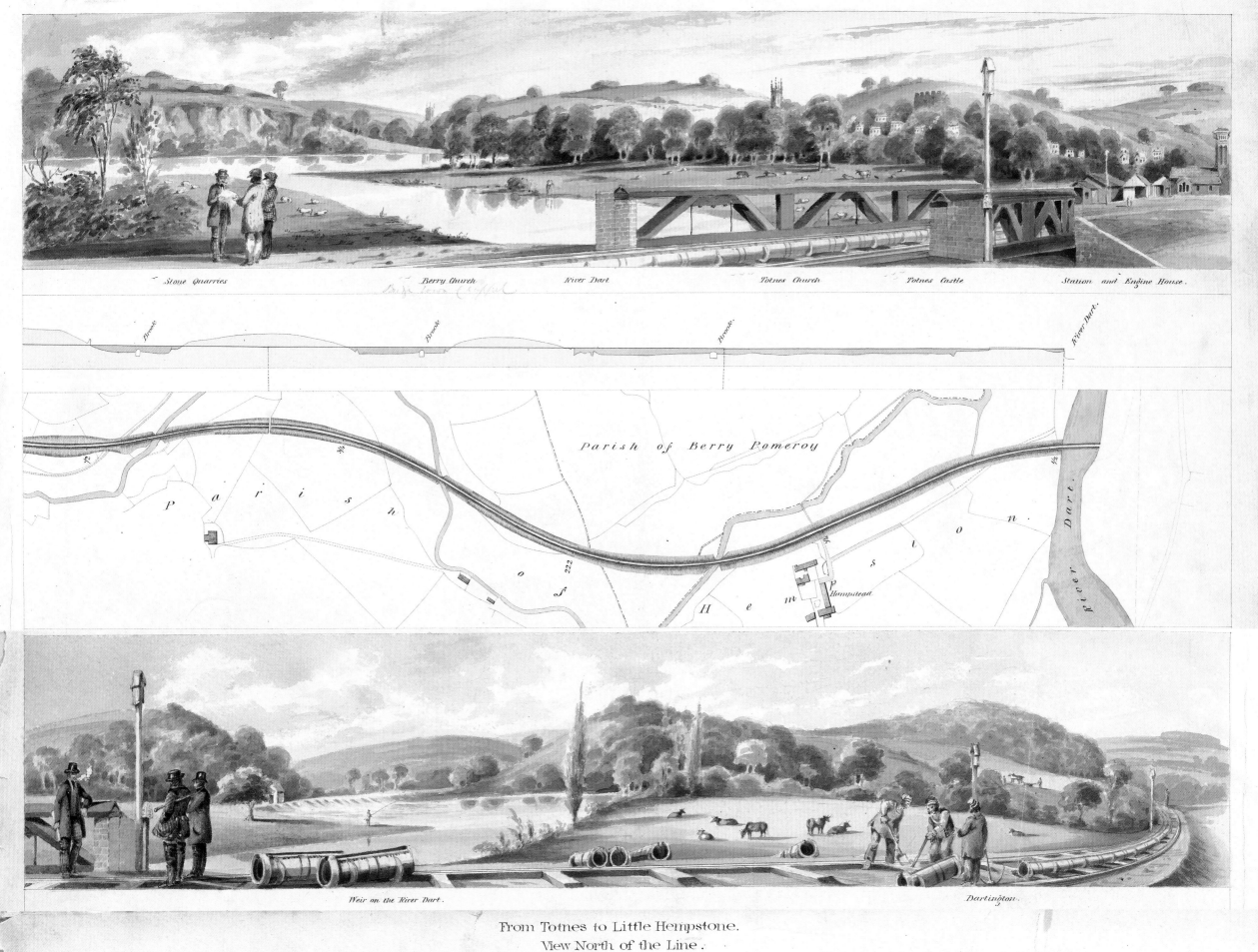

Stone Quarries   Berry Church   River Dart   Totnes Church   Totnes Castle   Station and Engine House.

Brook   Brook   Brook   River Dart.

Parish of Berry Pomeroy

Parish of Hempston

Hampstead

River Dart

Weir on the River Dart.   Dartington.

From Totnes to Little Hempstone.
View North of the Line.

Dawlish

It is a little surprising that Dawson did not include a high level view of Dawlish from Lea Mount in his atmospheric watercolour set, as it was a popular viewpoint for artists. This was rectified soon after the end of atmospheric operation and this fine view below was issued in the series of lithographs of Dawson's work made by William Spreat. Lea Mount owes its formal, straight-cut outline to the anxieties that followed the falling of a portion of the cliff on August 29th, 1885, when over fifty tons of rock buried a party of seven women and children, killing three of them. To prevent further accidents, all overhanging portions were cut away. Evident in this view is one of the pedestrian tunnels through the cliff, which existed before the collapse.

The Georgian elegance of Marine Parade was still largely unspoilt at this date. Beyond the breakwater can be seen the original nine-span classical form of Colonnade Viaduct, the station trainshed, the atmospheric engine house, the coastguard station with its footbridge and boathouse and then Sea Lawn House. In the distance a train is coming along the sea wall.

Lithograph reproduced by kind permission of The Newton Abbot Town and G.W.R. Museum.

Photographed by Kate Green.

Dawlish Engine House

The superb painting above by Nicholas Condy (1793-1857), ref AE185.49, shows Dawlish Engine House in its heyday. Although all of Brunel's engine houses featured Italianate styling, each one was unique in detail.

The narrow site also resulted in the longitudinal layout, with the chimney located between the boiler room and engine room. The tall signal with its double discs, climbing steps and policeman's platform is prominent. This governed the turnout into the trainshed in the centre of the view, whilst there is a single disc and crossbar signal beyond.

The white and black colours used for S.D.R. signals show up very clearly. Like Starcross, the trainshed served a single platform on a loop, was closed in on the town side and open towards the sea. The short length of pipe laid to the right of the track in this view, is the starting pipe for up trains. On the seaward side can be seen the vacuum distribution pipe, with a branch connection.

Eastcliff, Teignmouth

This fine painting by W. P. Key below illustrates the Heathcoat works outing to Teignmouth on 10th August 1854, just six years after the end of atmospheric operation.

It can be appreciated at Knightshayes Court near Tiverton, built for the grandson of John Heathcoat, owner of the lace factory in Tiverton at the time of the outing. It is surprising that the train was allowed to discharge its passengers alongside the sea wall, rather than in Teignmouth station, and getting over the wall cannot have been easy for the smartly dressed visitors. Apart from the Heathcote party, the uncluttered length of the promenade is noticable. Eastcliff tunnel was opened out between 1882 and 1884, being replaced by the familiar lattice girder bridge seen on page 52.

The train is hauled by an ubiquitous S.D.R. saddle tank with brass splashers and safety valve casing. The blue-green paintwork of the nearest coach is interesting, in comparison to the brown or varnished ones nearer the locomotive.

Coryton Cove

The Sheet 12 North view was another one which Dawson re-worked as an individual painting *just* after the end of atmospheric operation. It is reference 14/1929/3 at the Royal Albert Memorial Museum and Art Gallery and features a steam-powered train heading eastwards across Coryton Cove. The semi-circular arched portals of Coryton and Kennaway tunnels stand out clearly.

The picture was again made into a lithograph and issued by William Spreat illustrated above, endorsed by a signature from William Dawson (and 'Septr 1848' date). Dawson's interest in geology is very apparent here, with Coryton Breccia (including quartzite and pink feldspars) and Teignmouth Breccia (including Devonian and Carboniferous slates, cherts, and igneous rocks) both in evidence. These were laid down in an alluvial fan. A major fault at Coryton Cove brings these and the Dawlish Sandstone, which overlies them, together.

Lithograph reproduced by kind permission of The Newton Abbot Town and G.W.R. Museum.

Photographed by Kate Green

Ivybridge Viaduct

Possibly the most beautiful of Brunel's timber viaducts, the one over the River Erme at Ivybridge consisted of eleven bays giving a total length of 252 yards. It was an imposing 108 feet 6 inches in height. William Dawson was one of a number of artists who attempted to capture its splendour. His painting, above, Entitled 'Viaduct over the River Erme', executed in Watercolour, gouache and pencil and signed and dated 29th August 1848, is held by the Royal Albert Memorial Museum and Art Gallery, reference 14/1929/1.

The South Devon viaducts differed from the later Cornish ones, as they were designed to carry the relatively light loads of atmospheric trains. A pair of trussed timber beams supported the decking, but additional trussed timber balustrades were added to accommodate the weight of locomotive hauled trains. A four-coach train is shown passing over the viaduct, hauled by one of the South Devon's many saddle tanks.

The painting is signed and dated 29th August 1848, so any passengers travelling beyond Newton will be changing to Atmospheric traction for the next stage of their journey, this being the last full month of the system's operation.

Shaldon Bridge

View 14 South was also repainted by Dawson as a stand-alone work, reference 14/1929/2 at the Royal Albert Memorial Museum and Art Gallery and distributed by William Spreat in lithograph format as illustrated below.

Before the opening of the bridge, travellers had the choice of making a crossing by ferry or, if they had horses or a vehicle, of making the long detour via Newton Abbot. In 1827, the Shaldon Bridge Company opened the first bridge, which was designed and built in wood by Roger Hopkins.

It was claimed at the time to be the longest wooden bridge in England with a length of 1,632 feet and 34 arches and the second longest bridge in Europe. It had stone abutments at both ends and a swing bridge at the Teignmouth end to allow passage for tall masts. As early as 1838, some of the spans collapsed due to the actions of shipworm, entailing considerable rebuilding.

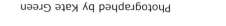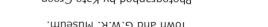

Introduction

In August 1846 the S.D.R. Board ordered six pairs of 68hp engines from Boulton & Watt, intended for the new engine houses west of Newton. These were to be of an improved more modern design, featuring steam cylinders and vacuum pumps mounted horizontally at floor level, resulting in a much more robust installation altogether. The arrangement was to follow the 50hp and 82½hp engines which Boulton & Watt were currently building for the London & Croydon's extension to Epsom.

In June 1847, following the abandonment of atmospheric working on the Croydon, the S.D.R. agreed to take the three pairs of engines which were under construction for them. One pair from the original S.D.R. order was subsequently cancelled, whilst two further pairs were ordered from Harvey of Hayle. The final total would therefore have been ten pairs, sufficient for a second pair at Newton to cope with its additional workload, plus new engine houses on the branch line at Torquay and on the main line at Dainton, Totnes, Rattery, Wrangaton, Ivybridge, Hemerdon, Plympton and Plymouth.

The 40hp vertical engines used between Exeter and Newton had originally been intended to extract air from 13" diameter pipes, but ended up having to create vacuum in 15" pipes instead. For the 22" pipes installed west of Newton it appears that the 40hp was erroneously multiplied by 22/13, resulting in the order for 68hp engines. It should have of course been multiplied by $22^2/13^2$, which would have called for 115hp engines. It would appear therefore that underpowered engines would have remained a problem if the second phase had ever been put into operation.

At the time of writing the Boulton & Watt collection held by Birmingham Central Library is inaccessible for an extended period, pending relocation to the new Library of Birmingham. Therefore it has not been possible to gain access to Portfolio 669 and select drawings of the horizontal S.D.R. engines to appear in this work. From a previous visit it was apparent that the S.D.R. engines were very similar to those of the Croydon & Epsom, apart from the altered dimensions, so one of the latter will be sufficient to illustrate the general layout. The Croydon & Epsom engines were purchased by the S.D.R. in any case, so it is not inappropriate to include a pair here.

The two engines were mounted at 21 feet centres, with the two flywheels located side by side in the space between. This would have allowed the flywheels to be coupled together when required to enable the two engines to work together.

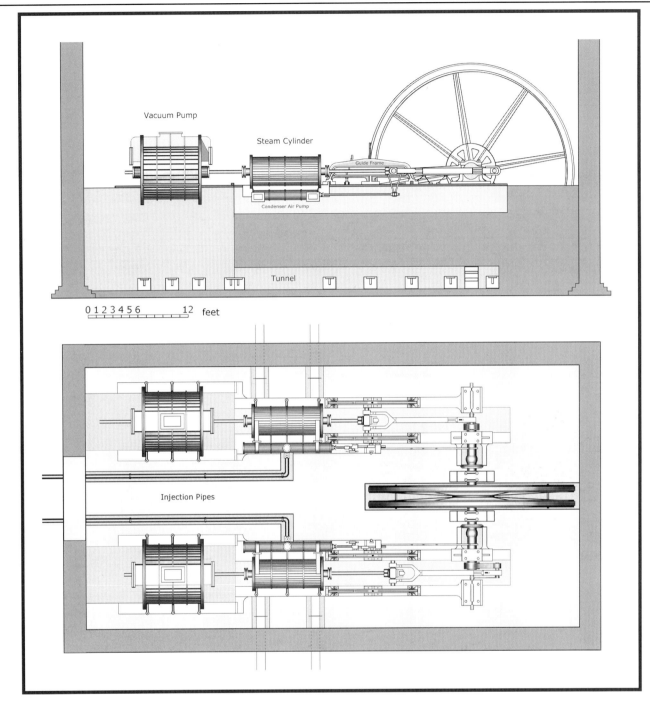

Croydon & Epsom Railway: Pair of Boulton & Watt 50hp Engines. Arranged to Facilitate Coupling, Later Purchased by S.D.R.

The steam cylinders were 3' 9" diameter, with the air pumps following usual practice in being double the diameter at 7' 6". They were connected in tandem to the same piston rods, with a common stroke of 6' 0". The two flywheels were of 25' 0" diameter with the centre line of the engine units 1' 6" above floor level. The crank shafts were much shorter than the earlier design at only 12' 0" each. Likewise the connecting rods were also only 12' 0" long, the whole assembly being much more compact and practical. The 68hp engines ordered by the S.D.R. were probably very similar in appearance and layout. They may have only differed in steam and vacuum cylinder diameters, which would have increased to about 4' 4" for steam and 8' 8" for vacuum.

A longitudinal pit, 2' 6" wide by 3' 0" deep ran under each engine unit, which comprised steam cylinder, crosshead, connecting rod and crank shaft. Two long iron mounting plates, each a minimum of 18" wide and increased locally where necessary, were mounted on the floor below the centre line of the engine, one each side of the pit. The steam cylinder, crosshead guide frame and crank shaft bearing were all fixed to the same plates, so the engine assembly would have been very stable in operation. Two similar but much shorter floor-mounted plates supported a third bearing for each crank shaft adjacent to its flywheel. The two flywheels ran in a single pit, approximately 2' 9" wide by 11' 6" deep.

The two vacuum pumps were mounted in the same fashion on iron base plates each side of a well. In view of the greater cylinder diameter, the vacuum pump pits were much larger, each 6' 3" wide by the full 11' 6" deep like the flywheel pit. 2' 6" square tunnels also ran at this lower level under the engine units.

Beside each steam valve cylinder was its associated steam cylinder, on the same centre line and mounted on the same base plate. The valves were actuated by valve gear driven by cams on the crank shaft. Most interestingly, this was an early case of the use of piston valves, which had been a feature of the Swannington Incline winding engine on the Leicester & Swannington Railway in 1833; they did not come into general use until the end of the nineteenth century.

Underneath each steam cylinder was a condenser air pump, driven by an arm hanging from the crosshead. The exhaust steam was all condensed and re-used in the interests of efficient operation, so only smoke from the boilers passed to the tall chimney. The engines in each new building totalled 136hp (two at 68hp), compared with 102hp (two at 40hp plus two at 12hp) in the older pattern. Boiler capacity was increased by the same ratio, so four boilers were provided at each new engine house, instead of three each at the earlier installations.

The new engine houses followed a similar Italianate styling to their predecessors. The boiler rooms were again long and low, but wider than before with four arched openings in the end instead of three, one opposite each boiler to permit installation and replacement. As previously, the chimneys were designed as campaniles, but each one to a different design. Brunel had visited Italy in the 1840s in connection with his consultancies to the Genoa-Allesandria-Turin Railway and the Maria Antonia Railway. The latter ran from Florence and would have permitted opportunities for sketching campaniles. The engine rooms were of course much lower than their earlier counterparts, due to the revised machinery layout, and were not much taller than the boiler rooms. They again featured a large semi-circular arch to permit machinery installation and maintenance.

Torquay Engine House

Torquay Engine House was built to serve atmospheric trains for the original 1848 terminus station of Torquay. The engine house was about a mile north of the station at the top of a 1 in 75 gradient, on the up side of the line; the respective mileages from Paddington being Engine House 218m 16ch, and Torquay 219m 12ch. When the branch was extended towards Kingswear, a new 1859 station named Torquay was opened closer to the town, and the original station was renamed Torre.

Work commenced on building the Engine House in the summer of 1847, and it must have been complete by the following summer. However, on the 29th August 1848 the S.D.R. Board decided to discontinue atmospheric working, so the machinery was never installed and when the Torquay branch opened on 18th December 1848 it was worked by steam locomotives from the start.

Torquay Engine House survives as the most complete example of Brunel's remaining engine houses and is the only one which retains its full height chimney. Constructed with walls in local grey limestone in random sizes, the quoins are built in larger stones laid to regular course sizes. The engine room has three tall windows in the gable wall furthest from the railway, the central one having an arched head. There are two more in the side wall, but these have been bricked up. This part of the building would have housed the flywheels, which would have risen nearly 14 feet above floor level. The rear part of the engine room, where the steam cylinders and air pumps would have been installed has two storeys within the same roof height, with three windows on the first floor, over two windows and a doorway at ground level. The rear gable wall nearest the railway was not provided with the normal arched machinery doorway, being adapted instead for domestic use.

The boiler house is of similar construction, although not so tall. The gable wall furthest from the railway has one arched window either side of the central chimney, whilst the gable end facing the railway has four arched openings which would have allowed the boilers to be installed. Pan tile roofs were provided for both buildings. The chimney is built over a tapered base and features a semi-circular arched niche to each side. The dummy bell housing is defined separately and has a two-stage decorative corbel table each side, supporting the roof to the chimney head.

How the superfluous engine house was used between 1848 and 1882 is not certain, but in 1883 the Longpark Pottery Terra Cotta China Works commenced manufacture in the building. The owners Messrs Critchlow, Ridley & Taylor produced mainly terra cotta items and very quickly dropped the incorrect use of the word 'China' from their impressed mark. After 1903 a group of Aller Vale potters took over, producing decorative glazed pottery similar to that of Aller Vale, with the business later being recorded as the Longpark Pottery Co Ltd. The works finally closed down in 1957. The building was occupied by a fruit and vegetable warehouse for many years. Currently a florists is based in the engine room. The Longpark sign was still in place in the boiler room and a parcels distribution company in the boiler room at the time of the Broad Gauge Society visit in June 2007, but has since been taken down.

The engine house is shown in use by Longpark Art Pottery, the cutting to the area occupied by the wording suggesting that this was the location of the reservoir. The works is approached by a driveway in a cutting leading from Newton Road. The engine room is shown as approximately 80 feet by 40 feet, with the boiler room at 60 feet by 40 feet. The 1889 plan was very similar, but the building was labeled as Longpark China & Terra Cotta Works.

1906 Ordnance Survey Plan

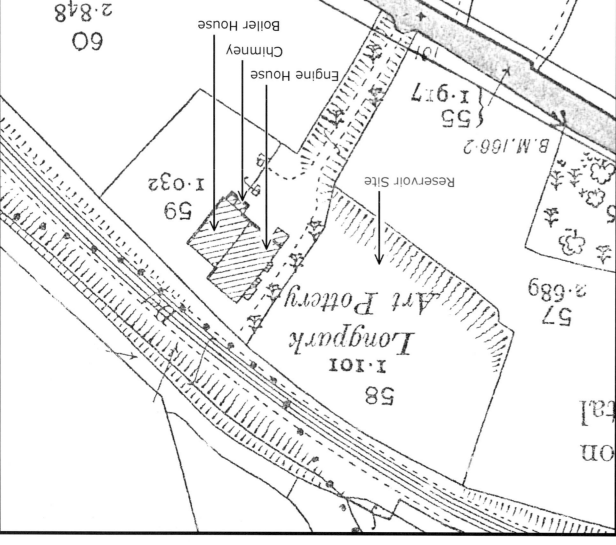

Photo: Keith Poole

Advertising Card and Decorative Plate Produced by Longpark Pottery

The growth of ivy on Longpark chimney is clearer in the advertising card on the left and more obvious in the colour prints.

Amongst the hugely varied products produced by the Longpark Pottery Co was this decorative plate on the right which actually featured their own works.

The boiler house has been extended by a lean-to building alongside and, most interestingly, two bottle kilns have been inserted into the boiler room and engine room. These were later removed, returning the building to its original appearance.

Torquay Engine House circa 1930

A rare view of the side facing the railway. The four arches to the boiler room on the left, one opposite each boiler, confirm the number intended for installation here. The engine room does not have a large arched opening like Totnes, and the usual upper floor of the central part has evidently been continued to the end of the building. The domestic scale windows appear to be original, so the design may have been altered before completion, when the fate of the Atmospheric was known. Chimneys have been added and there is also a basement at this end.

Torquay Engine House 2013

The engine room is located to the left, with three windows in the gable end, plus a shop front added during the Longpark years. The boiler house is to the right, with an arched window each side of the Italianate chimney.

The Engine Room 1927-1936

The Austin 16 tourer standing outside the engine room looks brand new and therefore dates the picture to 1927-1936. Longpark have added an entrance porch to receive these wealthy visitors and other potential customers coming to their works. The single-storey flywheel area of the engine room appears to be in use as a showroom, whilst a craftsman stands in the doorway of the actual pottery works, located in the intended boiler room.

Torquay Engine House 2013

The changes made since the pre-war photograph are mainly superficial. The porch has been removed, revealing the intact stonework behind. The domestic chimneys have also been taken down. The two goods entrances into the boiler room and the shop front to the engine room are the main alterations from the original layout. The tapered base to the chimney shows clearly, this being the only Atmospheric chimney still completely intact.

Dainton Engine House

Construction of the second phase engine houses with their new improved horizontal layouts commenced at Dainton in May 1847. The Engine House was strategically placed at the summit of both the 1 in 36 gradient from Newton and the 1 in 37 gradient from Totnes. This would have been the first opportunity for the atmospheric system to really demonstrate its advantages over steam locomotives. It is notable that the two atmospheric railways which operated over an extended period, the Dublin & Kingstown and the Paris à St Germain, both featured steep gradients.

The building was constructed on level ground, with a small cutting down to the main line which was beginning to fall towards Totnes here. The available land tapered towards the overbridge at the south-west end of the site, leaving little width for the building which was squeezed into the gap between boundary and railway. As a result, the coal siding was unusually carried on a timber trestle above the bank of the cutting. Similarly, the boiler reservoir curved away from the railway following the site boundary, as opposed to the neat rectangles elsewhere. It is not clear how the water was supplied to this elevated location. Perhaps the engine house pumped water as well as creating vacuum.

Constructed in grey Torbay limestone, the building comprised four parts. The engine room was nearest to the summit and Dainton Tunnel. This featured the usual large semi-circular arch facing the railway. Next came the boiler room, which inexplicably appears to have been built with space for just three boilers like the first phase engine houses. This is demonstrated by the three arches for their installation and maintenance shown in the watercolour on page 71.

It was soon realized that increased boiler power would be required for the new larger engines, and so a fourth boiler was added. This was given its own narrow bay with a single arch, rather than alter the works already under construction. Fourthly came the chimney, still in Italianate style but noticeably simpler than the earlier engine houses, given its isolated location. A pair of 68hp Boulton & Watt horizontal engines had been installed in the engine room by the summer of 1848, and must have been

almost ready for test running by the time of the decision to abandon atmospheric working in August. Sadly, this was never to happen. The engines were sold in August 1849 and the redundant building probably came down in the 1850s, there being no alternative use for it in this remote location. The main line was doubled here in 1855, which involved laying a new down line through the vacant part of Dainton Tunnel. This second track continued close to the Engine House, requiring the cutting to be reduced and provided with low retaining walls. These works would have required the removal of the timber trestle, if it still existed.

The former engine house siding was retained but of necessity slewed across onto solid ground and therefore passed through the engine house site. Demolition must therefore have occurred at some time between 1849 and 1855. The reservoir may have been filled in with spoil from the widening works.

Dainton Engine House in 1848

The proportions of the Engine House illustrated in Dawson's View South of the Line on page 71 do not correspond with the plan on the same page, an extract from which is shown here. The accompanying sketch is an attempt to adjust Dawson's view to correspond with the plan. The engine room to the left has been made more prominent, the three arches in the boiler room re-spaced to suit the boiler layout, and the right-hand bay narrowed to match the plan. It would therefore appear that the two bays housed four boilers between them.

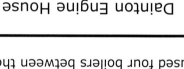

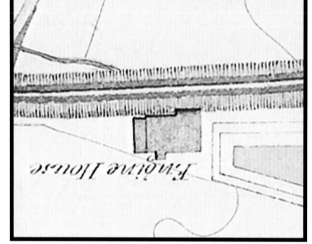

Engine House

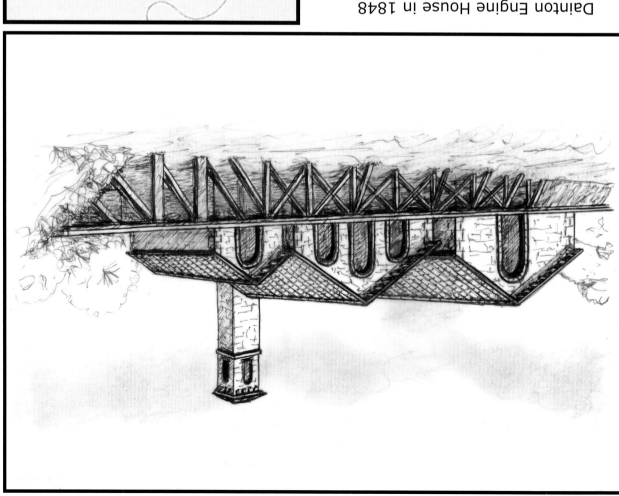

1888 Ordnance Survey Plan

The former location of the Engine House has been dotted on the plan, by reference to Dawson's drawing. A siding runs round the northern side of the former reservoir, below its bank. This may have been used to fill the pond in and progressively slewed across. An area of marsh is indicated adjacent to the southern bank.

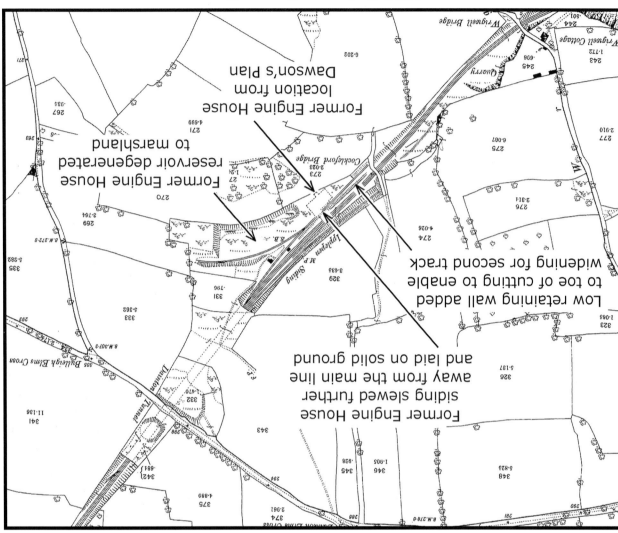

Former Engine House location from Dawson's Plan

Former Engine House reservoir degenerated to marshland

Low retaining wall added to toe of cutting to enable widening for second track

Former Engine House siding slewed further away from the main line and laid on solid ground

Newton Road Showing the Atmospheric Railway 1848

This engraving by G Townsend of Exeter shows Totnes Bridge, St Mary's church and a partial view of Bridgetown. To the right can be seen the timber viaduct carrying the railway over the River Dart, with the goods shed beside the line and the station buildings behind. The Engine House is by the right margin, with its reservoir beyond.

Totnes Image Bank & Rural Archive ref RD/0217

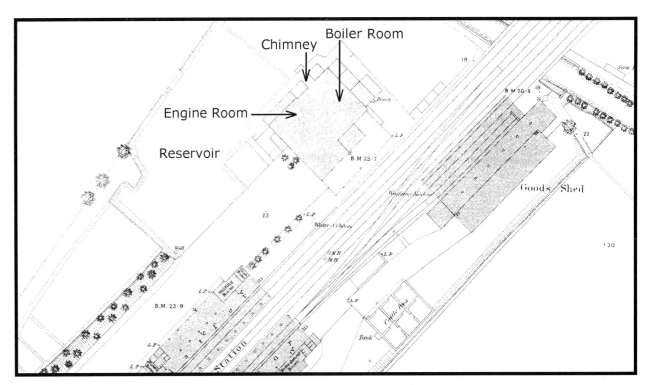

1888 Ordnance Survey Plan

Totnes station had timber train sheds covering the up and down platform lines, whilst two through lines ran through the centre. The goods shed had two internal tracks. The Engine House is set back a little from the railway and would have originally had a coal siding in front. The flat area surrounded by banks indicates the site of the former reservoir.

Totnes Engine House

Dawson's set of watercolours stopped just short of Totnes at the Dart River bridge. The Engine House is only seen in the distance in the page 77 South View. Construction of Totnes Engine House commenced in the summer of 1847. By the summer of 1848 the building was finished and most of the machinery had been installed at the time of the decision to discontinue atmospheric traction. The unwanted equipment was sold to a Mr West in January 1853, for the modest sum of £850 which implies that it only went for scrap.

The building walls were built of local grey limestone in squared random sizes, the quoins and window surrounds being emphasized by larger stones laid to regular course sizes. The elevation facing the railway, which was next to the station and exposed to public view, was adorned with red sandstone features. These included rusticated voussoirs to the large semi-circular arch to the engine room, a string course right across the façade and a high level circular window to the boiler room. Queen-post timber trusses carried the purlins and rafters, which were lined with diagonal timber boarding. Externally, the roof was originally covered in Roman tiles in natural red clay, but these were later progressively replaced by slate, with the engine room itself being the last to retain the originals. A water pump room was built on the side of the boiler room, in stone to match the main buildings. This was an original feature, which is visible in the Dawson watercolour. Over the years several other additions were made, all in relatively lightweight materials. The usage of the building in its early years is not known.

Symons Cyder Mills were established by the River Dart by 1884, and by the early part of the twentieth century they were making use of the former Engine House as a distribution warehouse. In 1934 the site was acquired by Daws Creameries, which opened in the following year after the erection of new buildings and a tall circular brick chimney. For a time the new chimney and Brunel's original one stood together, before the historic structure was demolished, The Italianate chimney had been 95 feet high and it is said that the redundant stones were used to build a compressor room for the main factory. In 1937 the site was acquired by Cow & Gate. At that time milk was collected every day from 350 local farms, taking in and processing 7,000 gallons of milk per day. Cow & Gate merged with United Dairies in 1959 to form Unigate.

Totnes Station on 11th May 1892

Just ten days before the Gauge Conversion, much preparatory work has been undertaken. An up broad gauge goods has been diverted through the platform line to avoid an engineering train on the up main. The Engine House was partly covered in ivy at this stage.

1466 at Totnes 1894-1914

517 class 0-4-2T no 1466, dating from 1883 and in immaculate condition, is seen at Totnes between 1892 and 1914, with the Engine House behind. The train is standing on baulk road converted from Broad Gauge. Third class coach no 2741 was built to Diagram S9 in 1894. The large arch in the gable wall of the engine room has been bricked up, but the roof retains its Roman tiles.

By 1966, at the site's peak as a processor of dairy products, it was taking in milk from 1,300 farms, over 65,000 gallons per day. In May 2007, Dairy Crest, who had taken over the site from Unigate in 2000, announced that they were closing their operations in Totnes, with the loss of 162 jobs, which came as a major blow to the economy of the town.

With an eye to selling the site to developers, Dairy Crest began moves to demolish the Brunel Building, but following a fierce community campaign, English Heritage's original decision not to list the building was reversed. The building finally received its Grade II Listed status in March 2008. Slate roofing was reinstated during 2012.

The Atmos Totnes project continues to campaign for community use of the listed buildings when the site is redeveloped and has commissioned ambitious architectural proposals for the site.

The Engine House 1918-1933

Noticably grubbier than in the previous image, the Engine House is still in use by Symons' Cyder. A tripod for lifting barrels stands in front of the engine room and a lean-to addition covers two of the arches of the boiler room.

Totnes Image Bank & Rural Archive ref RD/1119

The Engine House 1918-1933

Taken at the same time as image RD/1119, the engine room still boasts its original Roman tiles, but the boiler room and pump room have been re-laid in slate. It can be seen that the boiler room arches have also been bricked up.

B.G.S. Archive

The Engine House 1935

The Daws Creameries buildings and their associated tall brick chimney are nearing completion, with builders' materials still on site. The atmospheric railway chimney is still standing as well. The allotments to the left occupy the site of the former reservoir.

Totnes Image Bank & Rural Archive ref CM/001

The Engine House 1935-1939

Two G.W.R. 4/5 ton Associated Daimler lorries, fitted with Swindon-built flatbed bodies, stand outside the engine room, one loaded with milk churns and the other with boxes. Two smaller 2 ton Fordson lorries are loading beyond. The engine room has lost its original roofing.

Totnes Image Bank & Rural Archive

Inside The Engine Room 1986

The milk powder room being renovated in 1986, looking north away from the railway. This was located in the former engine room, with the arched windows to the exterior on the left and the wall to the boiler room on the right.

Totnes Image Bank & Rural Archive ref UG/243

The Engine House 1997

The engine house was in good condition and apparently well maintained at this time. Good use has been made of the engine room archway, formerly bricked up, to install a large window to provide daylight to the powder room.

P.R.G.

Rattery Engine House

The historical record of Rattery's short-lived and never-used Engine House begins with a reference in Peter Margary's diary for 26th May 1847 (Margary, later S.D.R. engineer, was at this date a junior engineer under Brunel):- "Met Mr. Brunel at the Dawlish office at 7. Went with him by the first train to Newton and from thence to Ivy Bridge. He settled the position of the Engine Houses at Totnes, Rattery, Wranggerton and Ivy Bridge....." And then on 2nd June 1847:- "Went with Samuda and Hensman to Ivy Bridge. Settled the position of the Engine Houses at Rattery and Ivy Bridge".

Joseph Samuda, the atmospheric patentee and supplier of much of the materials, clearly had to be placated in these matter, as well as Brunel in these matters! Margary's diary continues to the end of December 1847 and contains no reference to work at Rattery. It seems that work began in January 1848, as the local paper Woolmer's Gazette noted on 15th January that "Rattery Engine House foundations are just commenced". Subsequent references are found in the Western Times on 22nd April "There is an Engine House in erection four miles below Totnes", and Woolmer's again on 13th May, noting that Rattery Engine House "is in a forward state" but "it is very doubtful it will ever be used for its intended purpose".

Right up to the decision to abolish Atmospheric traction altogether in late August 1848, it had been the policy that, whatever might be done generally as to the Atmospheric, it would still be used on the inclines west of Newton as "assistant power". Thus it is most likely that work at Rattery continued until the end and, judging by the time it took to build the previous Engine Houses, it must have been pretty complete by then, structurally. Nothing was ever done at all on the proposed S.D.R. Engine Houses west of Rattery, so Rattery was in fact the last Atmospheric railway Engine House ever built anywhere.

The engines for Rattery were made by Harvey's of Hayle and parts of them were deliverd to Totnes (presumably by sea) where they remained until 1853. The S.D.R. Board being advised on 15th January 1853 that Margary had arranged for their sale to a Mr. West, who bought most of the S.D.R. engines at this date. The remaining parts were still at Hayle, and in March it was reported that they had been resold to the makers. There is no evidence of any equipment at all having actually been installed at Rattery. The land on the opposite side of the road, including the reservoir, was soon sold off, but the Engine House site remained in S.D.R. ownership.

From study of the 1888 and 1904 editions of the Ordnance Survey 25" plans, it was evident that the cramped site would not have contained the standard Engine House layouts used at Torquay and Totnes. Also, with a different machinery manufacturer, some differences might have been expected in any case. A site visit in 2012, a chance meeting with the owner of two of the cottages which occupy this site, and an invitation to look around provided some of the answers.

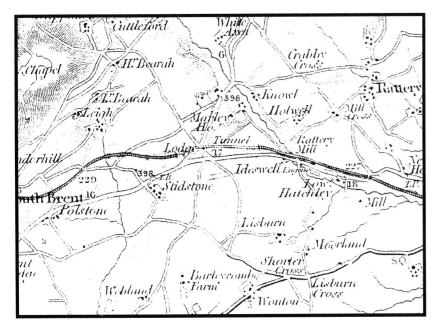

Ordnance Survey 1" Map 1865

To the east of Marley Tunnel and below the annotation for Rattery Mill, the reservoir is clearly shown as a small rectangle south of the road and the Engine House as a black building between the road and the railway, with the name 'Engine' appearing.

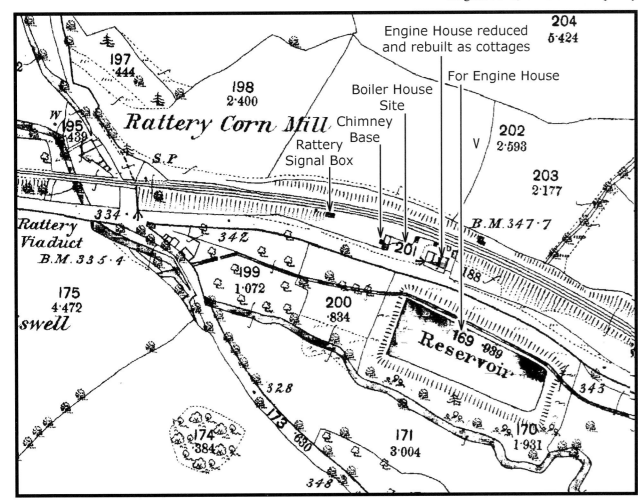

Ordnance Survey 25" Plan 1888

The L-shaped site shows up clearly, with some detail features visible, together with the Engine House reservoir on the opposite side of the road. Rattery Signal Box was located on a short stretch of level track at the top of the 1 in 65 incline from Totnes, although the climb did resume more gently at 1 in 200 as far as Marley Tunnel.

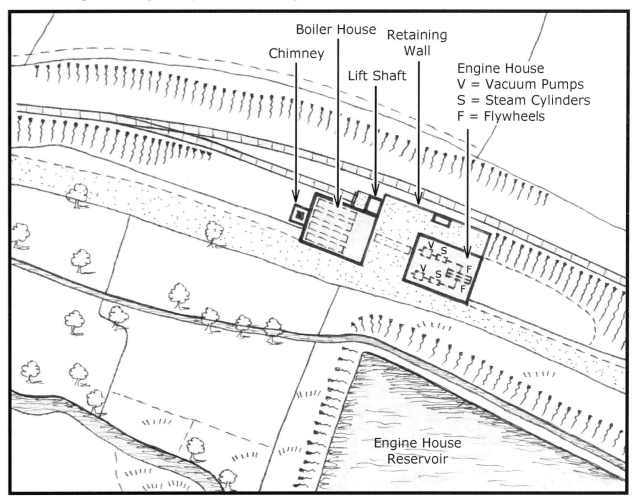

Estimated Layout of the Site in 1848

It appears that the boiler room occupied the narrower part of the site, with the chimney to the west end and a lift shaft to the north. The full extent of the Engine House is shown, before its later reduction. The intended positions for the equipment are indicated, together with space for boiler withdrawal between the two buildings, the yard being some 25 feet below the railway line.

Rattery Signal Box c1904

A 'Duke' class 4-4-0, believed to be no. 3321 Mercury, is returning light-engine to Totnes, having assisted a train up Rattery Bank. The down line still retains bauk road, converted from the Broad Gauge. The rendering of the gable wall to the cottages conceals the secret of its alteration. It previously continued past the front gardens (with resident standing by the gate) out to the edge of the lane, when it was still a full Engine House. In front of the cottages the cut-down stump of the boiler room chimney is visible, with a mono-pitch roof following the slope of the embankment.

P. J. Garland Collection, Kidderminster Railway Museum

To begin with the easy part, the reservoir is still in existence on the opposite side of the road and has found a very suitable new use as part of the Hatchlands Trout Farm. The lane shown on the 1888 plan was much narrower than the current road, with the verge shown about 40 feet from the retaining wall to the narrower part of the site, which is about 60 feet long, 60 feet by 40 feet equates to the boiler rooms at Torquay and Totnes, so identifying this part of the site. Adjacent to the north-east corner of the boiler room, the owner opened the arched door into what appeared to be a lift shaft, boarded over with railway sleepers high above. It appears that the coal siding was located immediately north of the boiler room, either carried on a trestle at railway level, or cut into the embankment at intermediate level. An end dock adjacent to the lift would have enabled tubs of coal to be taken down to ground level.

The west wall of the cottages is fairly nondescript and covered in render, so turning the corner and seeing the rear wall of the building for the first time, tucked away from public view in the narrow chasm facing the high retaining wall, came as something of a shock. There it was; in similar style to Torquay and Totnes, the rear wall of the Engine House was unbelievably still there! The wall has three bays of windows over two floors, so corresponds with the two-storey portion at Torquay. From west to east, the three cottages must occupy the space allowed for vacuum pumps, steam cylinders and connecting rods respectively. The fourth bay, which would have been single-storey double-height to cater for the large flywheels, has been demolished, to provide access to the rear of the end cottage. This wall is in line with the rear wall of the boiler house, and so would again have permitted a 40 feet wide building originally. The cottages are little more than half of that, so the rendering of the west wall must conceal how it was cut back.

ABOVE: The big discovery of the visit – The surviving north-west corner of the engine room, with the unmistakable features of random squared limestone walling, large limestone quoins and Italianate window surrounds in Bath stone.

LEFT: The arched doorway gives access to the lift shaft, now roofed over with railway sleepers. The wall is continuous with the retaining wall to the right and former east wall of the boiler room wall to the left, now cut back to just a buttress.

ABOVE: In the yard between the retaining wall and the rear wall of the Engine House. Three-quarters of the rear wall survives – all the two-storey part over the cylinder and pump positions, which was suitable for conversion to cottages.

ABOVE: The site of the boiler room. Stone buttresses have been added to shore up the surviving north side wall, which acts as a retaining wall to the embankment.

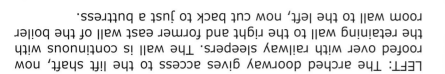

Site Investigation 2012

The new south-west corner would have come part-way through the end arch, so a good deal of masonry alteration would have been required. From this wall to the eastern retaining wall is about 60 feet, suggesting an original engine room size of 60 feet by 40 feet. Torquay and Totnes were 80 feet by 40 feet, but the design drawing on page 73 was only 63' 6" feet long, so the size is not unreasonable. Harvey's machinery layout may have varied from Boulton & Watt's in any case. The owner of the central and eastern cottages stated that the Deeds of the properties dated from about 1850, which equates very well with conversion soon after the Abandonment. The layout of Rattery Engine House would have been unique, due to the engine room and boiler room being separate freestanding buildings, with a 45 feet gap between them, sufficient space to manoeuvre 35 feet long boilers in and out. All the Engine Houses featured deep tunnels for vacuum, water and steam distribution, so the separation would not have been a problem. The owner opened up a manhole cover in the rear yard and we were able to look down into one of these deep spaces.

LEFT: Inside the boiler room, with traces of whitewash still visible on the stonework and showing the buttresses which replace the support once provided by the building. The bushes above the wall mark the line of the former coal siding.

ABOVE: In the rear yard, with the high retaining walls to the railway on the right and embankment in front. The arched doorway and square hole indicate the position of the lift shaft. The manhole cover to the deep chamber is between the two plant pots.

LEFT: The Engine House reservoir still survives, at lower level on the opposite side of the road. It now forms one of the Hatchlands Trout Lakes, set in 16 acres of picturesque valley, with one fly and two coarse lakes fed the River Harbourne.

ABOVE: Inside the lift shaft, looking up at the deck which has been installed to close it off, made out of old railway sleeepers.

South Devon Railway Piston Carriages

I was slightly surprised to discover that it was as long ago as April 24th 1993 that the Broad Gauge Society held its Annual General Meeting at the City of Bristol Museum, courtesy of the then curator, Paul Elkin. After the meeting we had the opportunity to browse through the Woodfin Collection (now moved to 'Steam' at Swindon), which contains substantial rolling stock records, including register copies, tracings and photos of drawings. Much of the collection is indexed, but a lot of it is not. It would certainly make an interesting retirement project for somebody, and is perhaps the last location where any significant quantity of unknown broad gauge rolling stock may be discovered. Browsing through the collection of photographic negatives, some 20,000 in total, we stumbled across a real bombshell.

Research

Negatives 14471, 14894-14896 and 16141-16150 actually recorded drawings of one of the elusive South Devon Railway piston carriages.

The following year's A.G.M. was also held in Bristol on Brunel's birthday April 9th 1994, and I spent the morning looking at the piston carriage negatives in more detail. It turned out that some of the photographs were of an original drawing dated November 23rd 1846, whilst others were of a tracing made of this by Woodfin in April 1956. I obtained prints, courtesy of Andy King, and made a start on the painstaking task of composing accurate C.A.D. drawings of the vehicle. The prints of the original drawing were rather faint, and whilst Woodfin's were sharper, his tracings did not reproduce all the details appearing on the original. Progress was therefore very slow. During the following years, whilst we were trying to get the atmospheric facsimile project off the ground, I was in regular correspondence with Peter Ramsden. He provided the text on farming, livestock, geology, building materials and horse drawn vehicles which did so much to bring the book to life. It turned out that Peter had known Dick Woodfin, who had been very helpful to him when he was starting out in the hobby. Not only that, but Woodfin had actually bequeathed the piston carriage tracing to Peter, who kindly lent it to me for copying. Mike Jolly and Eddy Brown (who are sadly no longer with us) spent a long time with Peter and myself trying to make sense of it all.

Close-up of Newton Piston Carriage Shed depicted in Dawson Watercolour Plate 18.

Situated conveniently opposite the Engine House, the timber-clad Piston Carriage Shed has five openings in its side wall. Two appear to be doors and the others windows. The Piston Carriage standing inside has at least two oil lamps. The glazed panels to the conductor's platform are apparent, together with the piston head. A starting tube commences in the foreground.

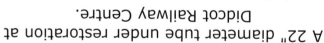

A 22" diameter tube under restoration at Didcot Railway Centre.

The ironwork has been treated, primed and undercoated. Picture taken from the Plymouth end showing the socket and the seaward side featuring the fixing points for the continuous valve.

Close-up of the Piston Carriage depicted in Dawson Watercolour Plate 15

At first glance quite different from the "Woodfin" piston carriage, the vehicle in Dawson plate 15 could really be quite similar. The main difference is that the timber body framing is only lined on the inside instead of double skinned. The open sided conductor's position is there, misdrawn with the opening over the buffer beam, the running board with step up to the door with glazed droplight and side lights, and an oil lamp shared between the second and third class compartments.

There were a surprising number of patent applications concerning atmospheric railways, and Roger Langley helpfully sent in copies of several of these which were very useful, often as much for the details which they took for granted as the actual items covered by the particular application. The final area of research thankfully enabled us to (literally) obtain some cast iron information. Graham Drew arranged for Mike Jolly and myself to spend half a day in an inspection pit at Didcot, measuring up their three lengths of atmospheric tube. Nowadays the tubes are on display out in the open with easy access, but where is the challenge in that? They are 22 inch diameter, as installed west of Newton but never used, rather than the 15 inch used between Exeter and Newton, but very informative nonetheless.

The accompanying drawings are the result of the assemblage of all this data, and are as accurate as I can make them. However, there are bound to be errors because we just do not have full information on the prototype. In addition, whilst we may appreciate the basic principles of the atmospheric railway, when it comes down to everyday operational details we are dealing with a technology which nobody alive today fully comprehends.

General Arrangement

The first problem is that the original drawing comprises a series of partial or split views, typical of the period, whereas I wanted to prepare full views. This opens up several pitfalls straight away! For example, the long view is half side elevation and half longitudinal section, it being normal for the half section to record the inside elevation of the same half illustrated from outside. It is therefore necessary to decide to what extent symmetry is involved in the design of the vehicle. For simple waggons and many coaches there is not too much difficulty. For something like a horse box disaster can ensue; there was a classic case of an exquisite model of a Gregory B.&E.R. horse box accidentally being constructed with a groom's compartment at both ends! For the record, the original drawing includes the following.

1. Half side view / half longitudinal section.

2. One complete end elevation.

3. Half cross section through centre / half cross section through box.

4. Half frame plan from above / half frame plan from below.

5. Half body plan from end to centre.

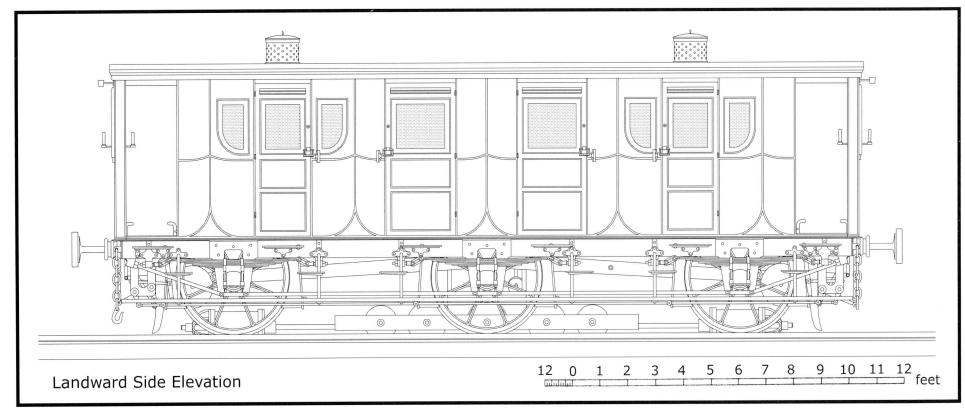

Landward Side Elevation

12 0 1 2 3 4 5 6 7 8 9 10 11 12 feet

The brakes were fitted to this side of the carriage. Single sided brakes were normal at the time and the only unusual feature is the fitting of brake handles at both ends, slotted so that the train could be stopped from either cabin. Before starting from Newton or Exeter it would be necessary to check that the leading brake handle was applied and then the rear one released before finally releasing the leading brake handle, otherwise various interesting scenarios present themselves!

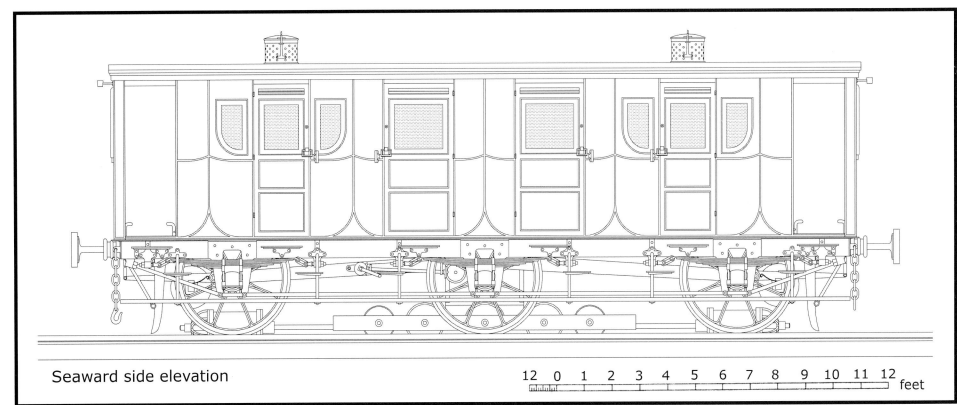

Seaward side elevation

12 0 1 2 3 4 5 6 7 8 9 10 11 12 feet

On this side a winding handle could be fitted, as shown, between the first and second wheels to swing the piston frame assembly up towards us when it was necessary to move the carriage over non-atmospheric lines. The handle could perhaps have been kept in the seat box in one of the cabins when not in use. No doubt a variety of other tools were in daily use in connection with manhandling the vehicle.

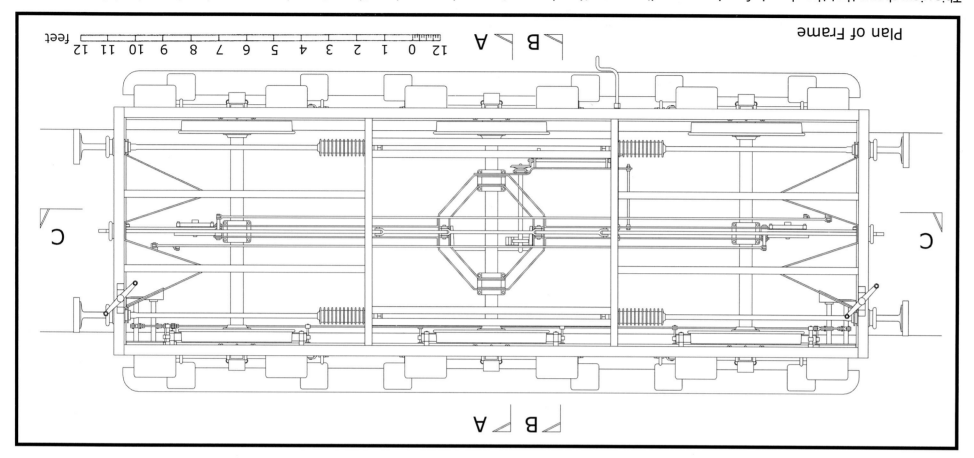

Plan of Frame

12 0 1 2 3 4 5 6 7 8 9 10 11 12 feet

This view shows that the chassis framing was quite conventional, except for the middle bay, where there were two pairs of longitudinals in line with the buffers, leaving a wide space for the atmospheric frame. This has four bearings, two on the central axle mounted on the octagons, and one each on the outer axles, mounted at the ends of the suspension frames. The connections between the coupling draw rods and the octagons can also be seen.

The carriage ends each had two glazed droplights plus one open bay to clear the brake handle. The Plymouth end was arranged for right hand drive, and the Exeter end for left hand drive. The body was only 8 ft. 4 in. wide, the footboards projecting well to either side with two small steps up to the doorway. The protective streamlined bars to the piston faces can be seen and above these, the narrow wheel which kept the continuous valve seated on its mounting.

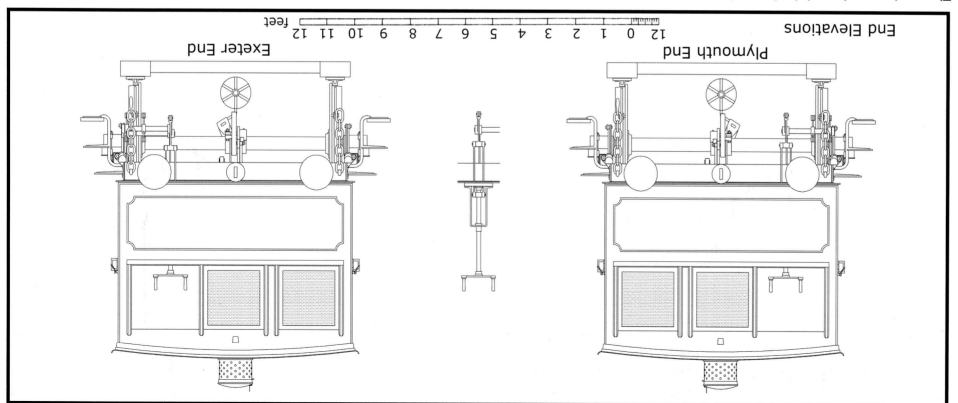

End Elevations

Exeter End   Plymouth End

12 0 1 2 3 4 5 6 7 8 9 10 11 12 feet

The basic decisions made on symmetry and general arrangement were as follows. Firstly the atmospheric tube would always have the valve flap facing the same way, common sense suggesting that it would have its back to the sea. Plates 18 and 25 of the Dawson watercolours shows unfixed lengths of tube standing at Newton and Totnes, with their sockets facing in the down direction. From our investigations at Didcot, this would confirm that the valve was indeed fixed on the seaward side. The fixing bolts are visible in several of the Dawson prints, but he merrily sprinkles them everywhere, rather than just facing in one direction.

Secondly, the hanging plate connecting the piston frame assembly to the carriage was bent over at an angle to match the valve. Therefore it always had to face the same way, and could not be turned round at the end of each journey. As a consequence, the vehicle itself could not be turned either, so it must have had a conductor's cabin at both ends. The interior plan was therefore almost certainly symmetrical - conductor / second / double length open third / second / conductor.

Thirdly, the piston frame was designed to hinge up out of the way towards the seaward side, so that the carriage could be towed over non-atmospheric lines when required. As a consequence the brake gear had to be mounted on the opposite landward side. The two ends of the vehicle were therefore handed, with right hand drive at one end and left hand at the other. I use the word "drive" euphemistically, as apart from winding the brake handle and hanging on (maybe blowing a coaching horn) there was little that the conductor could do to regulate progress. The South Devon atmospheric was not the straightest piece of railway in the world, and points of the compass are consequently not very useful. I have instead used "landward side", "seaward side", "Exeter end" and "Plymouth end" to describe the four basic directions for the different views.

Fourthly, a piston head would be needed for each direction of travel, the weight being balanced at the opposite end. It seems unlikely that the heavy fittings would be unbolted and barrowed round to the opposite end several times a day at Exeter and Newton. I have therefore shown piston heads at both ends. The cup leathers may not have taken kindly to being reversed repeatedly, and it is possible that the ring segments carrying these could have been removed from the trailing piston head - a much lighter task than dealing with the whole thing. There may also have been a valve to allow air to pass through the trailing head, although if it were even as much as say 10% of the area of the piston, the air would rush through it at around the speed of sound when the carriage was at speed. It seems more likely that the entry valve at the beginning of each length of tube would be left open until the train had cleared the section.

The chassis of the various piston carriages would probably have all been the same, due to the design being so specialised, but there is no reason why there should not have been some variation in body styles. Certainly a vehicle more suited to freight work would have been useful. The fact that the close-up of half a piston carriage in Dawson plate 15 is of a different style is not necessarily a problem. The basic layout appears similar, with a conductor's cabin followed by a second class compartment with fixed glazing either side of a glazed droplight.

Eddy Brown and myself both attempted a perspective view of one of the carriages, and both are reproduced here. There are minor differences between the two, but we agree on most points. The remainder of the chapter will deal with the construction of the vehicle in more detail, introduce the remaining drawings, and attempt to identify the number and history of these piston carriages.

The Chassis

The chassis appears to have been surprisingly conventional for such an extraordinary vehicle. The wheelbase was 9' 2" + 9' 2" = 18' 4", and wheels 4' 0" in diameter, all typical of other iron-framed vehicles of the era.

Railway Machinery, Volume Two, by Daniel Kinnear Clark, 1855 illustrates some very similar chassis. Plates XXXIV and XXXV cover a G.W.R. Third Class Carriage, and Plate XXXVI a G.W.R. Luggage Van. These drawings include a schedule of the various iron sections used, which can be readily identified from the Woodfin drawings. B.R. / O.P.C. drawing 2698 also illustrates a very similar iron frame for a G.W.R. Second Class Carriage. The solebars and headstocks were of 8" deep iron, ½" thick, set at 26' 6 ¼" x 7' 11 ¼" over the faces. The upper flanges projected 3 7/8" outside this, whilst the bulbous lower flanges were only 1 3/8" overall. Nevertheless, they came perilously close to the wheels (7' 7 ½" over wheels / 7' 8 ½" between solebar flanges according to my calculations), and may well have been ground away locally, although the drawings do not show it. Transverse members of 6" x 3" T sections divided the chassis into three bays, the outer bays also being divided into three by similar longitudinals, which were strapped to the headstocks by flat plate. In a normal vehicle these longitudinals continued through the middle bay, but an alteration was necessary to suit these piston carriages. Two pairs of L sections were used instead, spaced at 5' 10" centres to align with the buffing gear. This left a wide space in the middle for the atmospheric apparatus.

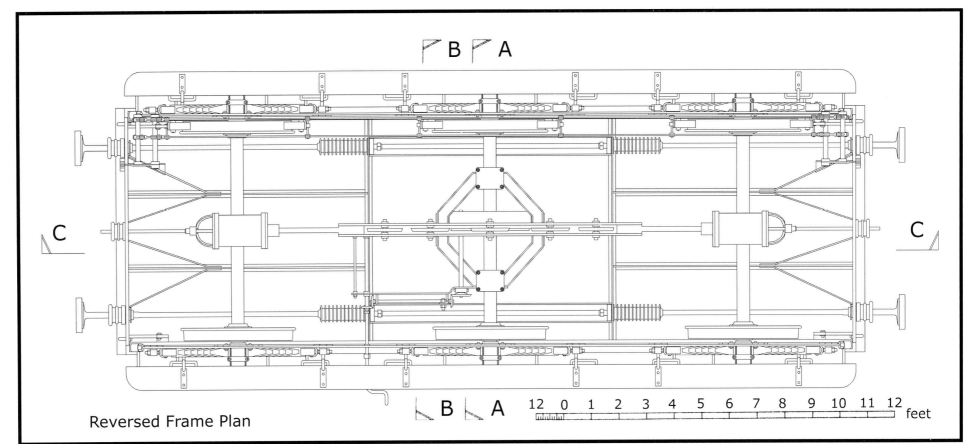

Reversed Frame Plan

A reflected view from below shows the piston frame, with its five roller wheels, and a piston under each outer axle. The removable winding handle is shown in place, between the first and second wheels, and the geared linkage that swung the piston frame assembly up to the seaward side, when it was necessary to move the carriage over non-atmospheric lines. The brake gear can be seen on the landward side, and the undersides of the axleboxes and springs.

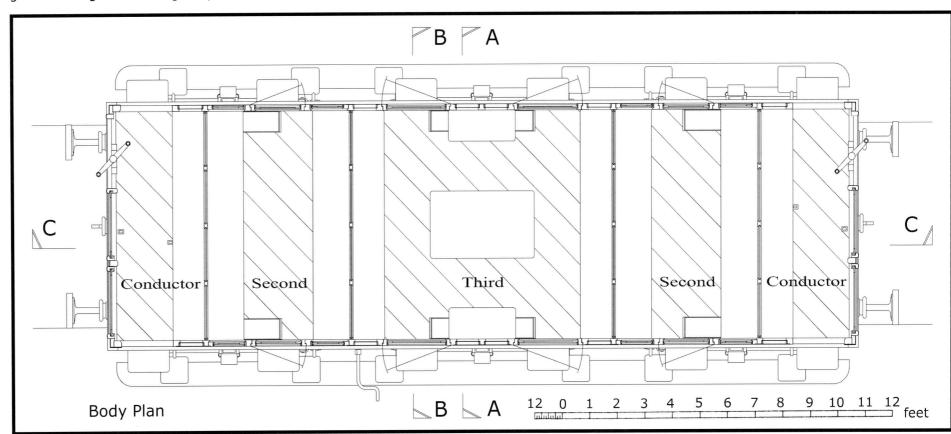

Body Plan

Conductor   Second   Third   Second   Conductor

This view gives a good impression of the pairs of iron footsteps, leading up to each entrance from the continuous wooden footboards below. The two droplights can be seen at each end, with the open bays to clear the swings of the brake handles. Wooden partitions separate the compartments, and wheel splashers interrupt the diagonal floor boarding in every doorway. The accommodation was certainly Spartan, to say the least.

Atmospheric Down Goods at Dawlish

This delightful drawing by Eddy Brown captures a down goods re-starting from Dawlish. The auxiliary tube has been used to start the train and the rope has been released, possibly endangering the watching gangers, although they seem quite relaxed about it.

The piston is about to enter the main tube above the section leading to Teignmouth. The wheel above it might perhaps have been raised to avoid the impact before being lowered onto the continuous valve.

The axleguards and axleboxes appeared to be the same pattern as those on the D. K. Clark drawings, with flat iron tie bars between the axleguards, and diagonally up to the solebars. The springs were labelled as 4' 10" long on the Woodfin drawing, which ties in well with the waggon register entries. The D. K. Clark ones were very similar, labelled as 5' 0" long. The wheels on the Woodfin drawing clearly match those of D. K. Clark, being typical 4' 0" diameter fabricated split-spoke wheels of the period. The buffers were completely normal, at the usual 5' 10" centres, 3' 0" above rail level, with push rods leading to four stacks of India rubber rings mounted on the chassis transverse members. No safety chains were shown on the Woodfin drawing, so I have copied these fittings from the D. K. Clark drawings, placed outside the buffers.

Footboards were omitted from the Woodfin drawing for clarity, so I have again followed Clark, with a continuous timber footboard hung from six iron bars, and a pair of iron steps leading up to each door and conductor's entrance.

The Atmospheric Apparatus

The atmospheric apparatus was hung from a substantial frame composed of pairs of iron plates, tapering from 5" deep at the extremities to 6" deep at the centre. An irregular pair of central octagons had two bearings on the middle axle, whilst the connecting longitudinal pairs had single bearings located centrally on the outer axles. The whole arrangement was un-sprung, but there must have been allowance for movement in it somewhere, to take account of irregularities in the track.

Perhaps the two octagons could move separately, with the longitudinal plates from one outer axle connecting to the inner one, and from the other outer axle to the outer octagon? This would result in two separate three-point suspensions.

Coupling hooks were provided as usual, but no couplings, as these would have interfered with the atmospheric apparatus when not in use. Instead of being sprung immediately behind the headstock as in normal practice, the drawgear rods were extended the full length of the carriage, and actually drew on the front and rear of the central octagons, which transmitted the load from piston to train extremely efficiently.

From the front and rear of the octagons, on the centre line of the carriage, two hangers suspended the carefully shaped plate, which actually passed through the slot in the tube. These hangers would probably have included relatively easily broken links to enable the carriage to break free from the piston assembly, in the event of it colliding with an obstruction. The suspension arms and hanging plate were pivoted at the mountings in the octagon. This enabled the whole assembly to pivot up towards the seaward side of the carriage, when it was necessary to tow the vehicle over non-atmospheric lines. A removable winding handle between the first and second wheels on the seaward side acted through two sets of spur gears, to turn a threaded rod, which engaged with the hanging arms. Section B-B shows the final stage of this gearing, with the piston in its raised position. The total movement was about 45°.

The hanging plate was cut away to clear the middle roller, dropping vertically in front of and behind it to pass between the twin 6" deep 11' long piston frames. Between these were mounted the five roller wheels which opened the continuous valve. Three were 16" in diameter, whilst the outer ones were of 14" diameter, to allow for the gentle curve in the line of the raised valve. The roller treads were also tapered to varying degrees, to allow for the angle of the open valve. The Woodfin drawing shows piston rods continuing beyond the outer wheels, but does not show the actual piston heads. No doubt these were covered by a separate specialist drawing, which does not seem to have survived.

The pistons which I have shown are slightly diagrammatic, and based on the Samuda and Clegg patent drawing, which was not highly detailed. The main features were a central armature, end plates, outer drum, streamlined guidance bars to assist on entering the tube, and a large retaining nut. There were also two or more cup leathers, which acted as piston rings.

These might well have had some method of moving the cup leathers of the trailing piston away from the tube, to avoid damage when travelling against their natural direction. They might have been on removable iron segments, or have screwed inwards like the jaws of a lathe chuck. They might even have been automatic, hinged and normally sprung shut, but made to open by action of the vacuum. It would be necessary to prevent the trailing piston banging against the tube, so there was probably some centring arrangement, three little rollers for example.

At each end of the central suspension structure a hinged arm was fitted with an 18" diameter wheel, sprung to keep the wheel in contact with the top of the valve. This stopped the valve creeping up in front of the train, maintaining the vacuum, and also ensured that the valve was closed correctly behind the carriage for future use. Little was shown of the linkage on the Woodfin drawing. It is possible that the two arms were linked, but I have assumed that they operated separately. I have shown a lever at the front of each cab, for raising the nearest wheel, and one at the back of each cab, for dealing with the trailing wheel, via linkage under the floor. I have just suggested simple notched lifting levers on my drawings, but there could just as easily have been winding handles like miniature brake standards.

There was also some further lightweight rodding under the chassis, which was poorly drawn on the Woodfin plans, being inconsistent in position between one view and another. We could not make any sense of it, and I have left it off. It looked as if it might be related to a trip lever on the landward side, possibly for raising and lowering the flap closure wheels automatically in set positions. Alternatively it might have been associated with opening valves in the piston heads. Such valves would help to control progress of trains, and the London & Croydon Railway was known to have them. It is thought that the S.D.R. dispensed with such luxury however.

The Bodywork

The body was timber framed, with partitions dividing the layout into conductor / second / double open third / second / conductor. The sides were faced both inside and out, with the outer faces being beaded in the traditional individual stagecoach body style. There was no separate waist panel, and tumble home was non-existent. Perhaps because of this, the door framing was fully visible, and not partly sheeted over as was often the case. The body was only 8' 4" wide, by 26' 10 ¾" long.

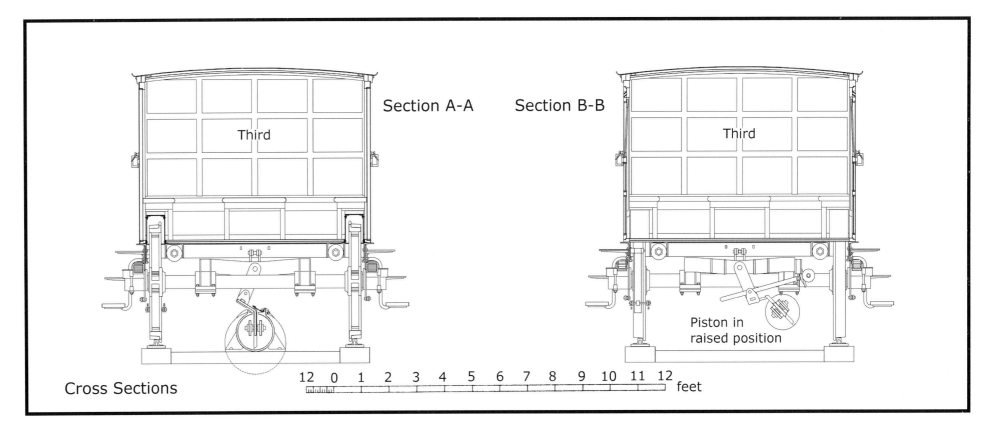

Cross Sections

Section A-A shows the bearings to the central axle, and the specially shaped hanging plate passing through the raised valve, to carry the piston frame running within the 15" diameter tube. The latter has large stiffening rings but, unlike the surviving 22" diameter tubes at Didcot, only requires the transoms to be set about 2" lower than usual, rather than scalloped. Section B-B shows the brakes to the central landward side wheel, and the piston wound up into its travelling position, for towing over non-atmospheric lines.

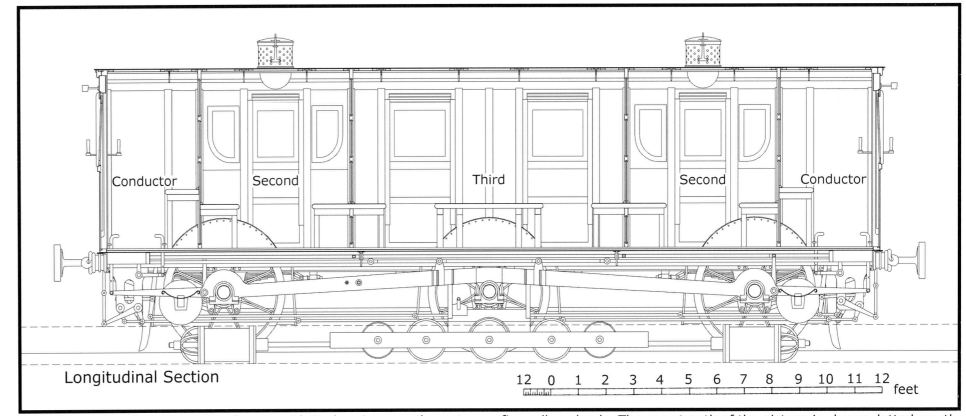

Longitudinal Section

This view shows the suspension frame, with its bearings on the outer axles, sweeping up to the central octagons, with their un-sprung bearings to the middle axle. The hinged arms to the sprung valve closer wheels are apparent, as is the split hanging plate to the piston frame, with its five roller wheels. The swept path of the pistons is shown dotted, partly below rail level. The trip hazards posed by the splashers are all too obvious. The lawsuits would fly thick and fast if anyone tried to operate a modern replica!

Perspective view. On the Sea Wall, East of Teignmouth.

I wanted a compact view featuring the cliffs, railway, sea wall and sea, which so define the line. Rather surprisingly, this curve between Sprey Point and Teignmouth is about the only point where it is possible.

The setting out was based on a 1959 photograph by David Marriott (Rails along the Sea Wall, page 39) with the clock wound back 111 years. Each length of tube had a carrying foot at the Plymouth end, just short of the socket, and three large stiffening rings.

The two second-class compartments were each 5′ 3″ long, and had glazed quarterlights, as well as glazed droplights in the doors, as well as one louvered vents over. Although styled with two coach body sides, the third class part of the carriage was one open space, with benches around the perimeter, and one in the centre. I have shown four doors, but there might well have been only two. The Woodfin half plan shows the two doors opposite each other, but we do not see the other half of the compartment. It might also have been used for parcels work, as the doors were 2′ 6″ wide, instead of the 2′ 0″ ones used for the second-class compartments. There were no quarterlights, but the wooden droplights shown on the original drawing were probably glazed before delivery. Splashers over the wheels formed trip hazards in all the doorways.

The conductor's cabins were open sided, except for the sheeting at each end of the bench. The timber-framed fronts appear to have been reinforced with small iron T and L sections. Two droplights were fitted, whilst one upper bay was left open, to allow room for the brake handle to swing. The lower panel was beaded in the familiar style of other S.D.R. carriages of the period. I have shown a lamp bracket above the droplights, as locomotives normally had one in front of the chimney. Eddy has shown his lower down, so you have a choice. From an artistic point of view, the beaded panel could certainly do with something in the middle of it. There were no fittings shown on the Woodfin drawing, so I have based door handles and hinges on other contemporary drawings.

Early South Devon Railway Goods Brake Vans

S.D.R. No:	G.W.R. No:	Body:	Length:	Width:	Height:	Frame:	Springs:	Wheels:	Wheelbase:	Buffers:	Drawgear:	Brakes:	Tare:	Load:	Builder:	Built:	Condemned:
1	10777	Iron	26' 6"	8' 2"	6' 0"	Iron	4' 10"	6 no. 4' 0"	18' 4"	India Rubber	India Rubber	Double	11-1-0	8 tons	Hennett	1845	1-11-77
(a) 2	10778	Iron	29' 0"	8' 10"	6' 0"	Iron	4' 10"	6 no. 4' 0"	18' 4"	India Rubber	Cradle	Double	10-0-0(?)	8 tons	Hennett	1846/7	31-12-92
(b) 3	10779	Iron	28' 0"	8' 3"	6' 0"	Iron	4' 10"	6 no. 4' 0"	18' 4"	India Rubber	India Rubber	Double	9-12-0	8 tons(?)	Perry	1846	31-10-92
4	10780	Iron	27' 0"	8' 4"	6' 0"	Iron	4' 10"	6 no. 4' 0"	18' 4"	India Rubber	India Rubber	Double	10-0-0	6 tons	Perry	1846	27-1-87
(c) 5	10781	Wood	27' 0"	8' 10"	6' 0"	Iron	4' 10"	6 no. 4' 0"	18' 4"	India Rubber	Cradle	Double	9-12-0	8 tons(?)	Perry	1846/7	30-11-92
6	10782	Iron	21' 3"	7' 10"(?)	6' 0"	Iron	4' 10"	6 no. 4' 0"	14' 0"	Browns	India Rubber	Double	9-6-0	6 tons	Hennett	Aug.1846	30-6-92

Notes: (a) Load changed to 6 tons 20th Dec 90. Tare changed to 10-16-0. (b) Load changed to 6 tons 4th May 89. (c) Fitted with end doors 16th Mar 88. Load changed to 6 tons 23rd Apr 89.

Early South Devon Railway Composite Second/Third

S.D.R. No:	G.W.R. No:	Frame:	Body:	Body:	Length:	Width:	Height:	Compartments	Frame:	Wheelbase:	Wheels:	Body:	Buffers:	Drawgear:	Brakes:
37	2nd. 364			Wood	27' 9"	8' 10"	6' 0"	2S-2T-1L-1G	Iron	18' 4"	6 no. 4' 0"	S.D.R.	India Rubber	India Rubber	Six Block

Notes: Composite 37 rebuilt from Atmospheric coach.

Early South Devon Railway Carriages Third Class

S.D.R. No:	G.W.R. No:	Frame:	Body:	Body:	Length:	Width:	Height:	Compartments	Frame:	Wheelbase:	Wheels:	Body:	Buffers:	Drawgear:	Brakes:
14	3rd. 249	1848	1848	Wood	27' 9"	8' 10"	6' 0"	4T-1L-1G	Iron	18' 4"	6 no. 4' 0"		India Rubber	India Rubber	Six Block
16	3rd. 251	1846	1846	Wood	27' 9"	8' 10"	6' 0"	4T-1L-1G	Iron	18' 4"	6 no. 4' 0"		India Rubber	India Rubber	Six Block
38	3rd. 271	1847	1847	Wood	27' 9"	8' 10"	6' 0"	4T-1L-1G	Iron	18' 4"	6 no. 4' 0"		India Rubber	India Rubber	Six Block
39	3rd. 272	1847	1847	Wood	27' 3"	8' 10"	6' 0"	4T-1L-1G	Iron	18' 4"	6 no. 4' 0"		India Rubber	India Rubber	Six Block
40	3rd. 273	1846	1846	Wood	27' 3"	8' 10"	6' 0"	4T-1L-1G	Iron	18' 4"	6 no. 4' 0"		India Rubber	India Rubber	Six Block
41	3rd. 274	1847	1847	Wood	27' 3"	8' 10"	6' 0"	4T-1L-1G	Iron	18' 4"	6 no. 4' 0"		India Rubber	India Rubber	Six Block

Notes: 14, 16, 38 - 41 "Old Carriages, straight sides".

Early South Devon Railway Meat Vans

S.D.R. No:	G.W.R. No:	Frame:	Body:	Body:	Length:	Width:	Height:	Compartments	Frame:	Wheelbase:	Wheels:	Body:	Buffers:	Drawgear:	Brakes:	
1 & 6		1846	1865	Wood/Iron	21' 6"	8' 0"	7' 0"		Iron	14' 2"	6 no. 4' 0"	S.D.R.	India Rubber	India Rubber	None	ex-Third
2 - 5		1847	1866	Wood/Iron	21' 6"	8' 0"	7' 0"		Iron	14' 2"	6 no. 4' 0"	S.D.R.	India Rubber	India Rubber	None	ex-Third
18 - 20		1847	1869	Wood/Iron	21' 6"	8' 0"	7' 0"		Iron	14' 2"	6 no. 4' 0"	S.D.R.	India Rubber	India Rubber	None	

Oil lamps were just beginning to be introduced at the period, and further evidence of this has come to light since the original articles were written.

In view of the Board decisions reported on page 98, the drawings have been updated to show lamps to the second class compartments only and the lamp previously shown for the third class compartment has been removed. Conversely glass has been added to the third class droplights.

The History of the Piston Carriages

It is not known for certain how many piston carriages were built for the South Devon, although calculations can be made from the main line timetables on pages 10-11, and from the opening timetable for the Torquay branch. For the service which actually operated between Exeter and Newton, four piston carriages with 15" diameter pistons would have been required, two operating from Exeter and two from Newton. For the projected opening to Laira, four piston carriages with 22" diameter pistons would probably have been ordered, two to operate from Newton and two from Laira. For operation of the Torquay branch, a further two piston carriages with 22" pistons would have been needed. As the lines beyond Newton never operated atmospherically, the orders for 22" piston carriages would have been subject to cancellation or delivery in modified form.

According to Margary's diary, the first piston carriage was delivered at Exeter on 25th February 1847, and at 6.00 pm on the same day was sent down to Turf, towing a locomotive behind it, to clear the water and dirt out of the pipe (* See note 10 page 24). A "ghost service" between Exeter and Teignmouth commenced on Monday 16th August 1847, with two trains in each direction. It became an advertised public service from Monday 13th September 1847, and further locomotive-hauled trains were progressively transferred to atmospheric working during September and October. The piston carriages remained in the train as far as Newton, to save station time at Teignmouth,

and also to avoid the need to detrain passengers travelling in the piston carriage. Test running to Newton began in November 1847, and those trains that were already running atmospherically were extended to Newton from 17th December. As from 10th January 1848, most trains were worked atmospherically through to Newton, and from Wednesday 23rd February 1848 the service was fully atmospheric. The problems of the atmospheric system have been described earlier in the book. Whilst they were steadily dealt with throughout the year, the rapid development of locomotive design during the long gestation period of the atmospheric railways had effectively removed any incentive to fully deal with the situation, which would have required large sums of money. The last S.D.R. Atmospheric train was the up goods that arrived at Exeter around 12.30 a.m. on Sunday 10th September 1848.

There is little evidence in the South Devon Railway minute books that directly refers to the piston carriages needed to operate the atmospheric trains. The first time that rolling stock seems to have been considered by the South Devon Board was in January 1846 when they approached the Great Western to arrange for them to provide the stock. Rather than just running their carriages through, they offered to transfer a contract for six first class bodies and six seconds that were under construction. This offer was accepted and Brunel was instructed to obtain four third class carriages "with high sides and means of covering". In April 1847 the Board agreed to comply with a request from the Railway Commissioners to put glass in their third class carriages, and five months later instructed that the second class carriages should be lit. This agreement post-dates the 23rd November 1846 drawing on which the piston carriage illustrated was based. It is possible that the vehicles may have been delivered with glazing to the third class compartments and that oil lamps were fitted after their arrival in Devon.

In March 1846 the Board noted that four frames were under construction by Mr Davis of Wigmore Street, London, and in April there is a payment to Mr Dell for two second class bodies, presumably part of the G.W.R. order. In early July 1846 there is mention of third class carriages under construction by George Hennet that would be delivered in 4-6 weeks. At the same time the chairman "averted to the disappointment of Mr Davis who had made preparations for erecting an order for first class carriages that had been given to him by the directors in London, and that had afterwards been countermanded". In September 1846 Joseph Ward offered to construct one first and one second on speculation for the company which they accepted, but soon after this Brunel recommended building ten firsts, ten seconds, and eight thirds. The contracts were tendered and awarded at the end of November as follows:-

G. Hennet:- five first and six second class frames, plus ten complete thirds.

Smith & Willy:- five first and six second class frames.

J. Ward:- five first and two second class bodies.

J. Perry:- five first and four second class bodies.

Shackleford & Co.:- four second class bodies.

G.E. Elliot:- two second class bodies.

In April 1847 Mr Ward requested payment for the carriages he had built. This was much too soon to be the new contract, and so must refer to the speculative build.

As regards the 22" piston carriages, it appears that these were all ordered and several of them actually built. On 4th December 1848 Ward was pressing the railway for further payments, which presumably concerned these second phase vehicles. It was resolved "that the First Class Body referred to be received and paid for: but that the Piston Coaches remain with Mr Ward subject to further directions". He made further requests in May and August 1849; on the latter occasion Brunel was requested to "endeavour by some arrangement to relieve the company from the order for coaches which do not appear to have been required". On 2nd November he reported that he had made arrangements to take only one of the two coaches ordered. The Board was pressed for money at this stage and were unhappy with this arrangement, and informed Brunel "that with reference to the great inconvenience of present payment and to the liability of damage during the winter they should now receive a first class coach without frame and for which there is no present use. Mr Brunel be requested to get Mr Ward to allow a postponement of the payment until March or April: or otherwise, if payment cannot be delayed that he will give the second class instead of the first class coach."

On 2 July 1850 it was reported that two second class piston coach bodies had been received from Ward. In November they decided to instruct the Superintendent to have them mounted on frames and converted to ordinary second class coaches. In July the following year, Ward tendered to alter three un-mounted piston coach bodies while, at the same time, Samuda Brothers offered "to complete three frames belonging to the company and supply wheels". The following September "Mr Margary submitted the expediency of mounting a second class coach body now at Exeter" which was authorised.

In January 1876, the list of stock transferred to the Great Western included one second class downgraded to a composite, no. 37, which was remarked to be an "old atmospheric coach". The only other reference that appears to have been minuted regarding the conversion of piston carriages was on 17th April 1849: "The Chief Superintendent was directed to require a third Piston Coach to be converted into a Goods Break Truck." The Minute Books appear to make no other reference to goods break vans at this period.

	First	Second	Third	Piston
1846 G.W.R. Contract	6	6		
1846 Hennet			4	
1846 Ward	1	1		
1846 S.D.R. Contract	10	10	10	
1847 Ward	1			?2
1848 Ward	?1			2
TOTAL	?19	17	14	?4

In 1876 the following early carriages survived:-

10 of 1846 build

4 x firsts (3 Shackleford, 1 Ward)

2 x firsts altered to 1st/2nd composites

1 x 2nd/3rd composite

2 x third (unknown)

1 x third altered to a mail van

---

16 of 1847 build

3 x firsts (2 Perry, 1 Ward)

3 x firsts altered to 1st/2nd composites

3 x third (unknown)

6 x third altered to luggage vans

1 carriage altered to a fish van

---

9 of 1848 build

3 x firsts (2 Ward, 1 Perry)

1 first altered to 1st/2nd composite

2 x third, 1 of which had been rebuilt

1 x third altered to a luggage van

2 carriages altered to fish vans

There were also 2 seconds (1 Ward, 1 Perry) and 1 mail van (Shackleford) of unknown vintage.

The redundant piston carriages are believed to have been converted into goods brake vans at Newton. The accompanying extract from the G.W.R. (ex-S.D.R.) waggons register lists the most likely candidates for former piston carriages. With removal of the atmospheric apparatus, the chassis would be almost ready for re-use. The drawgear would have needed conventional India rubber springing adding, unless the redundant suspension frames and octagons were left in place. The twin brake standards would have been removed, and the operating gear re-arranged with a single standard in a more central position.

From the list, it could appear that the unusual bodies were replaced with conventional iron van bodies. Perhaps more likely, the relatively new timber body frames may have been retained, modified and re-clad overall with iron sheeting. The table lists the first six S.D.R. goods brake vans, and there were no further additions until 1853. The piston carriages must surely have all been converted by 1850, however slowly they were dealt with; in which case the ex-piston carriages must be within the range 1-6.

Goods services were very limited on the South Devon in the early years, and followed quite a long time after the various passenger openings. Goods traffic commenced between Exeter and Newton in May 1847, and was extended to Totnes from December 1847. Goods brake vans no. 1 of 1846 and no. 2 of 1846/7 from the table would have been perfectly adequate for this limited service. The building dates of 1846, 1846, 1846/7 and August 1847 for the other four vehicles are compatible with the provision of piston carriages for the piecemeal development of atmospheric operations. With the commissioning of the engine houses being so delayed, the piston carriages would have arrived in advance of the service requirements. The existing pair of brake vans would still have been adequate following the extension of goods operations to Laira Green on 13th September 1848, just after the abandonment of atmospheric working on 10th September. It would seem likely that the redundant piston carriages were steadily converted to goods brake vans during the following year, prior to the next goods openings, from Laira Green to Millbay, and Newton to Torquay, both in October 1849. I would therefore suggest that goods brake vans nos. 3-5 and composite no. 37 were the ex-15" piston carriages. It is apparent that no two vehicles were identical, which would tie in with piecemeal introduction, and perhaps also explain the different appearance of the piston carriage in Dawson's watercolour. The shaded details in the table correspond with those of the Woodfin drawing, which would suggest that goods brake van no. 4 might well have been converted from the vehicle illustrated in this article.

The vans passed to the G.W.R. in February 1876, becoming numbers 10777-10782. Four of them, 10778, 10779, 10781 and 10782, the latter three probably being ex-piston carriages, lasted until the end of the broad gauge in 1892. They stood on the dump for some months, and may well even have been photographed there. With their rebuilt bodies however, there would be virtually nothing to distinguish them from the other vans without such an illustrious past. The 22" piston coaches were modified for general use before being put into service, so are not easily identified. The page 97 tables list surviving early coaches and vans which passed to the G.W.R. in 1876 and may well include them.

The Other Atmospheric Railways

The Atmospheric railway in South Devon is fairly well known, due to its association with Brunel, location in a holiday destination, seawall promenade and surviving buildings. Other than those with specialist interest, very few people today are aware that three other operational Atmospheric railways were also constructed to the Clegg and Samuda system. All were built in the 1840s, contemporary with the South Devon, which was in fact the last of the four to open. They certainly worked, and two of them ran for many years after the South Devon had closed. A brief account of these other three lines is given here.

The Dublin and Kingstown Railway

On the night of 18th-19th November 1807, the troopships Prince of Wales and Rochdale were driven on to the rocks between Blackrock and Dún Laoghaire, with the loss of over 400 lives. This led to renewed calls for a new harbour to serve Dublin, and by 1816 legislation had been passed authorising construction of the West Pier at Dún Laoghaire, which was then only a small village. George IV visited the port under construction in 1821, following which the fledgling town was renamed Kingstown, a name which it retained until 1920.

Communication with Dublin was obviously essential and the Dublin & Kingstown Railway, the first in Ireland, opened on 9th October 1834. Charles Vignoles was the engineer. This was originally 5½ miles in length, with a terminus at the West Pier. It was extended a further half mile in 1837, to a terminus near the packet wharf. Trains ran every half hour between Dublin and Kingstown, calling at Booterstown, Black Rock and Salt Hill. Unusually, the railway was laid to 4' 8½" gauge, as it pre-dated standardisation of the gauge in Ireland. The situation threatened to become more chaotic than on the mainland, with the Ulster Railway opening on 6' 2" gauge in 1839, and the Dublin & Drogheda Railway on 5' 2" gauge in 1844. The situation was brought under control in 1846, when the gauge in Ireland was standardised at 5' 3" for new construction, and the existing lines were eventually converted to follow suit.

The harbour commissioners conveyed granite for their works by means of a double-track horse-drawn tramway from Dalkey Quarry. Following completion of the works, one line was deemed sufficient for the stone traffic and it was decided to convert the other for passenger use, as the area was becoming very fashionable. Vignoles had been amongst the first to visit the Atmospheric tests at Wormwood Scrubs and recommended the use of the system for the Dalkey line. The Dublin & Kingstown board agreed, thinking that the Atmospheric might provide Ireland with low-cost railways, and the harbour commissioners consented to the conversion of their line for the experiment.

The Kingstown to Dalkey Atmospheric Railway was 1¾ miles in length, with an average gradient of 1 in 110. It commenced operation on 19th August 1843, with an official opening on 29th March 1844 after the short tunnel at Kingstown was completed. Atmospheric trains left Kingstown on the hour and half-hour, with return departures from Dalkey at 15 and 45 minutes past the hour. The contractor for the line was William Dargan and the trackbed was formed below ground between retaining walls, to avoid the need for level crossings.

The line commenced immediately beyond Kingstown station, and passengers walked from one platform to the other. A single Engine House was constructed at Dalkey, on what became known as Atmospheric Road. A reservoir adjacent to the building supplied water for the boilers.

An Atmospheric Train at Kingstown Harbour Station

The view is looking south-east, under the elegant bridge to Marine Road. The stone balustrade still survives, separating the station concourse from the road and is more extensive than shown here. The station building is just visible to the left. The crowd on the bridge, station platform and Crofton Road are welcoming the first Atmospheric train to arrive from Dalkey.

The Engine House at Dalkey

The view is looking north-west across the Engine House reservoir. The low boiler room, tall engine room and circular chimney appear quite bleak in comparison with those on the other Atmospheric railways. Looking out across the Irish Sea, Kingstown Harbour can be seen in the distance.

Vacuum power for the ascent was obtained via a piston running in a 15" diameter tube, connected to the piston carriage at the front of the train. The speed was said to be much the same as the locomotive driven trains, from 30 to 40 miles an hour. The pipe ended about 100 yards before reaching Dalkey, the momentum carrying the train into the station, and a look-out man at the Engine House stopped the pumping engine when he saw or heard the train approaching. The pressure was shown at the Engine House by a special barometer in connection with the tube. As the line was uphill the whole way to Dalkey, the return journey was performed by gravity; before leaving Dalkey station an attendant lifted the piston by means of a lever and hooked it up under the train, so as to run clear of the tube.

The Atmospheric railway ran successfully for many years and became something of a tourist attraction in its own right. The end came with the opening of the first stretch of the Waterford, Wexford, Wicklow and Dublin Railway on 10th July 1854. This ran from Dalkey to Bray and was laid to the Irish standard gauge of 5' 3". The Dublin & Kingstown lines were leased to the new concern to provide a through route. This required their gauge to be converted to match and so the Atmospheric had to be abandoned.

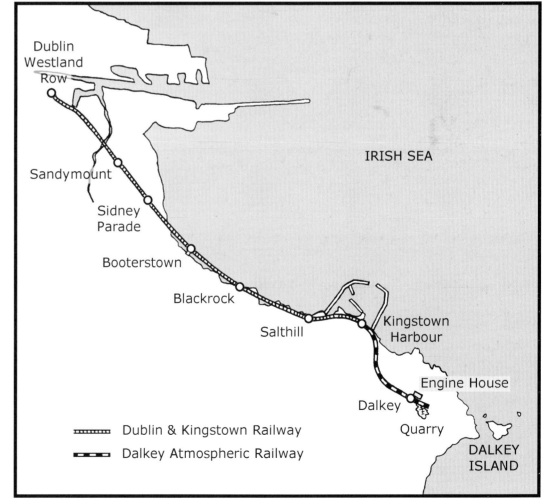

The Dublin & Kingstown Railway 1844-1854

The London & Croydon Railway

This Atmospheric railway had by far the most complicated history of the four which were built, which proved to be the main factor in its eventual downfall. The London and Greenwich Railway opened on 8th February 1836 from Spa Road to Deptford, extended at the western end to London Bridge on 14th December 1836, and at the eastern end to Greenwich on 24th December 1838. The total line length was only 3¾ miles, the line being carried throughout on 878 brickwork arches.

The London and Croydon Railway opened on 5th June 1839. It was 8¾ miles long, from a junction with the London and Greenwich at Corbett's Lane, to Croydon. The works included considerable cuttings at Forest Hill and New Cross, where 650,000 and 590,000 cubic yards of earth were removed respectively. The southernmost three miles were laid on the bed of the former Croydon Canal. Intermediate stations were erected at New Cross, Dartmouth Arms (Forest Hill), Sydenham, Penge, Anerley and the Jolly Sailor (Norwood Junction). The route was fairly level, except for the gradient from New Cross up to Dartmouth Arms, which was mostly at 1 in 100, with a short stretch at 1 in 85. At London Bridge, the London and Croydon trains had their own terminus

The South Eastern Railway obtained running powers between London Bridge and Jolly Sailor and opened the northernmost section of their own line from Jolly Sailor to Haywards Heath on 12th July 1841. The South Eastern Railway shared these lines as far as Redhill, where their own line diverged, with the first stretch to Tonbridge opening on 26th May 1842. As a consequence of the greatly increased traffic into London Bridge, the viaduct to Corbett's Lane was widened on the south side to four tracks in 1842. The Greenwich and Croydon companies also sensibly exchanged termini at London Bridge in 1844, to avoid unnecessary crossing of trains. The Croydon and South Eastern companies jointly built a branch from East London Junction, just south of Corbett's Lane, to a new terminus at Bricklayers Arms, with a view to reducing tolls paid to the London and Greenwich. Half of the South Eastern and all of the Croydon services were transferred to the new terminus.

Against this already complicated background, in 1844 the London and Croydon successfully applied for powers to lay down an additional line of rails, and also to build the nominally independent Croydon and Epsom Railway. They were receiving tolls from the two companies using their main line and this would enable them to run their own trains independently, whilst also bringing further traffic on to the line. The board determined to use Atmospheric traction for these works, in order to connect with proposed Atmospheric lines to Chatham and to Portsmouth.

The railway ownership in the area was simplified by two amalgamations. On 1st January 1845, the London and Greenwich was absorbed by the South Eastern Railway. On 27th July 1846 the London and Croydon amalgamated with the new London, Brighton and South Coast Railway. Between these two dates, whilst the London and Croydon was still independent, the first phase of the Atmospheric railway opened between Dartmouth Arms and Croydon on 19th January 1846, a length of five miles. This involved a timber flyover at Norwood Junction, to carry the Atmospheric trains over the Brighton and South Eastern lines.

Engine Houses were constructed at Forest Hill, Norwood and Croydon. These were very ornate in Gothic style, to appease objections from local landowners. The tubes were 15" in diameter and several were uncovered at west Croydon in 1933 during track relaying work.

The piston carriages featured a conductor's half-cabin at each end, which were to opposite hands. The carriages were not capable of being turned and the brake handles were both on the western side of the vehicle, as were the cabins. They were fitted with a lever for opening a valve in the pistons, to assist in regulating progress of the train and were also provided with stick barometers, so that the conductors were aware of the pressure available in the tube. Both of these were features which the South Devon managed to do without. About 27th February 1847, the service was extended to New Cross, a further 2½ miles, but the Engine House at New Cross was not brought into use.

By this time, the Croydon was part of the larger L.B.&S.C.R. concern, whose directors quickly made it clear that they were not in favour of continuing Atmospheric operations. The authorised extension of Atmospheric working to Bricklayers Arms was not carried out, nor that to Epsom, although machinery had been ordered.

All existing Atmospheric services ended on 3rd May 1847. The Croydon to Epsom line opened just a week later, on 10th May 1847, and was locomotive worked from the start.

A London & Croydon Railway Piston Carriage

The piston carriage is seen from the southern end, with the conductor winding the brake handle. He also has a stick barometer in his little cabin and a lever which presumably operated a valve in the piston head. From the side windows, it is apparent that the carriage has three passenger compartments.

Railways in South-East London - February, May 1847

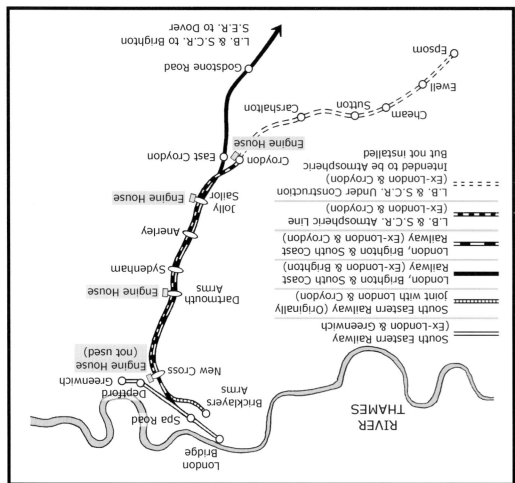

Legend:
- South Eastern Railway (Ex-London & Greenwich)
- South Eastern Railway (Originally joint with London & Croydon)
- London, Brighton & South Coast Railway (Ex-London & Brighton)
- London, Brighton & South Coast Railway (Ex-London & Croydon)
- L.B. & S.C.R. Atmospheric Line (Ex-London & Croydon)
- L.B. & S.C.R. Under Construction
- Intended to be Atmospheric But not installed
- Engine House
- Engine House (not used)

Stations and features shown: Epsom, Godstone Road, Ewell, Cheam, Sutton, Carshalton, East Croydon, Croydon, Engine House, Anerley, Sydenham, Dartmouth Arms, Engine House, Jolly Sailor, New Cross, Bricklayers Arms, Deptford, Greenwich, Spa Road, London Bridge, RIVER THAMES, S.E.R. to Dover, L.B. & S.C.R. to Brighton.

Atmospheric services were running between New Cross and Croydon, although the London & Croydon had now become part of the London, Brighton & South Coast Railway. It was planned to extend the service into Bricklayers Arms and out to Epsom, but the system was abandoned before this could happen.

Dartmouth Arms Station and Engine House (Forest Hill)

The view is looking north-east, across the original London & Croydon main line in the foreground, now mostly used by London & Brighton trains to Brighton, and South Eastern Railway trains to Dover. A down London & Croydon Atmospheric train stands in the station, drawing two open third class carriages and four covered ones. The barn-like engine room seen behind the station and boiler room were constructed end-to-end. Evidently horizontal machinery was in use.

Compagnie du Chemin de Fer de Paris à Saint Germain

The Paris à Saint Germain opened from the Gare Saint-Lazare in Paris to Le Pecq on the banks of the Seine on 26th August 1837, with a length of 19km (11¾ miles), and laid to the gauge of 143.5cm (4' 8½"). This was the first railway serving the French capital. Originally single-track, a second line was added in 1838 and intermediate stations opened progressively at Nanterre, Chatou, Rueil and Colombes. The railway was laid across flat country, but was not able to attain its final objective of the gardens and woods of the Chateau de St-Germain-en-Laye, a favourite Sunday destination for Parisians, due to the steep slope from the river up to the castle.

The development of the Atmospheric system in Britain attracted the interest of the French government, who granted a subsidy for an Atmospheric trial. This allowed plans to be made for extension of the railway from Le Pecq up the steep gradient to Saint Germain, as this system effectively separated tractive effort from adhesion. The western part of the existing line was also to be converted. Four sets of machinery were ordered, one each for Engine Houses at Nanterre and Chatou and two for Saint Germain. Tubes of 38cm (15") in diameter were ordered for the section from Nanterre to Le Vésinet, and of 63cm (24¾") for the climb to Saint Germain, the largest of any ever cast for an Atmospheric railway. Engines were ordered from Hallette of Arras, Meyer of Mulhouse and Seraing of Liège, boilers from Cail of Lille, and tubes from Chagot et Brunet of Blanzy.

Work on the extension commenced in 1845; it consisted of the erection of a wooden bridge over the Seine, followed by a stone viaduct of twenty arches. The route reached the centre of Saint-Germain-en-Laye by passing under the terrace of the Castle in two successive tunnels. The terminus was constructed in a cutting in the Castle grounds, thereby spoiling the symmetry of the formal gardens laid out by André Le Nôtre in 1669 to 1673, but without, it appears, giving rise to protests. The railway, which opened on 15th April 1847, was 1.5 kilometres (1 mile) in length, and laid to a gradient of 35 mm/m (1 in 28.6), which was considerable for a railway.

The line was double-track, but only the line for trains climbing the gradient was fitted with an iron tube on its centre line. In this case, the continuous slot at the top of the tube was kept airtight by means of two leather valves. This meant that the coulter which joined the piston to the driving car could be vertical, unlike those of the previous Atmospheric railways. The coulter itself separated the valves, doing away with the usual lifting wheels and permitting a much more compact vehicle than those across the Channel. A pair of small wheels at the rear, set on the diagonal, closed the valves behind the piston.

In the Engine House, located between the two tunnels, the vacuum pumps were driven by two steam engines of 200hp each. Each engine comprised two horizontal steam cylinders of 0.8m (28¾") diameter by 2 metres (6' 6½") stroke, mounted on a massive masonry base, which drove a flywheel crank shaft. These were geared down 5 to 1 by gear wheels to a separate crank shaft for two massive air pumps of 2.53m (8' 4"), with the same stroke as the steam cylinders. The drive for the pumps was vertical, with the pumps being located at lower level. The steam cylinders ran at 2m/s (6' 6½" per second) and the vacuum pumps at 0.4m/s (1' 4" per second).

St. Germain Engine House

Between the two tunnels near the head of the climb, the chimney of St. Germain Engine house can be seen to the right, with the low boiler room next to it. Beyond that, and at right angles to it, stands the taller engine room, which had horizontal engines at the upper level and vertical pumps at low level. An acending Atmopheric train is approaching the terminus

Engine House: L'Illustration, 17th April 1847.

Between them, the four enormous pumps were capable of exhausting four cubic metres (35 cubic feet) of air per second, sufficient to draw a train up the gradient at a speed of 35 km/h (21mph). For the return journey, the train descended by simple gravity to Le Pecq, where a steam locomotive would be waiting to take the train on to Paris.

In response to delays in receiving the Engine House machinery, the company had built the powerful long-boiler 0-6-0 locomotive 'l'Hercule' in its own workshops in 1846, ostensibly for transporting construction materials. This succeeded in climbing the incline with a working load, so the Atmospheric was doomed even before it opened. Construction had to proceed, due to the government subsidy, but the low-level section was never completed, even though the engines had been installed at Nanterre and Chatou.

The system functioned reasonably well ("tant bien que mal") and the Saint Germain line ran for a longer period than all the other Atmospheric railways, eventually totalling 13 years and 3 months. Atmospheric traction was finally discontinued on 2nd July 1860. As from 3rd July 1860, 'l'Hercule' took over the traction duties on the fierce incline. Steam power was eventually supplanted by electrification in 1920.

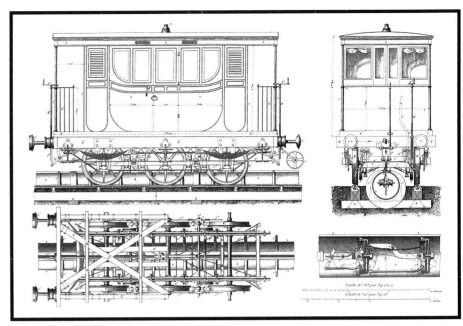

The 'Voiture Directrice' of the Paris à St. Germain

The P. & S.G. driving car was more compact than the piston carriages of the other Atmospheric railways. The outer four wheels were sprung to carry the weight of the coach, with its single saloon and two semi-open conductor's platforms, whilst the piston frame hung from the central axle. The car suffered a brake failure on 6th September 1858 and crashed into a steam locomotive at Le Vésinet, killing its conductor monsieur Lacôte and two passengers. A replacement to similar layout but simpler design was built, but Atmospheric working was discontinued within two years.

Driving car: Publication Industrielle, 1848.

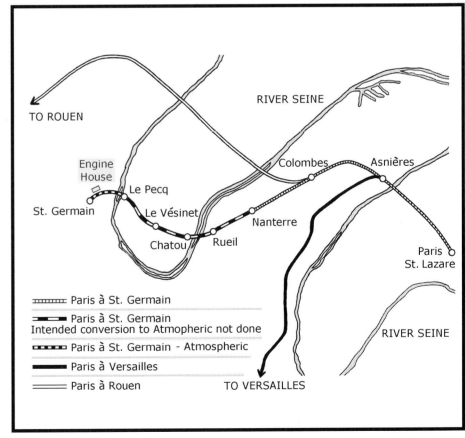

The Paris à St. Germain, 1847 - 1860

Atmospheric services were running between Le Pecq and St. Germain, but the planned conversion of the line between Nanterre and Le Pecq to Atmospheric working had been cancelled.

Map: Paul Garnsworthy.

The Atmospheric in Retrospect

Looking back from the 21st century, it is easy to dismiss the Atmospheric railway as a bizarre idea, and wonder why anyone would contemplate the construction of such a thing. However, to understand how this came about, we should try to see transportation in the 1820s through Georgian eyes.

When George Medhurst and Henry Pinkus were carrying out their experiments, nobody knew that the steam locomotive was going to conquer the world. Locomotives of the period were small and slow machines of limited power output, and were only used on level track over lightly-built colliery lines. To transfer waggons from one adit level to another, cable-worked inclines were necessary. Long distance journeys across the country were measured in days, rather than hours, and only very few people were in a position to travel in any case. Travel by stage coach involved frequent stops to changes horses and to take meals. The canal network was extensive over the industrialised part of the country, but again goods only moved at the speed of a horse, and negotiation of lock flights was very time consuming.

When the first main line railways were being planned, nobody was thinking of a national network, and each route was considered on its own merits. The first trunk lines involved heavy engineering to keep the track-bed as near level as possible, whilst changes in level were deliberately concentrated at specific locations, such as the 1 in 37.7 Lickey Incline on the London & Birmingham Railway and the 1 in 100 climb to Box Tunnel on the G.W.R., which both opened in 1841.

It was intended to use rope haulage on the inclines, despite all its limitations. Much thought was given to alternative means of propulsion which would alleviate these problems. The Atmospheric Railway seemed ideal in this respect; it would separate the tractive power from the gradients on the inclines, and it would also do away with the need for locomotives on the rest of the line. The Atmospheric system was sometimes referred to by its advocates as the "Rope of Air", which gives away some of the thinking behind its development.

The development of a workable continuous valve by Samuel Clegg, Jacob and Joseph Samuda, patented in 1838, finally made the Atmospheric Railway a genuine possibility. This was demonstrated by a test model at Samuda Brothers in 1839 and the test installation at Wormwood Scrubs in 1840 – 1843. The four vacuum-powered railways which came to fruition opened in quick succession after that over the next five years. As with any new technology, detail development was required to perfect it, and a pool of only four working railways was a very small base from which to carry it out.

By contrast, the number of locomotive-worked railways had snowballed between 1825 and 1848. Engineers the length and breadth of the country were working on individual detail improvements, which steadily and collectively built up the capability of the Iron Horse. The machines which were running at the end of this period bore little comparison with those available at the beginning of the atmospheric era. The period of introduction of Atmospheric Railways coincided with that known as the 'Railway Mania'. As the price of railway shares increased, more and more money was poured in by speculators, until the inevitable collapse followed. The mania reached its zenith in 1846, when no less than 272 Acts of Parliament were passed for new railways, over a third of them Atmospheric, which would have totalled 9,500 miles of new railway line.

Railway development for the next decade inevitably proceeded much more cautiously. Risks were kept to a minimum and excessive expenditure avoided. Compared with the great works of architecture and engineering associated with the early lines, the eighteen-fifties saw much more basic installations, sufficient to get the railways up and running, until sufficient income could be generated to commission more imposing works. Rolling stock and locomotives were often hired, or the operation of the railway let out to contract, which could be paid out of a proportion of the revenue, rather than as a drain on capital. In this new financial climate, there was no way that the huge capital investment required for further Atmospheric Railways could be justified, and with the rise in power of the steam locomotive there was no technical justification either.

The New Order at Newton

Rover class 4-2-2 'Balaclava' stands in front of the former Atmospheric Engine House chimney at Newton. Such a machine would have been unthinkable when the Atmospheric was originally conceived.

With all this railway development came two other consequences. Firstly the railways of Britain could now be regarded as a single network. Anything which caused a break in this network, be it a non-standard gauge (however technically superior it might be), or a need to change between methods of propulsion, created an impediment to the smooth running of the overall system. People's expectations had increased immeasurably during the brief span of years from 1825 to 1848.

Railway investment had become a self-promoting cycle, based solely on over-optimistic speculation. With a greater number of railways in operation, it had become apparent that they were not always lucrative and often posed substantial construction difficulties. As a result, the supply of funds for new railways quickly dried up and most of these speculative lines were not built. The more worthwhile projects were bought out at bargain prices by established railway companies, expanding their networks.

Secondly, the number of people travelling had increased exponentially, as had the tonnage of goods being carried. As a result, train weights had also become much larger and peak flows more variable. The Atmospheric system lost out on both counts. It was an efficient system when train weights and frequencies were fairly constant, but if more people travelled it could only run more trains at its ideal weight until line capacity was reached, rather than increase the weight of trains. The Atmospheric system was not therefore prolonged any further. The London & Croydon went over to locomotive working as early as 3rd May 1847, largely due to the political situation involved with its amalgamation with the larger London & Brighton Railway. The South Devon also terminated Atmospheric operation with undue haste, from 9th September 1848. It is a pity it was not introduced between Newton and Plymouth, where its capabilities would have been of great benefit over the steeply graded route. Much expense has been incurred over the years providing supplementary locomotive power, train crews and engine stabling, to haul trains over the Dartmoor foothills. The Atmospheric Railway could have obviated this for a while. The Dalkey Atmospheric ran on for a number of years, up until 10th July 1854, when the gauge of the railway was altered to connect to the expanding Irish system. Only the Paris à St. Germain ran for a reasonably natural lifespan, the last working bringing the whole Atmospheric era to an end on 2nd July 1860.

The fact that it was decided not to continue further with Atmospheric propulsion is not the same as stating that it was a complete failure. At the time of writing the annual performance figures for rail services in Devon are 95.7% punctuality and 99.5% reliability. By comparison, the figures given on page 15 for South Devon Railway Atmospheric workings over four winter months show 97.5% punctuality and 99.9% reliability. On the modern railway, problems with doors and couplings have taken years to resolve. In the 1840s, Pearson and his hard-pressed staff had only months to get brand-new technology running efficiently. The fact that they achieved what they did should be regarded as something of a triumph on their part. If it was not the technical failure that it is normally described as, the enormous cost of the Atmospheric installation and its premature abandonment on the S.D.R. certainly imposed a massive financial burden on the small company. Thomas Woollcombe kept very tight control of the S.D.R. commercial operation over the remaining years of independent existence, saving it from the failure to restore modest profitability. However, the straightened circumstances did reflect well on the next phase of the Brunel's work in the West Country. For example, the numerous timber viaducts erected during this period were models of economic design and elegance.

Atmospheric Personalities

Samuel Clegg 1781-1861

Image: Mechanics Magazine 1835.

Samuel Clegg was born in Manchester on 2nd March 1781, received a scientific education under Dr. Dalton and was then apprenticed to Boulton and Watt. He was much involved in the introduction of gas lighting, and in 1814 became the engineer of the Chartered Gas Company. He was later employed by the Portuguese government, reconstructing the mint at Lisbon, amongst other public works. Returning to England he joined the Samuda brothers in developing Atmospheric traction. He died at Fairfield House, Adelaide Road, Haverstock Hill, Middlesex, on 8th January 1861.

Jacob Samuda 1811-1844

Descended from a Portuguese Sephardic family, Jacob was born in London on 24th August 1811. After an engineering apprenticeship under John Hague, Jacob set up in business with his brother Joseph. Working with Samuel Clegg, the Samudas obtained a patent for a 'new improvement in valves' in 1839, which finally made Atmospheric propulsion possible. Jacob also developed an improved form of marine engine, which was fitted to the 500 ton iron boat 'Gypsy Queen'. Moored at Brunswick Pier, Blackwall, on 12th November 1844 the main steam pipe burst, killing Jacob and six others.

Joseph d'Aguilar Samuda 1813-1885

Image: The Engineer 1899.

Joseph was born in London on 21st May 1813. After gaining business experience in his father's counting house, he set up Samuda Brothers with Jacob in 1832, with workshops at Blackwall. Initially involved in developing marine steam engines, followed by their work on Atmospheric railways, they subsequently concentrated on ship building. A total of 145 ships were built by Samuda Brothers between 1844 and 1893. Joseph helped to establish the Institute of Naval Architects in 1860. He was M.P. for Tavistock 1865-1868 and Tower Hamlets 1868-1880. He died on 27th April 1885.

Thomas Gill 1788-1861

Thomas Gill was born in Tavistock in 1788. With income from quarrying, he set up the Millbay Soap Works in 1818 and was agent for Tavistock Iron Works, owned by the family. He erected a pier at Millbay, became Mayor of Plymouth in 1836 and M.P. from 1841 to 1846. Chairman of the South Devon Railway, he resigned in 1849 in protest at the decision to abandon the Atmospheric system. He was active in setting up the town of New Plymouth in New Zealand. He died at Ferrum Hill House in Tavistock in 1861.

Isambard Kingdom Brunel 1806-1859

Image: Engraving by T.O. Barlow (1824-1889), based on the painting by J.C. Horsley.

Brunel was born in Portsmouth on 9th April 1806. After study in France, he assisted his father on construction of the Thames Tunnel. He pioneered the Broad Gauge on the Great Western Railway and its associates. In 1844 he was appointed Engineer to the South Devon Railway. An approach from the Samuda brothers led to a visit to Dalkey and subsequently to Brunel's recommendation to use the Atmospheric on the S.D.R. In addition to railways, he designed bridges, steam ships and even a prefabricated hospital for the Crimea. He died on 15th September 1859.

Thomas Woollcombe 1800-1876

Thomas Woollcombe was born at Ashbury, Devon, on 6th March 1800. He was a solicitor, who became town clerk of Devonport. He was a director of the South Devon Railway, Chairman from 1849 to 1874. He guided the S.D.R. to financial recovery after the Atmospheric débacle, and was presented with £500 of new shares in 1852 for his exertions. He promoted the Royal Albert Hospital in Devonport. He was again associated with Thomas Gill in founding New Plymouth. He died on 12th August 1876, not long after the South Devon had become part of the G.W.R.

Peter Margary 1820-1896

Peter John Margary was born on 2nd June 1820 in Kensington. He was articled to William Gravatt, Brunel's chief assistant on the Bristol & Exeter Railway. He later assisted William Froude on the B.&E.R. before becoming Brunel's assistant on the South Devon Railway. Upon Brunel's death in 1859, Margary succeeded him as Chief Engineer, designing several branch lines, docks at Plymouth and rebuilding timber viaducts in stone. After amalgamation in 1876, he continued as engineer for the Western Division of the G.W.R. He retired in 1891 and died in London on 29th April 1896.

James Pearson 1820-1891

James Pearson was baptised on 29th March 1820 in Blackburn. He was put in charge of the Atmospheric engines on the London & Croydon Railway, under Hensman their Atmospheric Manager. In September 1847 he became Atmospheric Superintendent to the S.D.R. In May 1850 he was appointed locomotive superintendent of the Bristol & Exeter Railway, although he was still involved in disposal of S.D.R. Atmospheric equipment up until November 1852. Pearson set up workshops at Bristol and designed an innovative range of locomotives for the B.&E.R., including the extraordinary 4-2-4Ts which are always associated with him. He died on 30th August 1891 in Ealing.

Bibliography

Atmospheric Railways, by Charles Hadfield, David and Charles, 1967, Alan Sutton Publishing, 1985 - ISBN 0 86299 204 4

The Atmospheric Railways, by Howard Clayton, Published by the author, 1966

A Beast Book for the Pocket, by Edmund Sandars, Oxford University Press, 1937

The Book of Dawlish - A History of, by Grace D. Griffiths, Barracuda Books, 1984 - ISBN 9780860232018

British Rail - Main Line Gradient Profiles, Ian Allan Ltd. - ISBN 0 7110 0875 2

A Broad Gauge Album, by Iain Rice. Newton Abbot Town & G.W.R. Museum, 2000 ISBN 9780953353712

Brunel's Cornish Viaducts, by John Binding, Atlantic Transport Publishers, 1993 ISBN 0 906899 56 7

The Churches of Devon, by J.M. Slader, David and Charles, 1968 - ISBN 7153 4255 X

A Country Camera, 1844-1914, by Gordon Winter, 1966, David & Charles 1971

Discovering Horse-drawn Carriages, by D.J. Smith 1974, Shire Publications, 2011 - ISBN 9780852637203

Discovering Horse-drawn Vehicles, by D.J. Smith 1994, Shire Publications, 2004 - ISBN 9780747802082

Discovering Carts and Wagons, by John Vince, Shire Publications, 1970 - ISBN 9780852632840

The Exeter Canal, by Kenneth R. Klew, Phillimore & Co. Ltd., 1984 - ISBN 0 85033 544 2

Exeter - Newton Abbot, A Railway History, by Peter Kay, Platform 5 Publishing Ltd., 1993 ISBN 1 872524 42 7

A First Book of Geology, by Albert Wilmore Macmillan & Co, 1914

Geology for Beginners, by William Whitehead, Watts Macmillan & Co, 1898, 6th Ed., corrected reprint, 1935

The Haytor Granite Railway and Stover Canal by M.C. Ewans, David and Charles, 1964, revised 1977 - ISBN 0 7153 4020 4

A History of Forde House, Newton Abbot, Devon. by Mary O'Hagan, Teignbridge District Council, 1990

The History of the Great Western Railway, Vol. Two by E.T. MacDermot, 1931, revised C.R. Clinker, 1964, Ian Allan Ltd., ISBN 0 7110 0412 9

History of the Southern Railway, by C.F. Dendy Marshall 1937, Revised by R.W. Kidner, 1963, Ian Allan Ltd., ISBN 0 7110 0059 X

History of Teignmouth, by Grace D. Griffiths 1965 - ISBN 0948578173

History, Gazetteer and Directory of Devonshire, by William White, 1850, Reprinted David and Charles, 1968 - ISBN 0715342762

An Illustrated Handbook of Vernacular Architecture, by R.W. Brunskill, Faber & Faber, 1971

Bibliography Continued Page 104.

Bibliography continued

Iron Horse to the Sea, - Railways in South Devon
by John Pike, 1987

The National Archives RAIL 631/1 & RAIL 632/2
South Devon Railway Board Minutes.

The National Archives RAIL 631/84
Valuation of Locomotives, Rolling Stock etc.

The Newton Abbot to Kingswear Railway
(1844-1988) by C.R. Potts. Oakwood Press,
1988 - ISBN 0 85361 387 7

A New Survey of England - Devon,
by W.G. Hoskins. Collins, 1954

Parish Church of St. Michael, East Teignmouth by
Beatrix F. Cresswell. T.H. Aggett, Teignmouth, 1924

Rail Centres: Exeter, by Colin G. Maggs.
Ian Allan Ltd., 1985 - ISBN 0 7110 1564 3

Le Rail en France,
Les 80 Premières Lignes,
1828 - 1851
By François & Maguy Palau Gautier-Villars,
1995 - ISBN 9 782950 942104

A Regional History of the Railways
of Great Britain, Vol. 1 - The West Country,
by David St. John Thomas.
David & Charles, 1960, revised 1981
ISBN 0 7153 8152 0

The South Devon Railway, by R.H. Gregory
The Oakwood Press, 1982
ISBN 0 85361 286 2

Two Thousand Years in Exeter, by W.G. Hoskins,
Phillimore & Co. Ltd., 1960,
revised 1963 - ISBN 0 900592 01 x

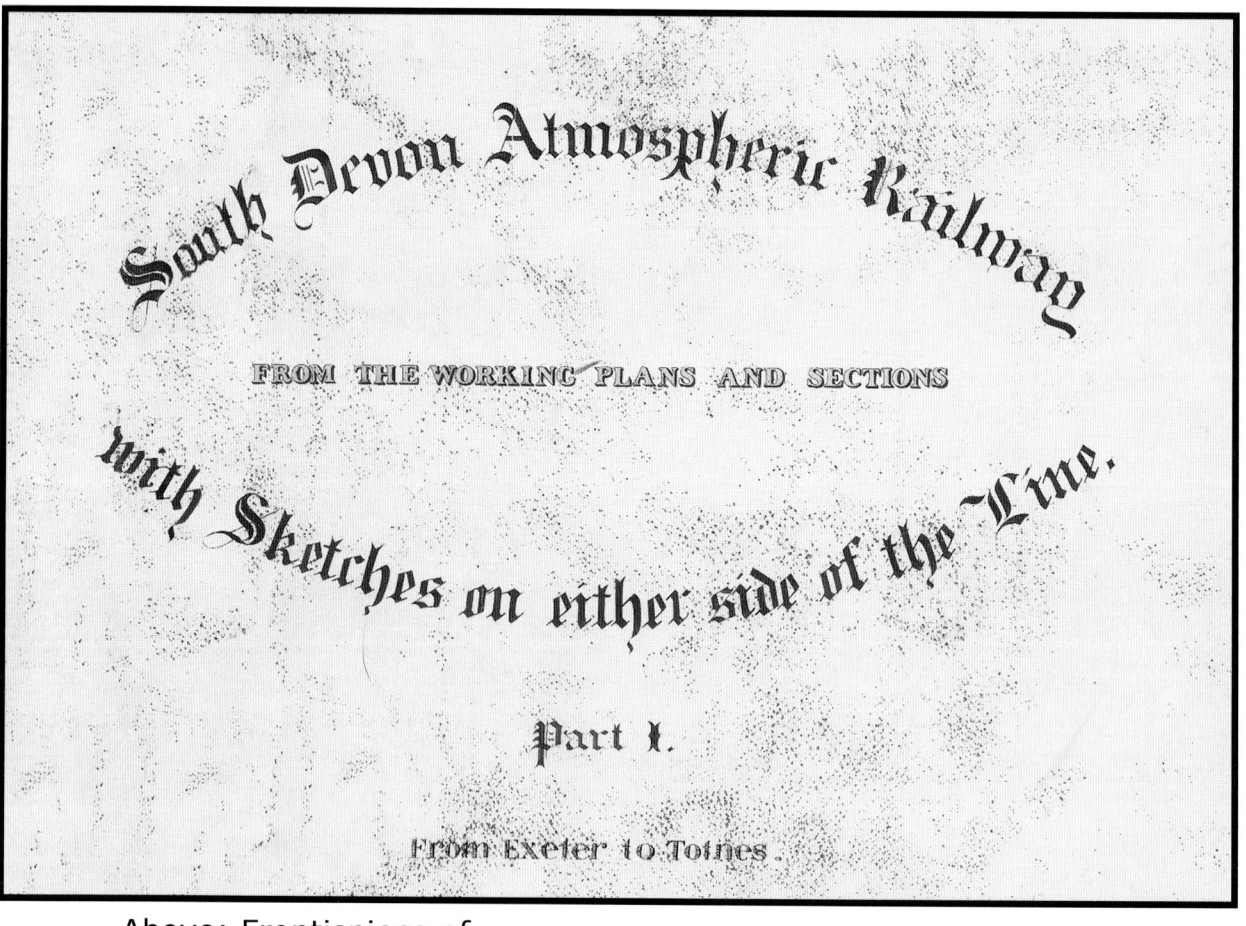

**Above: Frontispiece of
William Dawson's Book**

South Devon Atmospheric Railway, from the
working plans and sections, with Sketches on either
side of the Line.
Part 1. From Exeter to Totnes.
By William Dawson.
Published by the author, 1848.

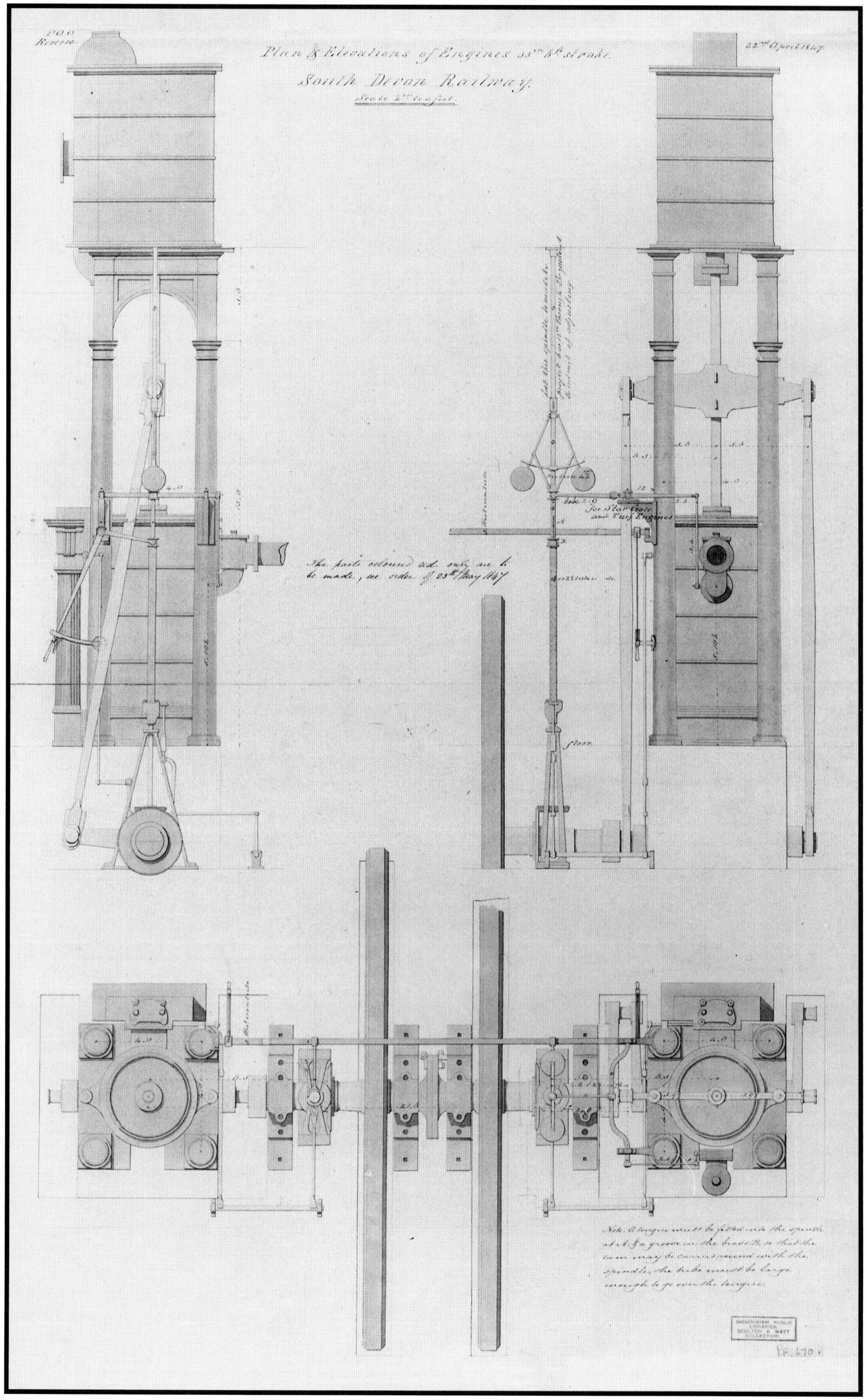

Image: Institution of Civil Engineers.

Right: Boulton & Watt Drawing

Dated 22nd April 1847, for modification to the
governors of the engines at Starcross (first
run 23rd March 1847) and Turf (first run 4th
February 1847) the new parts were ordered on
25th May 1847. It is not known if the Exeter
engines were also modified.

Plan & Elevations of Engines 35 H. stroke.
South Devon Railway.

Birmingham City Archives. Bolton and Watt Portfolio 670.